Born in Aba, Nigeria, Ernest Chetachukwu Anudu was raised in a traditional Christian family. Owing to his childhood dream of becoming a priest, he pursued his studies from the minor seminary to the major seminary, where he studied philosophy.

In 2018, he left Nigeria for Germany, where he earned his Bachelor's degree in Intercultural Theology and his Master's degree in International Migration and Intercultural Relations.

His experience, which the reader would readily read, inspired this work. This began simply as a process of writing down his thoughts, memories and reflections–each to understand the events unfolding around him. Still, it quickly grew into an accumulated narrative that tells a story about vocation, identity and purpose of living between two continents and cultures.

Ernest was able to demonstrate the inherent duality of the priestly vocation from the moment the individual became conscious of the calling to his development, humanly and psychologically, to become like Christ, the eternal priest and, at the same time, he reflects upon the shortcomings of the formation to the priesthood to meet its rigorous obligations, whilst reflecting on its dangers failing to fulfil the demands of our modern world and other social issues which are eroding the Christian values found in our civilisation. In these pages, he covers a wide range of critical topics, including racism and anti-racism, colonialism and the abolition of God in the human condition.

Written with a personable tone, intellectual and spiritual insight, *Note from Solitude: Childhood, dreams and Reflections* emphasises the sense of obligation essential to our world today.

To my parents, who—unwittingly gave me the most profound gift of all: the freedom to grow in distinction to them, yet holding me close. To my siblings, with a thankful heart.

To God, these words are written that You may mend what is broken in us, save what is left of our weary soul and world, and by so doing, betray us to your truth.

Ernest Chetachukwu Anudu

NOTES FROM SOLITUDE

Childhood, Dreams and Reflections

AUSTIN MACAULEY PUBLISHERS
LONDON * CAMBRIDGE * NEW YORK * SHARJAH

Copyright © Ernest Chetachukwu Anudu 2025

The right of Ernest Chetachukwu Anudu to be identified as author of this work has been asserted by the author in accordance with sections 77 and 78 of the Copyright, Designs and Patents Act 1988.

All rights reserved. No part of this publication may be reproduced, stored in a retrieval system, or transmitted in any form or by any means, electronic, mechanical, photocopying, recording, or otherwise, without the prior permission of the publishers.

Any person who commits any unauthorised act in relation to this publication may be liable to criminal prosecution and civil claims for damages.

All of the events in this memoir are true to the best of author's memory. The views expressed in this memoir are solely those of the author.

A CIP catalogue record for this title is available from the British Library.

ISBN 9781035883721 (Paperback)
ISBN 9781035883738 (ePub e-book)

www.austinmacauley.com

First Published 2025
Austin Macauley Publishers Ltd®
1 Canada Square
Canary Wharf
London
E14 5AA

Writing this work would not have been possible without the support, encouragement, and love of many individuals.

Many thanks to the memories of my friend, Ogochukwu E. Ibeh, who believed in my capacity to harness the depositories of my memory and transform them into meaningful achievements. To Ikenna B. Jideofor, Chukwulee Iheanacho, Emmanuel Ezeala, Gerald Aguwa, Theodore Iheme and Wisdom Chukwuma, thank you for walking through the manuscript and offering the most real critique and support that formed the basis of developing an authentic story.

I am immensely grateful to my editor, whose keen eye and insightful feedback have been invaluable in shaping this book. Your dedication and expertise have helped bring clarity and depth to my narrative, and for that, I am genuinely thankful. I extend my deepest gratitude to Bro. Alphonsus Onyekachi Eze, my spiritual director, and my teachers, Prof. Erna Zonne-Gätjens and Prof. Gabriele Beckmann. They have imparted their wisdom and guided me with their vast knowledge and experience. Your dedication to the vocation of teaching has shaped my intellectual journey. Through your rigorous instruction and encouragement, you have pushed me to reach my fullest potential, fostering both my scholarly abilities and my critical thinking skills. Thank you for your enduring commitment to my education and for inspiring me to pursue objectivity in all my endeavours. I also extend my deepest gratitude to my readers. Your willingness to journey with me through the pages of this book means more to me than words can express. I hope this work resonates with you and inspires you to find beauty and meaning in your moments of adversity. And all men and women from whose wealth of experience I draw, whose intellectual prowess has been the shoulder on which I lean, thank you for your invaluable contributions to my life. Your insights and perspectives have enriched my understanding and broadened my horizons, allowing me to weave a narrative that is both profound and reflective. Your collective wisdom has been a beacon, guiding me through the complexities of introspection and creativity. May this light you have given us never dim, and may the lessons and experiences we have shared continue to illuminate our path and that of the readers.

Per aspera ad astra

Table of Contents

Preface	11
I: Early Years	14
II: School Years	31
III: Formative Years	56
IV: Stings of the Past, Loss of Inward Grace	110
V: Adrift in Us vs Them	135
VI: The Abolition of God	166
VII: Reflections	185
Selected Bibliography	190
End Notes	195

Preface

When it became imperative that I change how I write this book; no longer an educational book using the voice of an authoritative guide but a more personable voice developing a narrative intertwined with personal reflection and shared experiences, the entire project took a life of its own and at the same demanding a level of vulnerability I had not expect. It was as if the book itself had become a mirror, reflecting not just the ideas I wanted to share but the parts of my reality that the state of our world, in its relentless hardness and tendency to produce conformity and idiocy, sought to suppress. The question I kept asking myself was: how much do I have to know to engage in this adventure? Was it enough to have a plan for publication, or did I need to anticipate every possible twist and turn? Why am I doing this, and what do I stand to gain? I asked these questions, knowing full well that the burden of reality placed on me, although too heavy to bear, is also too heavy to ignore. Part of me burned with an uncontrollable urge to dive in, driven by an insatiable curiosity. In contrast, another part hesitated, paralysed by dread that I was woefully unprepared for this task.

I did not think I had something new to offer the reader except an ingrained conviction that in the conduct of human affairs, religiously and secularly, we have become detached from life and human activity. This detachment, I felt, was not merely a consequence of modernisation or technological advancement. Those have their own repercussions, which we will realise sooner or later. Beyond that, I speak of a deep, more troubling symptom of our collective disconnection from thinking and the willingness to accept impunity and constant indoctrination in the name of education.

Each day, either on the television, at church or at work, I am bombarded from all sides with thousands of lines and images that force their impression on me. Two questions, however, would be enough. All we need to is one simple answer and the intensity of our neurosis will disappear.

What are we doing?

Why are we doing it?

These questions, deceptively simple, seem to pierce through the haze of distraction and automation that governs so much of modern life. If we compare our contemporary world with the ancient times, its progress and achievements, its science, humanities and religion, one discovers the striking loss of human experience in our world involved in the striking development and spread of racial ideology. It is not an examination of conscience which has become entirely meaningless. Thought itself, as we have to reckon it now with consequences, has become utterly useless. One is only perceived as a thinker in the light of pleasing the mob, catering to the demands of popular opinion rather than fostering genuine understanding. The pursuit of truth has been replaced by the quest for approval, and the intellectual process has been reduced to a mere tool for maintaining the status quo. Because everyone must please the mob, we develop ways to control our thoughts so that—not to prevent harm to ourselves—but to carry out the harm with race and sexuality as the weapons of choice, forming the battlegrounds where these dehumanising forces are brutally unleashed. We begin by telling ourselves there is something wrong with the way we think about reality. We create this illusion, this narrative of deficiency, as if our perceptions and beliefs are inherently flawed, as if our natural understanding of the world is inadequate. We are taught to distrust our own senses, to question our instincts, and to see ourselves as broken and in need of correction. This illusion becomes so pervasive that it infiltrates every aspect of our lives—our relationships, our work, our very sense of self. We are told that reality is too complex, too abstract for us to grasp in its fullness, so we must rely on an oversimplification and the structures crowned with the responsibility of doing so to interpret it for us. In doing so, we surrender the profound gift of all—our capacity to question, observe, and think independently.

However, I cannot be spellbound by this illusion any longer. And given my many brothers who come to you due to your perceived importance, I think it is time some things were said. Things I am going to say to call them to consciousness. Therefore, this book is less about what I know now and more about what I have come to understand in the process of unlearning. It is less about the accumulation of knowledge and more about the dismantling of false constructs by showing the mechanism by which we estrange ourselves. This book is about getting to know ourselves in the light of truth and objectivity.

Unfortunately, I could not do that without first revealing aspects of myself, which involve the image of the vocation to the priesthood. This aspect is uncomfortable and unsettling. These are the parts of me that I have long kept to myself for fear of judgment and misrepresentation. Yet, to truly call others to consciousness, I must first confront my own shadows; I must admit the biases, the contradictions, and the sacred wounds that have shaped me. This is the price of awakening—the duty to lay bare the uncomfortable truths I carry within, knowing that only by doing so can one make room for real growth.

I do not suppose I possess sophisticated academic qualifications to argue in this book, nor do I understand myself as the bearer of ultimate truths, for the heavens know that I can only understand things within my intellectual capacity and things beyond the reach of my knowledge if it does please God. It is, instead, my belief that I have a duty to speak from the depths of my own experiences, my own struggles, and my own reflections. It is not knowledge for knowledge's sake that drives me but the urgency of confronting the illusions that dominate our thinking, systems, and lives. It is the sharing of a raw, unrefined truth that has emerged from my reckoning. This book is meant to be a conversation—a call to examine the inner workings of the self and society in a more honest, direct way. When the centre can no longer hold, we must return to the essence of who we are. We must return to simplicity, to the truths that anchor us now that our affairs here on earth are spinning out of control.

Suppose any theologian or psychologist comes across this work, particularly in the last three chapters, he will immediately discover that it is the work of a neophyte who has challenges finding suitable theories to prove raw thoughts of the realities unfolding around him. Sometimes, I appear to be stating things akin to the ancient instead of the modern. To the degree I have managed to locate references to my ideas, the reader must bear with me if specific thoughts appear to be speculative. These thoughts are either exclusively against my will and can only be stated as they are or a result of my ignorance to look further for proof. In any case, the force of creativity has taken its thorn on me, demanding more than I sometimes feel capable of giving. I hope I have done my best and to trace the easily recoverable quotations and those that are not.

I
Early Years

I grew up in Aba, a city in Abia state, the eastern part of Nigeria. It is a place where the country seems to pulse with the rhythm of life itself: commerce, creativity and industriousness have their sanctuary erected in the city. It was here that my story began and one I feel compelled to tell.

I was born into a family of humble means. My memories now begin at the age of three or four. I recall our yard with two opposites: the left and right-hand sides. The surroundings had no fence, but pavements bordered every backyard corner There was a farm in the backyard where we harvested snails and locusts. We also made nests to catch and raise birds. At the front is a patch of giant vibrant flowers with great ornament and colourful petals. It was our playground but also a source of conflict and an instrument for discipline. Growing up, it was an unspoken understanding that flowers concealed the potential for chastisement. It was very accessible and convenient as it was taken at no cost.

Another memory comes to my mind, which is perhaps the most vivid of my early years in our yard. This is around five to six years. Nearby, on the left-hand side, is a kiosk laden with different types of alcohol and beverages. It is a square of domestic tranquillity for those who have had a stressful day. There is a borehole there, where we usually buy our water in gallons.

On the right-hand side are another borehole and a kiosk. The borehole appears similar to the one on the left, with a sturdy metal casting protruding from the ground. A small concrete platform surrounds the borehole, and a GP tank on top provides three channels for fetching water. Nearby, empty containers such as jerry cans and trucks are often lined up for people to fetch water efficiently. Each truck, depending on its size, can contain at least five to ten jerry cans.

The boreholes are usually on so that anyone can practically fetch water at no cost. But that is never intended, and if caught, one would have to replace the water as punishment. This is common with the borehole on the right-hand side. I recall the day it happened to me. I think I was returning from school and had taken water from the tap with my water bottle before I was caught and asked to replace it, including the droplets.

I could not buy my way out with money. The idea was that I had to replace the water with a crook or any other means possible. This is the first time it occurred to me how unimaginably cruel human beings can be. When my punisher saw that I could not do it, he let me go, collecting the water from me. I remember contemplating the experience for a very long time.

Memories of the ordeal replayed in me every moment I crossed the borehole. I remember not being able to shake off the feeling of fear and helplessness and the enormity of what had transpired. The weight of what transpired pressed me down so much that I had to share it with my mother to find solace in the fact that that did not happen. But talking to her about it proved to be frustrating as she could not help curiosity. Each question I posed appeared to hit a dead end and with a vague response of *Hapuga* (forget or rather do not worry so much about it). But not worrying means that I have to worry and be afraid of my own proclivity to punish someone in the same manner.

Like every yard, conflicts often emerged in ours. Arguments usually erupt like sudden storms, fuelled by frustrations and jealousy that one is doing better than the other, that the music is too loud or that we are doing laundry or dishes in the yard… I recall a memory that shocked my imagination. My father was engaged in a verbal exchange because I was cleaning the dishes inside the yard instead of the backyard when it was not raining. I remember the words hurled at him that he is stinkingly poor and cannot afford to build his own house. Each insult seemed to chip away at my spirit. I stood helpless to witness what one may call verbal abuse. I struggled to comprehend the cruelty of it all.

But that is what I could do—contemplate things I could not change. I came to this consciousness as early as possible that contemplation is the only avenue through which I could come to terms with realities beyond me. It is also a means of controlling swirling emotions within me, knowing full well that these things are true in themselves and that my difference towards them adds nothing to their reality. Obviously, we were poor, and there was nothing I could have done at that moment.

If, for some reason, I do not like the situation, I could only accept their existence whilst changing my attitude towards them. As a consequence, I may have a good outcome. This is a deliberate and focused process of shutting the outside world into the background and developing the inner landscape to take the lead. My position in the family has a hand in developing such mindfulness. As the youngest, I was meant to be an observer and not the sayer, the listener and not the doer. I spent the majority of my childhood observing things and absorbing the dynamics and experiences of my older siblings and the world around me. I do not believe things because they have been imposed on me but because I have experienced them and can testify to them by virtue of my experience. This means that I had less intrusion on my personal affairs, but it does not follow that I get the affirmation that I had required of them during my adolescence. Then, no one could believe I had grown and could make my own decision and live with it.

I had a lot to wrestle with my eldest brother because I found it problematic to be dictated what was true if I knew that to be false and if what was true for him had no rationale but was a superiority complex. Sometimes, these impositions clash, leading to conflicts that linger. My mother, in particular, found it challenging to accept that her youngest offspring had transitioned into adulthood. Memories of my infancy and early years can cloud her judgment. In these circumstances, she will remind me of my first words as a child and days of sickness each time I assert my autonomy.

This reluctance to acknowledge the passage of time often creates a rift when I push against the constraints of her outdated role and imagery of me. Ironically, she has been preparing me to distinguish myself from them, too. My mother will always tell me not to involve myself in their conflict. And I consider this to be an invaluable lesson to distinguish myself from them. However, the frustration is always the feeling of powerlessness in the escalating tensions between your loved ones and not interfering with alleviating the conflict. In any case, I think she was helping me to form my own personality aside from their own. As I grew older, the character of such personality became appreciated and, at the same time, abhorred. Then, criticising one parent and leaving the other means that you do love one and not the other.

But I think for one to be able to love his parents unconditionally, he must be able to develop some abhorrence for that love. I cannot recall in my boyhood when I failed to criticise what I loved because I was afraid to lose the ties between us. I have a very acute sense that to love is to suffer; otherwise, what would a thirty-two-year-old man named Jesus be doing on the cross?

Another memory that comes to my mind in that regard is in my nursery two about my form teacher whom I loved so much. It was during a break, and every kid had gone out to play. I went to my form teacher, Aunty Kate, to play because I was very fond of her. She was like a mother to us, blessed with the perfect height to meet us eye-to-eye. Then, she grabbed me and sat me on her lap.

Something happened, and she made a comment that I did not like. I remember challenging her; when she could not fight back, she pulled me down, and in the process, I mistakenly broke her bangle. She told me right to my face that I was possessed, which I understand now to be that I had progressed beyond my peers due to my steadfast demeanour. After school, I hurriedly left for my mother's shop and eagerly recounted the incident to her. At first, she showed her frustration and eagerness to dismiss my story as usual, but I remember insisting that she talk to the teacher for me.

The next day, she took me to school to see my form teacher. It was in the middle of the morning assembly, so we waited until it was over, and then my mother approached her. She was very flabbergasted. Her forehead creased with confusion and disbelief that the incident was the reason that brought my mother to the school.

. She explains to my mother and me that by being possessed, she meant what I understood it now to mean and not what one may have understood it to be culturally. For her, I had a level of maturity and understanding beyond my peers. Whilst I may not have been academically advanced and confident enough to speak for myself, she believes that I have the potential in me. The explanation appeared to be soothing even though it did not match the rage at which the word was spilt prior. On this note, I accepted it not because of what it was but because of what it had to say about my future; simultaneously, I apologised for breaking her bangle.

A few months later, she tested me based on her observation about me. In a candid conversation with my mother, she proposed a daring leap that would see me jumping a class. She discussed with my mother that I should be allowed to take the final exam for nursery three pupils instead of nursery two. The final school exam for nursery three, of course, could not have been so difficult, but it dared me to prove my mettle against pupils a year my senior. I tackled the exam gracefully and forwent my attendance at nursery three to primary one.

It was a quiet yet profound gesture from her. Although I was little, around six years old and very tiny, the encounter was so indelibly imprinted upon my mind and its memory is still told today in my family.

Indeed, her explanation resonated with me as if the very essence of my life became defined at that moment. I think in the quietness of my heart that through this experience, it was established that I have always had within me the capacity to argue for what is true, not because I know what truth is but because I think from the earliest moments of our cognitive development, we possess a pure conception of truth and understanding which is not affected by our experience in the world. Even if we are told what is true, we do not accept it except if it demonstrates a connection with some objective, pure and immutable truth. Such intrinsic inclination can only be true because somewhere, an ultimate truth exists from which all other truths take their position.

My parents were traders by profession and had no primary or secondary qualifications to take up professional jobs. My father is a man of few words but observant and calculative. As early as five o'clock in the morning, he will rise and say his rosary before preparing for morning Mass and eventually for the day's business. Saying the rosary remains one devotional prayer that my father has not stopped even after being dealt with illness at this later stage. There is a sense of reverence in his actions towards the rosary.

It is one prayer that I understood very well because of its power to bring one to sleep. Immediately after dinner, my father would call everyone to recite the rosary together. My mother would cite the biblical verse that a family that prays together stays together. As the first bead finds its place between my fingers, a serene tranquillity envelops My eyelids, heavy with the weight of reverence and prayer, begin to droop. And my mind, immersed in the timeless mysteries of the rosary, finds solace in the gentle embrace of sleep. But when I reached the age of seven, my attitude towards became different; I joined the block rosary. At the same time I became conscious of myself and my individuality. It is something that happened in parallel, and the reason for such an occurrence remains unclear to me. My father rides a bicycle to and from the shop. From the early hours after the morning Mass, he could be found at the busy market of Ehi Road, where he sells different kinds of used bottles and containers of relaxers. How he discovered that kind of business is something I have not understood to date, but it was what he did to put food on our tables. When it happened that made many sales, he would buy chin-chin for the family, a popular Nigerian snack made from dough. I often eat it with so much excitement because it is a sign that he has succeeded in navigating the complexity of the streets of commerce.

My mother was gentle, with steely resolve in her approach to things. She is an ardent member of the charismatic fellowship. As such, one could understand her reluctance as well as willingness to mediate in the matter concerning me and my form teacher. Her charisma for devotion and prayer makes her a triumphant beacon in the midst of uncertainty.

I always felt compassion for her—she was too poor to study and pursue her dream of becoming a nurse. She always felt like someone who wanted to do more with her life but was held down by poverty—a fate so unpleasant and heart-wrenching that it stained every single opportunity she had to move forward. The daughter of peasant farmers, and I am the grandson of peasant farmers. Like my father, my mother was a trader, too and the backbone of trading ventures in my family.

She peddles her way to the Nkwo-Ngwa market, a vibrant market in Aba where she sells tubers of yam. She was a familiar presence in the market, and everyone admired and respected her for her personality; her warm smile and infectious laughter are memories that come to me now. Both my parents built a life for our family of nine from the ground up, brick by brick, sale by sale.

Assisting my parents in their trade was a necessity for us as a family. Every Saturday morning, my sisters, and I would wake up early, do the house chores and head to the backyard to wash the containers my father had brought home from his shop. We would scrub, rinse, and sanitise them, depending on what they had previously contained. Washing containers every Saturday was not just a routine chore; it was a ritual that drew many of us together. Our friends from the neighbourhood on the right side of our building very much participated in it.

It was a space for telling stories and discussing what had been happening in our families. Because everyone would get a reward afterwards, it was crucial to take part. A similar case applies to my mother. On many occasions, my brothers and sisters would miss school to hawk yams in the market even though they raised us to admire education. For them, education was our ticket out of poverty.

My father sings it as praise. But at times, helping them out was more important than school. Making deliveries for those who had purchased items in bulk was a necessity to increase sales. I was little then; I was lucky to be in this regard and had not participated in deliveries. Apart from that, I fear missing school. I always thought that each time I missed school; I missed one single target to change my family's socioeconomic status.

On one occasion, I was beguiled by external circumstances into this situation. It was to fry grounded cassava to produce garri that would be partly sold and eaten by the family. On that early morning, I rose with a heavy heart after a series of deliberations with my mother about whether it was right that I missed school or not. My thoughts drifted to the classroom. I imagined my friends gathered around our teacher, their voices rising and falling.

I could not shake the vivid image of my classmates' faces contorted in surprise, perhaps even disdain, at the sight of me frying garri during school hours. The thought of their judgment, their whispered speculations about why I would take on such domestic chores meant for women during school hours, sent a shiver down my spine. I could already hear the incredulous questions echoing in my mind… "What's he doing?" "Look, he is frying garri. They can't buy it from the market because they are poor." The fear of being perceived as lesser and, of course, exposing my self-importance struck me as unfair and inferior.

But for me, it was a special duty—one that I could disobey but would not learn from. Possibly, I will never have a means of making amends. So, I squared my shoulders and walked with my mother to the production centre, where we fried our ground cassava. It was about two miles away from our yard, very near to the Nkwo-Ngwa market. We arrived there quite early in the morning, around eight o'clock.

My mother had carried out the important stages prior to frying, including the draining process of excess liquid. So, we began by pouring the coarse and gritty grounded cassava onto a wide, flat sieve to sift through the mound, separating the fine flour from the coarse remnants. Then, carefully transfer the flour to a sizzling pan where it is to be fried. After some minutes of steering the processed cassava in the frying pan, I felt somewhat satisfied and comfortable doing it. Equally, I longed to be seen and greeted by my friends.

I found myself alone with my mother, surrounded by people, both passers-by and people who came to the place for the same reason. I felt alone with her, working together and telling me stories about her life in the village before and after she met my father. There was a silent understanding between us; it was an unspoken acknowledgement of how well I did to help her out.

I came to admire her strength and dedication to duty. There were times before now when I felt this way, usually when I travelled with her to the village for the planting season. But this was different; a different image of her was created in my memory. A figure of someone industrious with unyielding dedication and not ashamed of her responsibility as a woman and mother to care for her family.

As I returned to school the next day, I felt the weight of curious gazes, my friends eyeing me with a mixture of intrigue and confusion. I could almost hear the whispers ripple through the room, questioning why I was not in school the previous day. But I could not help but smile to myself, knowing that beneath their curiosity lies an experience they could not possibly understand and a lesson I have learnt. I discovered a richness of experience, a connection to my roots and the everyday struggles that shaped me.

I felt a kinship with my ancestors, with those who had toiled and sacrificed so that I could stand where I was today. That singular gesture that I showed my mother, despite how important she knows school was for me, has ever since then remained in her memory.

From a young age, I was taught the importance of learning and knowledge, knowing that it was the key to unlocking a better future. Going to school was a sacred ritual of rebirth, especially for my father, despite the fact he attended little of it. My primary one to three was fraught with obstacles. My uniforms were often neatly patched together from scraps of fabric. I could only have two; more than that was a luxury.

This also means that whenever I washed any corresponding uniform that was supposed to be worn the next school day, I could not dry it but lay in wait by the wooden doors, often still damp to be absorbed by the wood. Otherwise, my father would stay awake till there was electricity to give it a hot massage till it became dry as if a dryer did it. Heretofore, he made it his venerable duty to prepare my school uniform for the week. Every Sunday, around six o. clock, he would attend to this duty, ironing my uniform and that of my sister.

I do not remember a day in primary school when I wore an unpressed uniform to school. He did it until I started secondary school and was allowed to handle the pressing iron. He had a kind of measured precision that he used to unfurl my uniform, laying it on the dining table with a meticulousness befitting only a tailor. At the end of the ironing, he would give my uniform a box craft that befits a craftsman. For him, it was more than ironing my uniform; it was his devotion to education and a tangible expression of dress the way you want to be addressed.

Books were a luxury I could scarcely afford. Purchasing books became a luxury that I could afford only when they had something to do with my school, such as the textbooks required in school. That, too, was not easy to acquire; my parents often told me to share with my classmates till they could make sales to buy me one. The prospect of adding to my literary arsenal was fraught with deliberation and restraint, as each acquisition demanded carefully balancing household needs and sacrifices elsewhere. But I could not blame them because one definitely has to stay alive in order to study.

Each time I found an interesting novel to read, I verily reminded myself that it had nothing to do with my school. To gaze upon the shelves laden with books was to confront the stark reality of my family's limitations. There was always a tension between what was required by the school and what was required for my personal development. I remember the thrill of receiving my first set of textbooks in primary one, verbal and quantitative reasoning and Ugo C. Ugo.

Verbal and quantitative reasoning, as their name implies, is just like studying statics and philosophy these days. The authors of the books neatly crafted them with precision so that the reader worked to crack the intricacies of the arithmetic, language, and logic, which weaved seamlessly together. I struggled with quantitative reasoning more than I did with verbal reasoning. For me, verbal reasoning was just me.

There was a certain ease to my reading and practising verbal reasoning, a fluidity that flowed through my veins… I found not only a playground for my small intellect but a sanctuary for my soul. Quantitative reasoning was more of a protagonist who stands as an ambivalent figure to sharpen and confuse my reasoning at the same time. To do that comes with a mathematical inquiry that pokes my mind and a determination to understand. On the one hand, I had a sense of admiration for the precision and logic that quantitative reasoning brings with it.

On the other hand, there was often a feeling of frustration that accompanied my practice of it, especially when faced with complex equations. I did not understand why, in one instance, $1 + 1$ should be 2 and in another example, $1 + 1 + 1 = 1$. Why would numbers not simply be numbers but also translated into letters? Could not they exist as mere digits without the need for translation into abstract concepts like 'quantities' and 'equivalents'? As a young pupil, it felt absurd, almost comical, that something as straightforward as counting could be transformed into a convoluted mental gymnastics… They could appear as mere symbols on my page, and just when I thought I was grasping them, they slip through like elusive phantoms.

It was as if I were trying to catch a shadow with my bare hands, reaching out only to find emptiness staring back at me. I could fathom the subject within other subjects but not the subject in itself. The teachers themselves were not smiling, always serious whilst scribing numbers and letters on the backboard and drawing conclusions that seemed evident only to them. I fought back many times, and thanks to my visual memory, I was able to scale through averagely. Other subjects like agricultural science, primary science, and so on, I found easy and excelled meritoriously.

Whilst I could not afford children's books meant for my age, I spent my free time from school reading through the pages of the Bible, Catechism of the Catholic Church, book of saints and other prayer books. Moreover, they were relevant to Christian Religious Education. These were books that could even be replaced, especially by my mother, when torn without weighing their worth against any other item. She bought me my first Bible without asking. For her, it was a necessity that now I am growing up; I should follow the steps of the faith into which I was born and raised.

I remember that first Bible, which was blue in colour and contains only the New Testament. I read through the genealogy of Christ thoroughly, the first opening page of the Gospel of Matthew, and instantly plunged into disarray. Poor me could not entirely grasp every name that has to do with Lord Jesus, but every narrative is woven from the threads of his history and my faith.

As I began to read through the names, Abraham became the father of Isaac, Isaac the father of Jacob, and Jacob the father of Judah and his brothers, I felt confused as well as connected to a thread going back to generations past to the present moment. I felt a stirring of curiosity within me. Who were these individuals, I wondered, whose lives seamlessly connected to Christ's and my lineage? There were heroes and heroines, saints and sinners, each one leaving an indelible mark on the world and shaping the course of history that would later be crowned with Christ.

But it was not just the names that captivated me; it was the underlying questions they raised about the nature of identity, purpose, and destiny and the period of time one's destiny could take to manifest. It was not also the stories themselves; it was the underlying mystery they hinted at—the mystery of God's plan unfolding through the generations, of redemption weaving its way through human history. What unseen forces had guided the footsteps of these men and women, shaping their lives and destinies in ways beyond their understanding?

And to what, the fulfilment of one purpose, the Son of God, Jesus Christ. One becomes even more confused reaching the story's culmination–the birth of Lord Jesus in a stable where animals are sheltered. I could not understand why the eternal and infinite God could choose to enter man's world in such humble, seemingly insignificant circumstances. Were there no actual hospitals?

I continued my study and realised that the genealogy of Christ was not just a record of the past; it was a living testament to the divine name as master planner and His providence that had guided man's journey from the dawn of time. Here, we have God's covenant promises, beginning with His covenant with Abraham. Through Abraham's descendants, God promised to bless all nations, and the genealogy traces the fulfilment of this promise through the lineage leading to Jesus Christ.

Each name in the genealogy represents a pivotal moment in God's plan of redemption, a link in the chain of events leading to the birth, death, and resurrection of Jesus Christ. From Abraham to David and from David to Jesus, we see God's faithfulness in preserving the line of the Messiah despite the trials and tribulations faced by His people. More interestingly, it shows how decisions made by individuals in the past had far-reaching implications for the future, ultimately, in this case, leading to the good implication of the birth of a Messiah.

That was relatively easy for me to realise, but introspectively, I continued questioning myself on what it was for me and what role I had to play. I remember not knowing where to proceed with this sudden confrontation of the story.

The uniqueness of Matthew's presentation could not be a simple organisation and presentation of the ancestral family tree. Who am I, and how is my identity connected to these people of old?

Added to my confusion were the words of Prophet Isaiah, *"For to us a child is born, a son is given to us; upon his shoulder dominion rest. They name him Wonder-Counsellor, God-Hero, Father-Forever, Prince of Peace"* (Isa. 9:5). And of course, in Bethlehem after 14 generations. Was I also born there, in Bethlehem? I found myself ensconced by perplexity, grappling with the intricate complexity of the story.

I recount, I picked fights with my older siblings, who dared to recount the story to me. It cannot be that the Messiah was born *to us* in Bethlehem. My major problem then was the preposition *to us* as if I had anything personally to do with Him. I considered that to be problematic; everything that had to do with the incarnation was a nightmare for me. Once more, I turned to my mother, the closest person I could vent to, this time in the kitchen whilst making dinner.

"Mother," I ventured, my voice tinged with uncertainty, "it is said that Jesus was born *to us* in Bethlehem. Was I also born in that hallowed city?" Am I truly a part of this grand narrative, or am I but a mere spectator? This time, instead of dismissing me as usual, she looked at me with an understanding tinged with a hint of amusement.

"Nwachukwu," she called me, with a voice so gentle and soothing, "you were born at Chinwe Hospital; Christ was born for us in Bethlehem; that's what the passage was talking about. These kinds of things," she continues, "are beyond human understanding… Maybe when you become a priest." She finished.

To some degree, her answer came as a gentle sway that calmed me down for a moment. But within that serene acceptance was also a subtle disquiet like a whispering wind stirring the depths of my soul. Priest? That startles me. How do I behave now? Like a priest? Not when I had not decided what my future was, albeit my admiration for the Mass then had no equivalence, especially the Latin Mass.

On another night, I picked up the Bible and read the same passage and more, and whilst I could not comprehend it, an unbridled rage developed within me, a storm I do not have a name for. Why was Jesus Christ born unto us in Bethlehem? Indeed, God could have done everything to stop it from happening—that His son may be born in the hospital instead. If God is capable of making a Virgin conceive without intercourse, then nothing cannot escape His omnipotence. And now I have to decipher what that means to me. Why do I have to think about this story all the time, and why can I not understand it? Was it the weight of my expectation, the burden of belief, or the clash of truths that I could not reconcile or stand with? I contemplated the story in such a way that it was known to everyone in my family that I was wrestling with that passage of the Bible–the paradox of it and the mystery of God-made flesh, the infinite embodied in the finite.

I brought it up in school during our Christian Religious Knowledge classes. However, my school had disdain for Catholicism, emblematic of the way the teacher responded to my question, even though my question was everything but Catholicism. It felt like a mere brush-off, devoid of depth or nuance, showcasing a pattern of superficiality ingrained in their bias. In the deafening silence that followed, I came to terms with the weight of my unanswered question, feeling adrift in a void of intellectual isolation. Painful it was, alone I felt.

I thought if all was well, I could have asked for books where I could comprehend what I found very uncomfortable in the Bible. Instead, I was left with this very book, and I could either understand it or throw it away. It became very important that I understood what this story was all about. My mother made an effort to send my immediate sister and me to their Charismatic Bible study every Tuesday—not mainly because of my curiosity but to get us occupied instead of watching television.

There, we were divided into children's and adult groups. However, I found myself drawn to the adult group, feeling that I could grasp a deeper understanding of the Bible there. That was never entirely successful, so I made the conscious decision to stop going.

My question continued for at least a year, relentlessly poking at the recesses of my mind. Whenever the topic of the incarnation arose in conversation, I could not help but feel compelled to engage and bring up my lingering question once more. It was as if the mention of this sacred mystery reverberated my curiosity in a new light. Whether during casual conversations or formal discussions, I found myself drawn to the subject at every mention of the incarnation. I did so without a clear understanding of my motivations.

It was as if an inner impulse guided me, prompting me to seek answers and engage in dialogue that I was too small for… Then, in my seventh year of birth, a subtle shift occurred within me—an event that would shape the course of my entire life. It was about saying the rosary and later having a dream where I found myself face-to-face with a figure clad in radiant white garments.

Except for the white figure, the rest of the content of the dream remains unknown to date. I reckon I woke thinking that I would see the figure again, but it disappeared. I went back to sleep, and the figure reappeared. I felt a stirring deep that indeed, I was in the presence of the divine.

The image I saw liberated me instantly from my shackles, the doubt and uncertainty that held me down. At first, I began to discern naturally a growing clarity in my reading of the biblical passage and many others. I felt the weight of my questions dissipate, replaced by a profound sense of clarity and peace. I understood that by being born in Bethlehem instead of any hospital and by a dispensation in which the Blessed Virgin Mary was the medium, Jesus Christ entered into the human condition to make reparation for my sins. This is the sin that has been prolonged to all human nature through the carnal act in which man (the first Adam) acts as the first principle.

As then, Adam was the cause of the prolongation, and Adam was formed from the ground; the second Adam (Christ) likewise was formed from flesh as in the first man but unstained to redeem man and restore him to his original innocence. The birth of Christ was a necessity for the salvation of man—a mission that culminates in his sacrificial death on the cross. For a dead man, nothing is needed but a living man to raise him to life again. I was reminded of my connection to this whole economy by my spiritual identity as someone from the same earthly origin of Christ. For it was by forming me out of dust that God would recover his own image and likeness, of which the devil had robbed him after the fall of man.

The apparent ultimate need to create me is not because he needed to create me, but because I needed to be created. If He who has everything chooses to need me, it is because I need to be needed by Him. I am a mere dust without Him. To understand myself is to submit myself to His will; only then can I be sure that I am going the right way. But this I cannot achieve without the medium through which the Son of man came to be born.

Even if I love Jesus, I must surrender to the maternal protection of His mother against the serpent. God elevated the Blessed Virgin Mary, pointing to her as the gate of heaven and easy access to the trinity. In the Catholic faith, this is well-defined. It is not an arbitrary invention of faith, as one may often think about doctrines and dogmas. The central idea of God in this regard is deeply rooted in the Scripture.

For humanity to have someone they could resort to for maternal protection and comfort, it was essential to have an amiable feminine figure close to Christ. The turning of water into wine at the wedding in Canna buttresses this. At the crucifixion, Christ also made it clear, "Woman, behold your son. Then he said to the disciple, behold your mother" (Luke 19:26). If I do not believe in this, then I will not be able to hear the salutation, "You are my beloved son; today I have begotten you."

Realising this immediately made me sweat… It is as if a chord is struck deep within me; a new spirit has been created within me. In the same year, I found myself drawn to the Mariam Association, the Block Rosary Crusade dedicated to honouring the Blessed Virgin Mary through the rosary. Later, I joined the

Legion of Mary. Today, the Marian Association stands out for me in the myriads of pious associations in the Catholic Church.

The decision to join the association was not merely a gesture of piety but a conscious commitment to embody the principles of faith I profess, obedience, and surrender exemplified by Mary herself. At the stroke of six in the evening, I make haste to the centre where our daily prayers are held. The suddenness of the decision struck my mother as a surprise. Initially, she had expected me to slumber on the way. I could sense her perplexity and consternation, her attempts to reconcile the image of the child she once knew with the person I was becoming.

But she could not dismiss the sincerity of my conviction nor the depth of my commitment. Additionally, my father became supportive in his own subtle ways. Once it clocks at 5:45, he would refrain from sending me on errands to avoid lateness to prayer. I felt a deep sense of encouragement. It was as if the universe was conspiring to affirm my chosen path, guiding me along the journey of faith with gentle nudges and subtle reminders. As far as I could remember, I never bothered anyone again after this encounter, nor did such rage grow within me.

The school continued its course gradually. Having joined the Block Rosary Crusade, I had a deep desire at some point to express my faith outwardly in school. I began wearing the rosary around my neck. For me, it was a simple yet profound act, a way of carrying the presence of the divine with me throughout the day. It raised a few eyebrows among my peers and teachers, prompting curious questions and segregation.

The school administration picked offence with it. I devised the alternative of wearing it inside my singlet before the school uniform. However, that did not go well, as the rosary slips out whenever I wear my uniform for physical education. Ultimately, the rosary was taken from me during one-morning assembly and torn. The scene unfolded so surreal as I felt that my faith had also been torn asunder, along with the beads.

I felt a surge of conflicting emotions—anger and grief all mixed together. The act itself seemed to mock the sincerity of my faith as if my devotion to Mary had been deemed unworthy or misguided. This came to bore me; the school entirely bored me. It took up far too much time for me to find peace going to the same school every day. Later, I resolved vehemently to cling even more fiercely to my faith and to do that; I had to change school.

Before completing my primary three, I made the solemn announcement to my parents: I would not be returning to Rapid Academy, where my rosary had been torn. The decision was heavy upon my heart as, now, I was not considering the economic hardship of my family. Even as I spoke the words indistinctly, I could sense the mixture of surprise and concern that flickered across their faces. They had witnessed first-hand the toll that the events at the school had taken on my spirit, yet uprooting me from the surroundings seemed daunting. Nevertheless, I maintained that I was not going back, not necessarily because of the event but also because I had felt intellectually unproductive there and would like a new adventure.

They understood, perhaps more deeply than I had anticipated, the gravity of my decision and the urgency with which it needed to be made. Of course, there were practical considerations to be weighed—the cost of finding a new school, adjusting to a different school environment, and navigating the complexities of social integration. Interestingly enough, I had made my choice of school before coming to tell them. I need them only to align with my choice and not debate it so much.

Therefore, we started an inquiry at different Catholic schools. One was very dear to me and was the cathedral's school. There, one is welcomed by a blissful environment and a serious climate of learning. The Cathedral itself is adorned with intricate carvings and stained-glass windows featuring the apostles and saints. Each wing is meticulously organised and decorated… I have always admired the cathedral since I learnt I was baptised there.

Now, I will have the chance to see it every day, I thought. We met with the gateman, who directed us to where the school was located. On reaching there and stepping foot into the school, I met some teachers whose countenances bear the weight of *fides et ratio*.ABruptly, I knew that I was going to stay there. I felt a sense of belonging—a feeling of homecoming so indescribable that it became.

My mother, too, found an instant affinity with the school environment. Its noble architecture and serene ambience resonated deeply with her. As we walked through the halls, her eyes sparkled with approval, mirroring my excitement that I did not make the wrong and that I would get registered in the school. I eavesdropped on the lessons and found inspiration in the teachers who nurtured both the mind and the spirit. I heard the pupils reciting their Catholic doctrine.

Instantly, I discovered a passion for learning. But perhaps most importantly, therein, I discovered the vocation to the priesthood, a calling that promised to sculpt my destiny. Yet, like a double-edged sword, it wielded the power to both elevate and render my soul naked.

II
School Years

It is my first term in primary four at the new primary school. The first term of primary four was a time of adjustment and exploration—a transition period from the familiar routines of lower primary to the more rigorous demands of upper primary. As a new student, I had my fair share of curious glances and whispering conversations. Because of my selective attitude, I did not easily make friends. Thus, for the first few weeks, I was an easy target, a newcomer ripe for ridicule in the eyes of those who had already forged their bonds of friendship.

The taunts and teasing wore on me. Each day became a battle to maintain my composure despite relentless scrutiny and derision. I thought friendship has to be a spontaneous connection where kindred spirits find each other through the natural ebb and flow of life. I did not believe I had to push to grow naturally. However, that did not go well for the first few weeks. Slowly and quite slowly, my expectations became a reality, and I made friends with whom I formed a tight-knit circle of friends. School life thus began.

Lessons were different and quite earnest. They became more demanding, requiring tutorials beyond the standard school hours, and they were not optional. The standard school hours were insufficient to cover the breadth and depth of the curriculum. Thus, additional hours were allocated on certain days of the week to ensure that each form teacher covered his or her curriculum. I had to ask my parents for extra money for food to sustain me during the extra hours.

Most of the time, they give, but other times, they did not sincerely have, and I had to save up from the ones given before. I accepted it with enthusiasm and determination because this was the choice I made and what I wanted, namely, to grow. With each passing lesson, I grew more adept at navigating the lessons and expanding my horizons.

Amidst the demanding school curriculum, one aspect of ours stood out as unique and distinct: The Catholic doctrine and prayer. As part of the curriculum, they appeared to be subjects that were not merely for studies but rather companions on our journey of faith. I found myself captivated by the profound wisdom and spiritual insights that lay within. From the questions, who made me? And the answer, God made me, that explores the stories of the Old Testament to the teachings of Jesus Christ, I understood the rich complexity of the Catholic faith. Everything is supported with references from the Bible and the Church Fathers.

I found myself immersed in discussions that challenged me to ponder the deeper meanings behind the tenets of my faith and to grapple with questions of morality, ethics, and the nature of God Himself. I recall boasting to my friends from my previous school about the depth of knowledge I had gained about my faith now that I had changed school. Indirectly, I was also advertising for them to leave their school and join me in my newfound home. I could not help but feel a sense of pride in how far I had come in school. Many of them did, but it was not until they were approaching to take the common entrance examination.

Besides the Catholic doctrine, our educational system observes the Church's liturgical calendar. One significant aspect was our weekly attendance at morning Mass and making sure that those in the state of grace receive holy communication. The sacrament of absolution was also administered to pupils who needed it. The observance of holy days of obligation was also implemented. This also meant that each feast day, like All Saint's Day and Feast of Assumption of the Blessed Virgin Mary, was a holiday.

Consequently, we did not go to school, unlike my previous school, where one, due to his faith, may decide on those days whether to attend school or not. The experience was always nothing short of fascinating. Now, my faith is no longer fraught with uncertainty and doubt, and I am no longer singled out as that Catholic boy who wears his rosary around his neck. No longer constrained by the fetters of anxiety or doubt, unafraid to make the sign of the cross during morning assembly. I found myself more willing to affirm my tradition, step out of my timidness, and embrace means for deeper engagement with my faith.

Whether reading the scripture, participating in retreats and spiritual gatherings, or engaging in meaningful conversations with fellow pupils, I noticed that each experience of mine was with an open heart and mind, unencumbered by the fear of judgment or rejection. There was this new sense of freedom and authenticity—a liberation of my soul from the mob. Here, everyone perceives each other on a higher level of being that is peculiar to the individual experience when he is alone. Indeed, there were people among us who did not share in the Catholic faith and tradition. One was my best friend, but they never felt that they had to deny themselves of their own faith and tradition. In the same way, I never felt that I had to intoxicate myself for the benefit of others.

Instead, what I felt was very problematic and clear at the same time. I would like to call it a limitation, but I am unsure if that word makes clear what I have in mind. I am not going to change the reader's mind about this. In the end, it is both clear and unclear. But I think it can be shown as phenomenal whilst the reader makes his critique.

Within me, I felt that outside the doctrine and dogmas of the Church, there is nothing new to experience. Everything has been laid down in writings; we only had to memorise and reproduce the same formulaic responses, never truly engaging with the depth and meaning of things. The P-value, whether significant or insignificant, does not strike us as surprising because, outside it, nothing else could be perceived. Then, there is the idea of *extra ecclesiam nulla salus*. The idea that those outside the Catholic faith are somehow condemned and excluded from accessing truth or experiencing Divine grace appeared somewhat arrogant and cruel to me.

There may be other interpretations of this saying, and I want to believe there are so many of them more reasonable than what I learnt, but this was how it was interpreted to me. Pondering on that, I thought that if God made all of us in His own image and likeness, how could it be that some of my friends would go to hell or purgatory for things they had no control over? What about those who have never had the opportunity to encounter the Catholic faith and, indeed, are Christians but never have had the chance of coming to experience the Catholic faith? Then, it seems to me that God's grace is the cruellest because a loving and omnipotent God could have done everything to prevent them from being in another Christian denomination. But instead, He did not because He wanted to see if they would obey Him.

Why should they be held responsible for something within the powers of the omnipotent God? What does God really want from them? Is it possible that God wishes to see whether they are capable of obeying His will even though that may lead them down paths unknown and challenge the very foundations of their understanding? The answer is incomprehensible to me, but it could not be anything other than obeying the will of God.

I thought about it over and over again and came to the same conclusion, even though it was not the answer I had expected. They cannot be held responsible for obeying the will of God, who knew and ordained them before their mother gave birth to them (Jer 1:4). It was God who called upon Abraham with a command to sacrifice his son, Isaac, upon the altar in the land of Moriah (Gen 22:1). Abraham did not falter God's message. Early the next morning, he embarked on the journey to Mount Moriah, where the sacrifice was to take place.

As he and his son ascended the mountain, Isaac, unaware of his impending fate, questioned his father about the sacrificial offering. Abraham cloaked in the mantle of faith, responded with a profound trust in divine providence. At the appointed hour, Abraham bound his son Isaac upon the altar. As the sacrificial blade poised to descend, an angel halted his hand. In this crucial moment, God unveiled His divine purpose—a test of Abraham's faith, a trial to affirm his unyielding allegiance not to Himself God but to Abraham himself.

This was not a deception, as one may think, but a lesson that obedience to God is not obedience unless it is perfectly offered back in unquivering obedience. Further, it was God who created Adam and Eve and placed them in the Garden of Eden so that they had to think what they thought and be tempted by the devil (Gen 2 and 3). He did not do that knowing that Adam and Eve would disobey Him; He did it knowing that Adam and Eve would be obedient to Him. Thus, He could also demand something from me that goes against my reason. He demands self-surrender and absolute obedience, and such obedience brings about grace which God bestows. Nothing should matter except doing the will of God. From that moment on, I changed my attitude towards how I reacted to certain knowledge.

The experience instilled some 'epistemological humbleness' in me. By the same token, it left in me a sense of inferiority—a sense that I could never know it all, even when I desired to. No longer did I ruthlessly defend everything I knew to be true; rather, with a deep sense of introspection and awareness, I encountered everything I believed and what others appeared to hold subjectively true. I understood that one may know a tiny speck of an avalanche of truth, but one cannot stop trying to know since we possess some level of knowledge about the truth.

Consequently, we are impelled to press forward in our quest for wisdom and understanding. In them lies both the beauty and the challenge of the human condition—the beauty of our boundless curiosity and the challenge of our inherent limitations. The quest must be to understand rather than to argue or prove one's intellectual prowess. In his *Critique of Pure Reason*, Kant described understanding more perfectly as that which calls into action the faculty of cognition. In these circumstances, various interpretations become apparent based on varying circumstances, revealing the capacity of this faculty.

They assemble into more or less comprehensive collections depending on the time or depth of contemplation devoted to them. For Kant, understanding goes beyond mere empirical observation and instead serves as a fundamental element of human thought. It is not just a passive absorption of information but an active process that organises and gives structure to our perceptions. Kant underscores that understanding functions through a set of innate categories or concepts intrinsic to the human mind. These categories, including space, time, causality, and substance, act as the lens through which we structure and make sense of our experiences. They are not acquired through experience but are essential prerequisites for the very possibility of experience.

But aside from Kant's intellectual sophistication, the Bible had made the importance of seeking understanding in one's life clearly unambiguous. Here, I reckon a chapter in the book of Proverbs says: "Buy truth and do not sell: wisdom instruction and understanding!" (Prov 23:23). It stands as a powerful acknowledgement that truth, as it were, can be bought from any medium or channel, but understanding cannot be purchased or acquired through material means. Going a step further, we also see that it is not enough to have understanding; we need the wisdom to make wise counsel and desist from a dogmatical approach to the phenomenon. This is shown more clearly in Solomon's prayer for wisdom in Wisdom chapter 9.

Here, wisdom is personified as a being, somebody that can be desired and embodied. The personification of wisdom gives us the notion that wisdom is a companion or guide, someone with whom we can interact. Wisdom is not simply an abstract concept but rather a living presence that can provide guidance, insight, and understanding to those who seek it. It is depicted as having her own agency, intentionality, and the ability to interact meaningfully with those who seek her.

To acquire her means humility and absolute dependence on God, in whom Wisdom is rooted.

The school became lively and enjoyable. I began making more friends, actively engaging with my classmates, and initiating conversations. Our discussions revolved around Catholic dogmas and doctrine, including the papacy, priestly celibacy, the Blessed Virgin Mary, and the children of Fatima. Each interaction for me was an opportunity to expand, learn from others, and strengthen my own perspective. We often discuss the intricacies of religion, swapping stories and sharing frustrations about things we cannot understand. The thought of becoming a priest resurfaced, this time personally to me, but I dismissed it out of uncertainty and a sense of inadequacy.

I wanted to enjoy this school and had already been doing that. As the first term came to a close, I found myself unexpectedly in the fourth position, a result that was far from what I had in my previous school. Initially, it was unpleasant, and disappointment threatened to overshadow me. My father, too, appeared to be disappointed. It was not what he expected, but he could not punish me for it either. I remember telling my family that it was my first term and there was still time to work hard. Thus, I still have the opportunity to meet up in school.

There was nothing much to do during the holiday. I tried to read books previously read by my siblings. I went to the centre every day and always led in prayer. My mother found support from my siblings as they worked together at her shop. My brothers were meant to take charge of sourcing the yams from local suppliers, whilst she handled the logistics, transportation and storage to ensure that the yams remained fresh and accessible for the customers.

Meanwhile, my eldest sister started thinking of starting up a business to help the family. She contemplated so many things and later settled on peeling melon seeds, drying them, and selling them on the market. The business was everything but the most fun I had during my childhood. The seeds are often tightly coated, requiring patience and precision to remove the skin without damaging the fruit. It is a delicate and time-consuming task.

But of course, she often rewards the effort by buying me snacks and Christmas toys and giving me some pocket money. I fondly remember the first toy gun bought for me, as a Christmas gift. I was filled with delight so pure as I opened the present, revealing a shiny metal with a combination of plastic designs... My friends and I would embark on epic battles against imaginary foes and defend our fortress. I remember shielding it from the public eye each time I used it. To see it is to lose its value and appreciation.

For such reasons, her business was more than just her business—it was my job, both during the holiday and throughout the school session. Each time I return from school, I dedicate time to it after doing my assignment unless there is no melon to be peeled. My immediate sister also joined the venture. It comes with a punishment, whooping, particularly if I do not. She has the support of my parents and older siblings.

Apparently, there was nothing neither I nor my immediate sister could do about it. Feelings of frustration and desire to do things other than peel melons were often there but they were frowned upon most of the time. However, I saw the value of supporting her instead of dwelling on what I could do for myself.

When school reopened after the holiday break, I was so excited to be back to my daily routine. The first day at school was an empty classroom cloaked in dust and cobwebs. Our desks and chairs sat in solemn silence, and the teachers, too, seemed to share in the quietude. That particular Monday, our classroom served as a stage for an unexpected lesson that did not come from textbooks or lectures but from brooms, mops, and buckets of water. No formal lessons were scheduled, and our task for the day was clear: to roll up our sleeves and restore our classroom to its former glory.

I felt a sense of optimism and excitement for that day and the days ahead. As the clock struck 12:00 pm, we stood still and said the Angelus. The Angelus almost marked the end of the day, as there were no lectures to be had. One hour later, we prepared to dismiss for the day. We took our rucksacks and went home.

In the weeks following the resumption of school, the normal school routine was set in motion. Many students had returned from the break, and teachers had drawn their curriculum for the term. There was lots of challenge and pressure to do better than last term. Outside the classroom, extracurricular activities were also provided. Opportunities for personal growth and self-expression.

We needed to start thinking about the education week. Whether it was joining drama clubs, participating in sports teams, or engaging in cultural dance. I took little interest in the drama club because I did not know how to wear another persona. But I did more recitations and debates. Later, in primary six, I joined the drama club, which was specifically created for that purpose.

There, I played the court register in D. Olu Olagoke's novel, *The Incorruptible Judge*. It was one of those moments that made a huge impression on me, especially on the importance of decency and accountability in building a nation. Further, it offered me the opportunity to explore myself and fasten my verbal eloquence.

The court register was, of course, a challenging yet rewarding experience for me. I look back in filial gratitude at how the literature partly contributed to my inquisitiveness. I had this character and sought to capture his essence on stage. From his mannerisms, speech patterns and verbal eloquence to his motivations and inner struggles. The literature spurred my interest in law and matters of justice, bribery, integrity and corruption.

I remember I began dreaming of a legal career where I could make a tangible impact on my country's legal system. I would position myself sitting on the bench and acquitting those who have been deprived of existential minimum. The corrupt and unjust practices that had long tarnished the reputation of our legal system had no place in my legal practice. I imagined myself as a champion, using the rule of law to hold the untouchable ones accountable.

Although I did not know much about Nigeria's legal system, the novel renders the notion that there could be some kind of bribery and corruption in Nigeria's legal system. I was engulfed with this fire to establish some kind of legality and ensure accountability like Mr Justice Faderin, the judge in the novel. My dream was to wipe out those incompetent, retrogressive elements who nourished themselves with the blood of the poor. One might say that a typical Nigerian childhood is reading those novels with moral instructions. In actual effect, they are a critical depository of wisdom and knowledge to help us conduct checks and balances on questions regarding our national identity and the progress of the most populated country in Africa.

Recently, as I observe how things unfold in the country, I feel that the morals of that novel have long been forgotten. Thus, I feel the same rage. Whenever I watch or read about them, I cannot fathom how evil could have become more bland than the transformation of our courtroom into a slaughterhouse for the common man. Clothed in their legal gown, I cannot but imagine how far Satan has gone to chart out condemnation of man in his natural givenness… Their actions not only undermine the very essence of justice but also erode the trust and faith that people place in the legal system.

It is not difficult to sustain this feeling based on the perspective presented by the so-called political elites. For we can no longer deny that the cases concerning the common man, be it a protester who stands at the bar for his life or a girl who has been violated by a political tycoon in which an advocate engages in Nigeria, are frequently devoid of the political interest of the ruling party to maintain the same dilapidated status quo. And with a system now so full of technicalities where rigid adherence to precedent dominates every argument in court, and in an era when, to avoid the reproach of being emotional or theatrical, advocates hardly venture into moral appeals or powerful rhetoric, much of the reverence once afforded to the dignity of their office and the eloquent of their speech now appear insignificant or exaggerated.[1] Perhaps none of them was ever truly called to the vocation of advocacy; thus, the consciousness of the contrast between the dignity of their profession and the ideals of politicians has become blurred. On the other hand, the upper and lower chambers, which are supposed to prevent this mockery of an extraordinary and reputable office, are, by their *modus operandi*, expected to examine any appointment of a Chief Justice. However, the two houses appear indignant at the encroachment of the ruling party's boss upon their privileges and obligations to the citizens.

Therefore, the necessity for justice lavishes on uncontrolled pleasures as they jubilate and furnish their earthly dwellings with indulgence. One explanation for this outrageous sacrilege is that a thorough investigation into any Chief Justice's or other advocates' sincerity and resolution might reveal that many of them have secured their office through dubious means or have received them as a safeguard to protect their own secrets and those of their allies. As a result, they may not refuse to confirm such appointments, fearing the loss of political favours after the people have cast their ballots.

It would be needless for us to dwell on the evils of such practices; they are too obvious to require further comment or your research. They operate not in the shadows but in plain sight, still devoid of the moral compass to navigate legal complexity. I wonder what Hortensius will think of them: that their minds, which were supposed to be filled with legal facts, have become a dungeon for every kind of dirty trick and underhanded tactics… I wonder if we shall still honour them *propter necessitate*, for even if every man stands in need of justice and of the law, at all times in all places, as Hortensius opines, we cannot be certain in the delivery of the justice. Surely, the law is no longer the rule of justice but the very instrument for doing injustice.

Then there are the so-called political elites–so-called because their actions reveal nothing about their class but rather the decay within the country. There are two reasons why the majority of them came to power: total domination of national wealth without any concrete, actionable plan for economic growth, or if any, not commensurate with the political class of their mother country. As far as this class is concerned, they are chiefly concerned with exporting our raw materials to Europe, functioning as its farmers and extractors, whilst importing finished products that reinforce that dependency cycle and underdevelopment. This arrangement ensures that their power and privilege remain intact, even as their actions undermine the long-term prospects of their own nations.

Yet, they consistently demand the nationalisation of the economy and trade sectors. From their perspective, however, nationalising the economy does not entail dedicating the entire economic system to serving the nation's needs. Nor does it involve governing the state in accordance with the new social dynamics that entail restructuring it to serve the nation's collective needs or prioritising the welfare of its people. Instead, for these elites, nationalisation merely represents the transfer of unjust colonial-era privileges into the hands of native individuals.[2]

The second reason is to pin the masses against themselves–*ruthlessly* by turning their attention away from the very mechanisms that have kept them in bondage. The Northern part has always been their weapon of divisiveness—supporting a different kind of agenda with some presumed autonomy they have to enjoy enormous patronage of power than the rest of the masses.[3] Perhaps, with the inclusion of the South-West in the current political landscape, their mission to induce divisiveness continues to flourish unchecked. Their animosity towards the Igbos, fueled by the resentment, continues to manifest as a reversed hatred towards the imperial rule, which has cost them national identity.

But although the country's partition makes it easy to prove that the northern part is the most disadvantaged region of the country, its people are less ready to heed a clarion call, which sets the fierce struggle for freedom in motion. Broadly, this reflects a larger reality: the masses lack a shared consciousness of common interest and the specific articulateness needed to pursue determined, limited, and achievable goals.[4] The term *masses* applies to them primarily in a quantitative sense—capturing their sheer number as casualties of political extravagance, apathy, or a combination of both.[5] This is not only true in Nigeria but can be observed across other African nations and globally. These masses have often been transformed into political thugs, devoid of valid political opinions, hardly ever go to the polls–simply disconnected from meaningful political action.

The psychology of such individuals, marked by a fragmented sense of self, makes them more susceptible to political manipulation. This allows them to absorb and permit the introduction of political propaganda into the political system whilst remaining indifferent to the arguments of true nationalists. These attitudes place them outside political discourse and actions and enable them to form a group of sympathisers within their own tribes. Their role is not to engage with opposing arguments and propose solutions but to pursue arguments that will end up destabilising the country and, eventually, destroy their opponent. They present their arguments not in a manner that is within the control of a healthy individual but as invariably originating from a profound social and psychological fragmentation. The degree to which such individuals have succeeded in Nigeria and elsewhere in Africa is not merely a product of the mutilation inflicted upon them by their colonial masters. As Fanon puts it, it is also the result of intellectual laziness, lack of vision, and spiritual poverty among the middle class, which wields political power in these countries and the global outlook that its mind is set in without being grounded in the reality of its own people.[6] One member encapsulated this deficiency, when, in mockery, he asked his opponent: "*Na statistics we go chop?*" mirroring that despicable weakness and lack of interest in acquiring scientific and professional knowledge to help them develop tools and transform their environment into a place where humans can thrive.

Indeed, not everyone possesses Ronald Fisher's statistical prowess. In fact, too much emphasis on STEM[1] education has contributed to a decline in political interest and engagement. We may owe this discovery to Arendt in her book, *The Human Condition*. Be that as it may, we cannot concur without making a fool of ourselves that our interlocutor's question is from a source which can at least answer the basic philosophical question: Why are there things rather than nothing? If one is not proficient in statistical knowledge, one ought to at least be skilled in oratory. Every man must at least have something in him that commands respect–some insight, expertise or talent that makes his presence substantial and meaningful. But the political class which took power at the end of the colonial regime has left us disillusioned.

In their blatant narcissism, they are easily convinced that by turning a blind eye to their people's broader needs and replacing collective will with their selfish gains, they can eventually become like the mother country. But that misguided arrogance, which literally characterises their every move, will not drive them to massive progress; instead, it puts them, to quote Fanon, in the corner where they

---

[1] STEM stands for science, technology, engineering and mathematics.

must send chaotic appeals for aid to the former mother country they position to replace.[7] This class has nothing more than the same transcripts with which their actual and potential resources will be mismanaged. Since independence, they have refused to follow the pathway of industrialisation. They find it impossible to set up profitable factories for themselves and the country, which can only mean they have doubts about their ability to develop and transform their God-given natural environment. At the same time, they are unable to give free rein to their genius but expel them to Europe and North America while importing expertise at a 'fantastic cost.'[8]

Whilst the political class has failed, the university class, which fashions itself as the vanguard of enlightenment, compounds this by perpetuating intellectual dependency that reflects their incomplete rupture with the colonial order. Their intellectual curiosity remains one of dependency shaped more by the mimicry of unscrupulous liberals than by a genuine engagement with the conditions and contradictions of their own society. They are rash to emulate the decadence of Western countries without ever having replicated their earlier phases of exploration and innovation—phases that, regardless of circumstances and our resentment, remain intrinsic achievements of Western countries.[9] From the outset, the university class align itself with the decadence of the Western university class. This is not a case of leaping forward but instead of starting at the endpoint, bypassing the youthful stages of intellectual innovation and growth that characterise a true evolution of thought. Instead of nurturing an authentic intellectual revolution rooted in the specific needs and shared struggles of their own societies and the human condition, they emulate a decadent system that prioritises conformity in worldview over the cultivation of independent critical thought.

The university class will be helped at large on their way to decadence by pulling their genius into the now shredded and commodified Western academic system, where pursuing knowledge is secondary to ticking the diversity box and profit. As Western universities rally around diversity to enhance their image, they attract inquisitive minds from across the globe, not to develop their intellectual and moral independence but to initiate them into networks of ideology and power whilst turning them into tools for maintaining the same structures of domination. We shall return to this point later and, with proof, dispel misconceptions boiling in the reader's mind. For now, the university class no longer cultivate leaders whose eloquence flowers like the force of nature but manufactures functionaries for a globalised oligarchy. The long-term result will be a system in which the true spirit of intellectual inquiry is lost, replaced by a superficial pursuit of credentials and titles, and where the future of *educare* and *educere* is determined not by the needs of the individual but by the interests of a global ideological oligarchy.

In these circumstances where proper political will has been replaced with the pursuit of power for its own sake and moral courage with opportunism, it is only natural for a superstructure similar to a political structure to bear the blame. In this respect, religion serves as that superstructure. Thus, immediately, Marx asserted that religion is the *opium of the masses*, all of them felt some alteration in their consciousness like people under the influence of a chemically induced experience, liberated from the chains tied around their feet and the mucous that clouded their sense of reasoning. They began to see a mechanism of control that had long dictated their reality.

For the first time, African countries began to see religion not as a means of comfort but for what it is: a tool wielded by the imperial master to maintain dominance over them. The biblical promise of eternal rewards for enduring suffering suddenly felt like a strategy to discourage their spirit of resistance and emancipation. Now, they have understood that the structure they had clung to for comfort was, in fact, complicit in sustaining the hardship they suffered and still suffer.

However, they will not understand that their problem is deeply entrenched in the collective mindset, manifesting as a pervasive malaise that breeds corruption, loss of societal values and stagnancy in innovation. On the reverse, it is not surprising because the religious narrative is the single story that everybody, including those in the mother countries, enjoy most.[10] It is convenient and economically productive to the core. It is the easiest way to abandon political and individual responsibility. For a country like Nigeria, where two forms of religion are often at loggerheads with each other, religion is the formula that interprets the country's history, determines its present and shapes its advancement into the future. Any objection is immediately stifled, and intelligent opinions are ruthlessly suppressed. Upon reflection, if religion were a Nigerian problem, as it has always been chanted, the Nigerian problem (whatever that is) cannot be solved by becoming irreligious. That in itself is religion and has disastrous consequences; then anything can pass, and the individual can map out his own morality. Jung has it more brilliantly when he says that the religious function "cannot be dislocated without giving rise to secret doubts, which are immediately repressed to avoid conflict with the prevailing trend towards mass-mindedness."[2] Instead, the problem is solved by turning towards the Ideal, the good of religion and man's purpose on earth, which is to expand on the goodness of that good.

In another instance, Jung writes:

> During the past thirty years, people from all civilised countries of the earth have consulted me. I have treated many hundreds of patients, the large number being Protestant, a small number Jews and not more than five or six believing Catholics. Among all my patients in the second half of life–that is to say, over thirty-five–there has not been one whose problem in the last resort was not that of finding a religious outlook on life. It is safe to say that every one of them fell ill because he had lost that which the living religions of every age have given to their followers, and none of them has been really healed who did not regain his religious outlook.[11]

In other words, religion is a vital framework for meaning and psychological health in human life. The loss of religious instinct is synonymous with the loss of meaning. While there is staggering evidence that religion has its excesses in Nigeria and other African countries, it is not the explanation for the pitfall in our national consciousness. We must stop this imitation complex of the West, which, in its quest to secularise, has lost the distinction between right and wrong for reasons we shall seamlessly explore. The blind adoption of secular ideals without proper contextual understanding is de facto the reason there is an exacerbation of the existential vacuum in the West, and for a society like Nigeria and other African countries, they risk eroding the moral and cultural bedrock that sustains their society. Instead, one must take the good out of the ideals whilst discarding elements that do not align even with universal human values.

Actually, what I am here unfolding phrase by phrase, sentence by sentence, are some reflections I have had but did not know how to express them… In fact, it is difficult for me to determine how far some of these books have shaped my

---

[2] Jung C.G *The Undiscovered self* (2014) p. 17.

aspirations and ideas of the world. At such times, I knew I was limited and could do more after encountering them. I would read those lines again and again until I felt they had drained me, and I could no longer contain them. If I had questions, I asked myself, for no one would understand me—I wrote them down.

But I tell you that this might resonate with anyone who has read the play as it portrays the pursuit of justice and righteousness, which are universal categories and aspirations. Thus, dreaming of becoming a lawyer didn't strike me as particularly unique or extraordinary.

Anyway, going back to the second term of my fourth year in primary school, I saw myself experiencing positive growth in school life. This term, my grades improved noticeably. It would never have occurred to me that such a thing would happen. Before the term was over, I could embrace multiple challenges, including participating in external quizzes. I pushed myself to reach new heights at school, surpassing my own expectations.

Even though there were lots of things to be done at home after school, I tried as much as possible to do extra homework and reading in school and outside school. At this time, I discovered my school library, situated towards the end of the classroom block. Therein were also our cultural artefacts and musical instruments; the major reason, why pupils often conflict about the utility of the library.

My first entrance felt like stepping into a wizard's chamber, left to the mercy of time. Cobwebs cling to every corner, shimmering with particles of dust. I wandered through the aisles, and my eyes widened in awe at the shelves filled with countless volumes of literature. It quickly became apparent that the library was well-equipped with literature that I could not afford. No one wonder one actor said that *the library is the most egalitarian aspect of society*. The shelves were lined with books covering a vast array of topics, from classic literature and history to science and philosophy.

Of course, liturgical books were not missing. Here, I found a wealth of resources, the *Ordo Missae* and books of saints. That day, it was more than discovering a repository of books—it was a safe haven where I could retreat from the chants and rants of our classroom building. The first book I picked up from the shelf was *Without a Silver Spoon*, a title that immediately captured my soul. As I flipped through its pages, I was drawn into the protagonist's world and thought it was fate that I read the book.

Set against the backdrop of socioeconomic challenges, Ure offers a glimpse into the lives of ordinary people striving to overcome poverty and pursue their dreams against all odds. Through him, I witnessed familiar struggles and aspirations. The book resonated with me on a deeply personal level, as I saw reflections of my own experiences and aspirations in the story. Like Ure, I, too, have had my own share of convoluted emotions, and I found solace in dancing against all odds with honesty. The book became more than just a story—it became my manual of prayer.

My entire fourth year in primary school could be summarised by this newfound passion for reading. In stark contrast to my previous school experiences, this year was marked by a significant increase in the amount of reading required. My poor parents had to adapt to the demand of continually purchasing books to support my education. I voraciously consumed whatever literature that came my way, eager to expand myself and deepen my understanding of the world. The same year brought significant changes as we relocated from our familiar yard to a new yard, where we rented three rooms approximately 20 miles away.

This transition marked a new chapter in our lives, bringing with it both challenges and opportunities. Here, we were fortunate to have relatively spacious rooms, a far cry from the cramped quarters of our previous yard. The modernised bathroom and toilet facilities added a touch of comfort and convenience to our daily lives, making our living space feel even more welcoming and accommodating for our visitors. But of course, the rent weighed heavily on our finances at about 60,000 naira yearly. My father had to save ten times more than he used to in order to meet his budget. This posed a considerable challenge to us, demanding careful spending to ensure that we could reach the rental agreement whilst still covering our living expenses.

However, despite their best efforts, my parents realised that there was little they could do. It dawned on them that their children were growing, and with that realisation came the understanding that they needed to adapt to the changing circumstances. Around the same time, my immediate sister had taken her common entrance exams and would soon be starting junior secondary school. A discussion arose in our family about the possibility of enrolling her in a school near mine so that we could commute home together after school each day.

As usual, money posed an obstacle initially. Providentially, our financial concerns were alleviated by the generosity of the school's principal, a Knight of the Church. His benevolence made it possible for my immediate sister to enrol, with my parents contributing little to it.

By the time I reached Primary Five, my family's situation had begun to show signs of improvement terribly. My eldest sister landed a job as a salesperson at a popular company in Nigeria. This marked a turning point for my family and my aspiration for education. For the first time, there was financial stability, and we could change meals and eat in-between meals. The financial stability provided by her job alleviated some of the strain we had felt in previous years, easing the burden on our parents and allowing us to breathe a little easier.

With a steady income coming in, we could afford to meet basic needs and even enjoy a few luxuries that had previously been terribly out of reach. I remember the first time she brought catfish home, and it felt financially liberated to me after having my first bite. I felt a sense of gratitude for the simple pleasures in life and the love that my eldest sister had poured into the family with that dish. I felt grateful for the love and support my family had enjoyed hitherto. In that instant, it occurred to me with undeniable clarity that the significance of little things cannot be overstated.

Meanwhile, I continued to excel in my studies. During the following years, I succeeded in becoming the class monitor and began running errands for my form teacher. These positions were absolutely terrifying, but they also shaped my interest in standing in the classroom one day and teaching other students. I will write the names of noisemakers and Igbo speakers in the classroom. There was a fine between 5- and 10-naira naira if I wrote one's name, and I also handled the finances.

I had the privilege of teaching the class, grading papers, and even doing the result work worksheet. I was privileged to know my result beforehand and could actually experience normal blood pressure, while our report cards were being handed to us. Nonetheless, below me were my classmates who were consumed by envy. It spoiled fun because I was not the type that liked engaging in competition. I was eager to show myself, my talents and skills, but not when it is seen as a competition.

This might contradict your reading about my hardcore interest in debate participation. But the truth is that those debates were not an arena to be competitive but to show and fortify one's verbal eloquence, at least the way it appeared to me. I prefer the competition to be unpronounced, by-product and unseen rather than seen and pronounced. In those times of envy, I also had the bitter sting of failure as my performance plummeted, dragging me to the bottom of the class.

To date, I have not been able to provide a reasonable explanation for how this happened. But it was fun for my competitors. I could no longer rely solely on natural intelligence to carry me through; I had to do extra schoolwork to climb up again. Interestingly, I settled somewhere in the class that was perfectly enjoyable. I remember that, in the third term, I held my report card in trembling hands, although I had seen it prior to the closure day.

My form teacher and a few other teachers, including my computer science teacher, whom I remember with the deepest gratitude, showed confidence in me. She was generally a teacher (*rabbi*) and a mother. She gave me much more responsibility to handle. She would give me her lesson notes to go home with after writing for the class on the blackboard. Under her guidance, I flourished, blossoming into a person capable of having ambitions.

I could say the same for all my teachers. There was something spectacular about going to Catholic school, and I got to experience the beauty of it. I do not know how it would have turned out had I not changed school. Writing this, I am filled with the deepest gratitude for their impact and the education I received through them. It is something more than gold, a treasure that God may want to have.

As was customary, this time, my mother began to talk me into going for catechism and receiving the Holy Communion before the end of the third term. I was eleven, then going to twelve in August of the same year. Receiving communion within that age bracket was a deeply ingrained tradition in my family. It was also a prerequisite set by the Church. Then, it is believed that you have attained the knowledge of good and evil.

Also, you would be able to understand the mystery of the Eucharist as the body and blood of Christ. At first, I hesitated, unsure if I was ready to take this step of faith before the end of the term. But the thought of being able at last to receive the white bread consecrated by the priest filled me with so much ecstasy. Around August 2006, during the holiday or later, I began my prayer class, which was the first preparatory lesson to undergo when one is in the process of becoming a communicant. This stage consists of learning about the method of prayer, the Our Father, the Hail Mary and the Creed. It involves learning about the mysteries of the Holy Rosary, joyful, sorrowful, luminous, and glorious mysteries, as well as the lives of saints.

As it happened, I had been taught most of these at our centre and in school. The only difference was that in school, I had thoroughly learnt the Catechism in English; I now faced the daunting task of mastering it in my mother tongue to prepare for my First Holy Communion. It was more of a repetition, although the one for the First Holy Communion appeared to be more extensive than the one I learnt at school. I knew the words even before the brother who was teaching us the catechism says it. Instead of sitting all the time listening to the same lecture, the brother teaching us catechism would call me up to teach the class and answer their questions.

The class often lasts two intense hours of exploring the teachings of the church without personal questions. They always leave that for the block rosary centres, where it is assumed that they have more time to deal with those kinds of questions. In contrast, there was not enough time to deal with deep, troubling questions that weighed one's heart. Whilst valuable for covering essential teachings and doctrines, the two-hour sessions sometimes felt rushed and constrained, leaving little room for in-depth exploration of complex issues. In the same breadth, the brothers, some of whom were seminarians, felt constrained in what they had to utter so that, I presume, they do not open scars of their ignorance.

Rather than focusing on providing doctrinal clarity, they were busy providing doctrinal instructions without delving into the ambiguities of our faith or the doubts and uncertainties we grappled with daily. It was somehow a beautiful nonsense, and I do not know how I passed through it without rebelling. More devastating was the weight of expectation from family to uphold the same standard of holiness whenever I come back home from catechism. It was as if my every action and word was scrutinised against an impossibly and invisibly high bar. My mother has an ugly way of reminding me about that.

Her constant admonitions to be respectful and holier-than-thou always suffocate me. Sometimes, it felt like I was constantly tiptoeing around her watchful gaze, afraid to express my thoughts and feelings for fear of falling short of lofty ideals and glory. It became drastic when I passed this stage in my Catholic faith and decided to join the seminary. Thereafter, her words were like a soundtrack and persuasive chorus of 'you should' and 'you must'. Each time I fall short, I must kneel in deep contrition, crying *mea culpa, mea culpa, mea maxima culpa.*

Indeed, I do not condemn her for her love and ingenuity. I knew her concern came from a place of love and genuine concern. But I wished I had been freer to explore rather than follow the rubrics of the law. When school reopened in September, my schedule grew more constricted as I had to find a balance between the catechism and the rigorous demands of schoolwork. I was now in primary six and had extra lessons organised by the school to prepare for the common entrance.

The catechism classes were often after school hours, adding an extra layer of complexity to an already packed day. This means that once I returned home, I only had to eat, rest for an hour, and rush to the parish for the catechism class. Sometimes, I would go to the catechism class directly from the school if going back home would cut short my time. The classes themselves had become intense, with a heavy emphasis on memorisation and rote learning. We would spend hours poring over our catechism book, reciting prayers, and memorising answers to catechism with so much precision and accuracy.

Making mistakes was a punishable transgression, punishable by the severance of one's place in the class. There was pressure to be flawless, as that might cause withdrawal from the class. Soon, we would take the first exam and move over to B1, where we would begin to learn about God, sin, the Eucharist and other sacraments of the Church.

The new academic session was intense. So many past questions to learn in order to prepare for the examination. Luckily, our form teacher was informed about the expectations that awaited us. This made life a bit easier. by giving us. It also happened that we started talking intensely about our play, which would take place during the graduation ceremony.

Above all, I found myself not alone because some of my schoolmates were preparing for the First Holy Communion same time I was. There was a sense of a shared determination to succeed, make the most of the adventure ahead and get into secondary school. Everyone understood the assignment. The zeal was that even though I may not want to complete secondary school, I could at least finish primary school successfully, as it determines whether one would attend secondary school in the future. I knew I want to attend secondary school, but I was unclear about the school I would attend.

Again, I wanted to go to the seminary, but I brushed it off because I was not sure about such an endeavour. But also because of the financial burden of training a priest in Nigeria. My mother was really concerned about the money, despite the fact that her aspirations for me were clear. If I became a priest, she would love to answer the mother of a priest and be blessed by her son. Contrariwise, my father's involvement was a more distant approach, and his expectations were less overtly communicated.

Nonetheless, he so much believes that God will manifest himself if that is true and if that is what He wants me to do. For him, it is always "Let not my will, but Thy will be done."

He had a totally unspoken imagination of me achieving higher education, which should manifest without knowing how or what it truly means. My understanding of his vision was undeniably irritating. Whose will, and how is this will different from the burning flame in my heart to do the will of God? Or was it simply the will of fate, an impersonal force shaping my destiny in ways beyond my canal comprehension? Meanwhile, where is this desire coming from? I asked myself all the time. These questions gnawed me, and I reckon simply embracing the uncertainty to be at peace.

Around November, I took my catechism exam and reached the top of the class. I was filled with excitement, and my family was, too. I was now going to the B1 level, and hopefully, it would be clear that I would be receiving Holy Communion on the coming Easter Sunday. This also meant that I could start sourcing what to wear for the momentous occasion of my First Holy Communion. While all of this was unfolding, I still had to maintain my focus on school.

As the days turned into weeks, the first term exam began to loom large, with heavy homework rolling in its coaster. The tasks were not only about the first term exam—more extensively, the final exam. In the weeks before the exam, I dedicated my time to burning my midnight lantern till there was no kerosene. When the period finally arrived, it passed as if nothing had happened. Significantly, my grade improved; I emerged second overall in the final year.

The gentle hand of fortune has graced me. Two heights have been achieved. The satisfaction was stimulating, and so was everyone in my family. I felt a profound sense of gratitude for the support and encouragement at the time, from teachers who had guided us with wisdom and patience to family members who had offered support. The holiday season came with so much excitement. As quickly as it had come, it seemed to vanish, leaving no trails of remembrance.

We returned to the familiar school environment to take on the final stretch of the academic year.

The atmosphere was electric, charged with a sense of anticipation. The mock exam was the forthcoming exam to prepare for. Also, it was time we started registering for the common entrance exam, which was our final year exam. So many emotions swirled thinking about life after primary school, especially where to attend secondary school, knowing full well that my family could not afford expensive secondary school. I vividly recall taking the registration form, not knowing what to fill in the column of prospective secondary schools.

I wanted to go to a good but not expensive school. I wanted to attend a school where I did not have to sacrifice myself for something else. My mother suggested the school that my older brothers had gone to, but I did not like them, all things considered. Mainly because it was a government school, and a lot happened at government schools as opposed to private schools. I approached my father, but his response was not different from that of my mother.

I told them that was not too fond of the school, but not vehemently. Each school represented a different path for a unique opportunity to pursue unique dreams and aspirations. I wanted to continue with Christ the King Cathedral Secondary School, but my parents did not have the finances. My eldest sister was being looked upon to contribute financially, but until then, she had not commented nor shown any sign that she would do something. It was a bizarre feeling that I would be forced into what I did not like because of finance. I ended up filling out schools they suggested with the hope that life would turn and do my bidding.

This would be the same period I would take my final exam before the culmination of my receiving Holy Communion. I immersed myself in this last phase, trying to understand what I would feel when I received the Holy Communion. There had been stories of how the saints felt when they received Him, but I was worried about how I would feel. Would my body change into another state? How would the Eucharist affect me? The answers to these have been given in the catechism, namely that the Holy Eucharist reduces the propensity to sin and gives us everlasting life.

But how and when would that take place, and how would I measure it? I spent each moment reading the catechism privately and reviewing the scriptural references. I was tempered by moments of contemplation and deep reflection of the presence of divine mystery in that white bread. One thing struck me as particularly profound, namely the definition of receiving the Holy Eucharist, which I never came across in the Catholic doctrine I learnt in school. Indeed, to receive the Holy Eucharist is to receive the Body, Blood and Soul of Christ and the *godness* of our Lord Jesus Christ in the form of bread and wine.[3] I found this explanation in my mother tongue to be more theologically profound.

The word 'soul', was something new and different. Obviously, it must hint at a mystery I have not considered before. Only recently was I able to understand that the soul points to the mingling of the bread with the wine after transubstantiation. This points to the union of our body and the soul as well as the union of Christ with the Church. Each time I receive the Holy Eucharist, I embody not only a theological concept that has been fashioned ages before my birth but a real person, his body, blood and soul—the medicine to my ailment.

To embody that means to fully internalise and live out the spiritual significance of receiving the body and blood of Christ. It is not enough to understand the theological concepts; those are ways through which God choose to have an immediate experience with us. The understanding is then shown by the integration of the mystery in our faith and daily lives.

At that moment, I reckon telling myself that I was unworthy to go into this blessed union. Would I be faithful? On the other hand, I thought that perhaps I needed to know what I knew in order to orient myself towards the ideal. Thus, I decided to attempt the exam and prepare for my Holy Communion. As I expected, I passed the exam, and every odd against me partaking in the Holy Eucharist that Sunday was ruled out.

Then, we had our sacrament of absolution, marking the conclusion of the catechism class. My family was happy. As custom demands, one person would have to be present during the Mass to light the candle for me. My mother would be there for the Mass and the lighting of candles. I had my white shirt and short neatly ironed and my shoes polished for Easter Sunday. On 8 April 2007, the long-awaited moment to partake in the Holy Communion arrived.

The first pews were sparkling in white sleeves and veils whilst our parents and guardians sat behind us. The homily delivered by the priest, although it was centred on the feast of the resurrection, was also centred around us and the significance of the sacrament. During the consecration, I tend to observe the actions of the priest in relation to what has been taught in the catechism classes.

---

[3] In Igbo: Inata Oriri di aso bu inata Ahu na Obara na mkpuruobi na abumchukwu nke Nna anyi Jeeso Kristi, no na Yukarisia. See Katikizim nke Okwukwe Nzuko Katolik n' asusu Igbo, pg. 90. 1996 edition.

When my turn to receive the Holy Eucharist reached, my heart started beating faster than before.

It all came back again, what I have learnt about the Holy Eucharist. I started making the act of contrition in silence till I slipped out my tongue and received a flat substance fell on my lips. Then was a sudden tranquillity within me. I prayed and then left to my sitting position.

After the Mass, I remember not knowing what happened and being eager to decipher if the Holy Eucharist had had any effect on me. In contrast to what was said in the catechism, I did not feel the mystery, but I felt my smile and some tranquillity. Those were memories that are vividly present whenever I reflect nostalgically on this day.

My mother and I took some photos and walked home. After a few hours of reaching home, she called, sat me down and began her own sermon with a litany of advice and expectations. I had expected it, even though not immediately. But here I am, listening to another sermon. It appeared to be a total frustration to me. The worst is how the sense of inadequacy would start creeping in and being judged by my proclivity for guilt. There was more to how I should behave than how I see and react to things. I could not help but wonder if she understood the turmoil that rages within me sometimes, the uncertainty and doubt that clouded my thoughts. Amidst the frustration, I took it heart to make sense of them.

When we returned to school after the Easter break, there were fewer activities for us except for our common entrance examination. Additionally, for me, was the play to be during the graduation. I felt somewhat happy that I could now participate in Holy Communion during our weekly Mass. It was an honour to stand up and join the cue, proceeding to the altar for the Holy Eucharist. In the same breath, I felt a bit weird within me, thinking that it was all going to end soon and that I did not know about the future.

What happens if I attend a school that I do not like? How do I find myself afterwards? Still, I made sure that I was not paralysed by my uncertainties. I made a silent vow to myself—to accept whatever comes my way and never lose sight of that dream. I knew that no matter what lay ahead, I had the power to carve out my own destiny and create a future that was uniquely mine.

In the days leading up to the exam, tension mounted as we performed the last-minute revision. Our form teachers did their best to see that we did not only stand out as individuals but also as a school. Time stood still as we held the questions in our hands.

Everything appeared to fade away: family, friends, and dreams, with only the stark reality of the exam before me. At that time, I could feel my breath and sense my heartbeat very gently. Within a few hours, the exam was done, and the burden was lifted. At last, I could sing my *Gloria in Excelsis Deo* .

I recounted this feeling to my mother during the graduation ceremony. I also told her that I was not sure about what came next and did not want to take the road. In fact, I cannot attend any other school, if not where I chose. Oddly enough, I have seen my future therein—not anywhere else. As understanding as she was, she did not have the resources to actualise the wish.

Providentially, my sister made it happen and I was registered at the same Catholic school. Meanwhile, the play of *The Incorruptible Judge* was a resounding success. From the time the curtain rose to the final bow, the reaction of the audience was electrifying, and the applause and cheers were so loud that they could cause an earthquake, shaked. There was a shared hope that Nigeria would be better—a yearning to wipe away impunity and for people to be treated not on the basis of their socioeconomic status but because of their natural talent. There were reflections on godliness whilst being human, and much wisdom poured out from grey hairs. How and when this would happen remains to me an open question hanging in the air like a tantalising mystery box.

But one thing is certain: in a very real sense, a society that has lost focus on what defines its existence cannot orient itself towards the good. For the existence of any society is derivative of something which is perfect, complete, lovable and eternal. Something which no one can reproduce or replace without upsetting the balance between chaos and order. The political process in Nigeria and by extension politics in general must be subjected to an ideal beyond the political process… If we assume that our leaders must cease their exorbitant lifestyles, stop displaying their dark proclivities, and prioritise the lives of the commoners, then perhaps we can begin to pave the way for a new society. Eventually, things will go sideways, but there will be advancement. There will be new problems, but the old ones will pass away. There would be leadership and service when self-aggrandisement is gone. There would be crime, but there would be accountability.

III
Formative Years

I set myself apart from my peers and was exposed to various social situations and societal norms. Simultaneously, the desire to join the seminary became stronger within me, a yearning that went beyond a mere subjective feeling. It was a profound calling to submit myself to God, much like the psalmist describes—'as the deer yearns for running streams, so my soul longed for you, O God.'

To some extent, I envisioned the priesthood as the ideal path to fulfil this profound call. I devoted myself to this calling with deep commitment, striving to answer it to the best of my ability. However, life soon took an unexpected turn, presenting me with new challenges and opportunities I could not have foreseen. In the following pages, I will recount these experiences, embracing both the trials and the growth that came with them.

Do not expect any explosive insight today—nothing I say here that others have not expressed with greater clarity. But, I invite you to consider them anew, as today is not about originality but deepening our understanding. I write this chapter not out of anger; my blood is not boiling, and I have no fever. Instead, I am compelled by an urgent sense of responsibility to confront our deepest fears—the demons and truths we often shy away from.

After my primary six, I was blessed by my sister who gave my mother some money to register me for my school choice. So, I continued with my junior secondary school at the same school to let myself be there whilst what is hibernating in me manifests properly. Our school was an uncompleted building, with rain splashing over our bodies from the window if it rained heavily. Nonetheless, I had a great time studying at the school. We were given fertile soil from science to art subjects to grow our seeds and flourish.

I was good at science, which has to do with the human mind and behaviour. I cherished so much guidance and counselling. The subject offered me the ability to see things clearly. Having completed my year 3 at the secondary school, I decided to leave and join the seminary. As difficult as the decision was to make, I also believed it was the right choice, given my time in discernment and how things had unfolded for me.

Moreover, I met a priest with whom I discussed my intention and who gave me some guidelines on how to proceed. Things were more apparent enough, and I was sure it was my own decision and never that of my family or peers. As earlier said, my father was ambivalent about the decision. For him, going to the seminary was like brushing one's talent under the carpet. He expected more from me, an academic.

Although he has not been educated himself, he has tremendous respect for educated people and has always believed education to be the way to manage the vicissitudes of life. I understood his worry, but at the same time, I wanted to allow things to unfold. If I did make it, I could study something that deals with human behaviour. I intended to do further studies in psychology to become a counsellor, which then I thought matched very well with the priestly vocation. So our worries may turn into achievements sometime in the future, I thought to myself.

With the help of my eldest sister, I procured the entrance examination form for the seminary, took the exam, and made it to the set. It was a blissful moment for my family, including my father, who had not primarily shown interest. I did not mind that I was demoted to my immediate class as the seminary did not accept candidates who had already taken the Junior School Certificate Examination (JSCE) in another school. Thus, I would have to repeat JSS3 and proceed from there. Hitherto, I had not repeated any class.

Rather, I skipped a class which you read from the beginning. I did not mind that I would now be called Ernest instead of Chetachukwu, which bears not only my identity as a person but also my heritage and my union with my ancestors. At first, this felt strange and unfamiliar, like a shedding layer of my identity.

But I told myself that things worketh for good for those who believe. This challenge is what I must overcome and abide by the rules of the seminary. Dedicating myself to this course, I will achieve whatever I want. How much I am willing to give into it will also determine how much I will take from it. Money was contributed, and my mother acquired all the properties for me to start school.

That morning, on a bike, my mother and I arrived at the seminary. Everywhere was green and bushy. The seminarians had been on a long holiday. In consequence, no one would cut the field. It would be our first manual labour the week after arrival day. I brought my matchet with me, which gave me a blister whenever I used it.

But I was told I would get used to it in the long run. And indeed, I did. Surely, there was no other option. To remain in the seminary formation, one must learn to do manual labour. Manual labour is part and parcel of the seminary formation. It is a form of prayer, *laborare est orare*, our superiors would tell us.

A seminarian who cannot do manual labour cannot also care for his parish if he becomes a priest. Such a person is not accepted into the major seminary. Even when accepted, he will be spotted and expelled. Thus, even if one does not care, he should care for the sake of his vocation.

Accordingly, when we arrived, a seminarian in his pastoral year was waiting for the new intakes. My mother and I were received together with other minor seminarians who arrived. We had some formalities done and then taken to our dormitories. Our parents did not follow us. It is forbidden for them to accompany us to the dormitory.

The same goes for visiting days and parents' meetings. No seminarian was allowed to take his family and relatives to the dormitory. Thereupon, it became clear to my mother the magnitude of my choice and future life.

Initially, it hurt, albeit we were mentally prepared. Although, I can only speak for myself and do not know to what degree my mother was mentally prepared. Emotionally detaching herself from her son suddenly came as a shock and must have hurt her. In any case, I believed she was fine and very well-ready. Of course, some of us cried in the arms of our parents at the very instance they bid farewell.

They had to let us go, as vital as it was, for no parent would want his ward to be spotted or nicknamed. For many of us, that was our first moment of being away from home and gaining independence. The living conditions were relatively new—and to the extent it was, some boys were bed-wetting after the first few weeks we arrived. I know of my classmate who was bed-wetting even in the senior class. He often feels ashamed when he does.

But apart from that, doing laundry was also a challenge for most of us. The dirty laundry from some boys was carefully stored and washed when the scent apprehended the natural aura of the hostel. One cannot help but wonder if they actually did anything at home at all. Interestingly, one of us had a maid before he entered the seminary. It is for this that I understand why the Church applies these rules to enforce emotional detachment and self-determination.

The reception could not have happened; otherwise, most of us would be attending day school instead of boarding school. More so, it was necessary to develop human and psychological stability to confront the ever-changing dynamic nature of the priesthood. I think the individual as a seminarian has his own fate to follow and the road other human beings trod before him. He must live his life there without disturbance and contamination.

Otherwise, he will likely grow defenceless and helpless, having no moral compass to navigate existential contingencies.

Here, the writings of Erich Neumann in the History and Origin of Consciousness also come to my mind as something that helped me understand the concept. He writes that once a child reaches the threshold of consciousness and can make a conscious decision, giving him the freedom to experience life from his own standpoint is necessary. According to Neumann, when the child is still in the mother's womb or the uterus, the 'round' of mythology, the *urobos*, and when he is still in the infantile stage, he is enwrapped, sheltered, nourished and protected from the devouring mother nature. He calls it the 'embryonic stage'[1] of human consciousness development because the maternal side of the uterus dominates this stage of a child's ego-consciousness development. All the positive maternal traits are present at this stage of development as the child has no activity of his own.

The mother and the child are one; she comforts and gives nourishment and pleasure to the child. The second stage, the 'alimentary'[12], is marked by self-gratification, hunger, and food. Here, the child's waste is used to provide his food; anything obtained is eaten. Then, in the third stage, when the mother has nothing to do with the infantile stage, the child begins to differentiate himself from his mother; he becomes distinct and can eat and excrete; it is a sign that the end of the 'uroboric autarchy'[13] or the maternal benevolence has come. This means detachment from the mother and entering the world to encounter universal principles, the essential individual development tasks. Self-formation is necessary, as it would determine how the child would stand against challenges.[14]

The same could be seen in the writings of Jung, where he talks about individuation, a process of psychological rebirth that is more evident in adult life.[5] He writes that nature itself necessitates a cycle of demise and renewal, as articulated by the alchemist Democritus. These natural transformations occur regardless of our awareness, exerting substantial psychological impacts. The mature man must, once more, free himself from the world and stand by himself.

I say this to clarify that all these were necessary to understand that the regulations are not intended to cause emotional damage.

Although it can hurt the child, he must understand the turn his life has taken and construct an ideal that will guide him throughout the journey. Such wisdom could be seen in the Church's documents on priestly formation. The alternative is that the individual becomes fractured and impotent.

When I finished unpacking my luggage, I returned to the reception and bid farewell to my mother. Then, I went back to my dormitories in the solitude of my heart, imagining my life in the next four months. Now, I have begun a new chapter and would settle into it to make it my own. My life will become fully grown if I work very hard. In the first few months, I will find my way exploring the halls of the seminary and listening to what it has to say to me.

Making new friends is definitely an option, and trying new hobbies, too. I will embrace the dorm life and teach my family what I have learnt when I get home. If I push through and abide by all the seminary rules and regulations, I will graduate, go to the senior seminary and become a priest.

These were my thoughts, and shortly, it was time for chapel.

We joined in the vespers to thank God for journey mercies and the gift of our vocation. A short speech was given by the bursar, who welcomed us to the seminary on behalf of the rector. This is not an official welcome by the diocesan bishop, who declares the academic year open. The opening of the academic year is performed simultaneously with the 'investiture', whereby the seminarian is clothed as a seminarian with the school uniform. Until then, he continues to wear his 'daywear', which is worn by every seminarian in the evenings, apart from causal wear.

In essence, the speech was a formality to kindle the seminary's life in us. "The seminary is your new home," he said in a calm and comforting voice whilst exalting us to be good seminarians and take our formation seriously. This stuck with me and gave me the courage to move forward.

Now, my dependence on my family will have to be reduced, and my love for the seminary be prioritised. I must do everything possible to protect my stay in this newfound home. Indeed, being able to stay also means having a thriving vocation. As I decided to come, I decided to stay until God decided otherwise, which I hoped he did not, but He did. In *bonus fidei, I accepted His decision because even then, He neither ceases to make me a figure among gentiles nor stops calling me out from my low moments and* into abundant grace.

Like the psalmist, I sometimes wonder what is in the mind of God that he gives me counsel, mortal man that he directs and perfects my plan, a man who is merely a breath and whose utmost desire has been anathematised by the irrational judgement of man. There must be something about Him that I cannot fathom even when I reach the depth of my knowledge. He cannot be confined to a system. He must be experienced, embodied, and lived.

After the welcome speech and exaltation, the orientation week regulation was read to us, and we departed to the refectory. The food was different—nothing like home. Looking at it, one sees the nature of the country's economic situation. We sat adjacent to each other with our plates and cutleries. We said grace and the meal was shared.

Some of us did not eat, including me, given the food we brought from home. However, I took some grocery, *soso* in the seminary vocabulary, a mixture of biscuits, cornflakes, golden moon or *garri* with milk and sugar and so on as best suits the person. Such groceries are necessary to sustain oneself, especially during Lent, when the quantity of meals is reduced. At the end of supper, we had recreation, where we got to know ourselves. It was a spectacular moment.

We questioned ourselves about what led us to this journey. Needless to say, it is not a one-time conversation, but for the first moment, one gets a glimpse of what motivates the other. For some, it was a personal decision based on personal experience, whilst for others, acquiring the education and formation was more important. Some did not entirely have a reason but were still in the process of discernment. Thus, they entered the seminary to discover their calling.

A while later, the bell rang. It was time for compline. Again, we all assembled in the chapel. The night prayer was said, and we retired to bed *in magnum silentium*. But people could still move around until the lights were eventually out.

The seminary schedule is such that it runs consecutively. The next programme begins with rising around 5:15 am on weekdays and 6:00 pm on weekends—and runs till the next day. Usually, after the Compline, there should be a night prep immediately. However, this regulation was relaxed since it was orientation week, as we have yet to be taught. Regardless of the stress and frustrations, the schedule was one of the things that could mould one into a perfect being or marr one.

It appears simple but is, in fact, full of complexities and quite easy to default. The defaulters are marked and punished severely with whipping and hard labour.

The exact type and weight of labour are indeterminate and rest heavily on the discretion of one's superior. If one is lucky, the person might get a field to trim, a farm to cultivate or firewood to fetch. Else, once could be knelt and flogged to bring painful elaboration.

At one time, my classmate was deeply wounded after an extreme whipping and was rushed to the infirmary. The seminarian who whipped him was neither cautioned nor told not to flog again. Such incidents are considered the actual act of discipline. They have acquired a moral legitimisation which constitutes a system of belief. Neither the parents nor the guardians have anything to say in that regard. Otherwise, their sons would be placed under surveillance or returned to their parents—not intact, but with bruises and sickness.

In my solitude, I always thought about the terrible nature of this punishment and how our lives could have been without it. Indeed, the importance of discipline in the seminary must be maintained. It is much easier to run into a crisis without a system of discipline to guide and regulate our behaviour. The seminary formation is divided into four aspects, according to the Church's Apostolic Exhortation on the Formation of Priests, *Pastores dabo vobis*: human, spiritual, intellectual, and psychological formation.[15] These four aspects are laid out to give the priest a necessary foundation to interact with the world and its changes, and one-in-the-line formation must take them seriously.

However, I came to the conclusion that what we were doing was no longer punishment. On the contrary, we were busy overturning the spirit of the exhortation—whilst allowing our dark proclivity to play out in the background. The discipline is a substitute for human interrelatedness. In turn, the seminarian fears his superiors instead of bringing out his real self, virtues, and vices to be formed. However, it remained challenging for me to draw such a conclusion, given our sophisticated way of perceiving and justifying the actions we take in the seminary and our tendency to attribute them as essential for our formation to the priesthood, regardless of its apparent cruelty.

Somehow, I thought this was caused by the lawlessness and some superiority complex of people vested with the mantle of shepherdship but see themselves as demigod incapable of error. Thereby inflicting a culture of brutality on their subjects. Worst still, there is always a biblical injunction, 'spare the rod and spoil the child', to back it up as if the Bible was meant for that particular purpose without knowing that there are other ways to discipline aside from corporeal punishment. Teachers brutalise their students in order to mould them into socially acceptable behaviour.

In the seminary, the use of bamboo, leather belts, and iron is prevalent. When given a post, the senior students rely on such punishment to dispense their authority. Rage, resentment, and verbal curses are sometimes what accompany such punishment. It does not matter if one cries or sheds blood; crying makes it more acceptable. It indicates that the punishment is effective on the punished person.

Sometimes, I imagine that we have forgotten that we are dealing with human beings, and this punished poor behaviour could reflect our own limitations. In several instances where seniors refuse to cane, they are threatened with a bad report or expulsion from the seminary.

In this case, one may ask the question of what the motivation to remain in the seminary should be. Another striking discovery for me is that it was not only an instrument for correcting wrong behaviour but also for differentiating age and status. For example, such punishments are not used in the senior seminaries. This is not to say that the seminarians there are incapable of discipline. Instead, another form of punishment appropriate to their age and status is used, such as trimming the field, keeling under the sun, mopping the corridors, or refectory.

Interestingly, we do not problematise it as our pandemic but rather as the effect of the colonial enterprise, thus a tradition that was handed down to us by colonial ancestors. Some say that the moment we encountered the Europeans, our magnitude of violence was expanded. This argument to follow means that the encounter awakened latent fears and insecurities, manifesting in aggression towards one's subordinates. Once we have power, we tend to exert it in ways that show dominance, often as a means of compensating our own vulnerabilities. This abnormality manifests in various forms, from heightened suspicion and hostility towards others to an internalised sense of inferiority that affects our social structures and relationships. The trauma of colonisation created a dissonance between our ideal self (who we think we are) and our real self (who we actually are).[16]

Indeed, I understand that such an invasion was and is morally despicable. No man should be forced to do something against his will or adopt a culture he will always feel alien to. No man should be forced to learn a language that creates a tower of babel whenever he opens his mouth to speak.

And no one should impose on a people a system of education that does not reflect how they perceive the world. Conversely, the colonial explanation appears to me as an escapee goat. It is a way to run away from the responsibility we owe to ourselves. Like the religious narrative, this, too, strikes me as though everything that befalls us could be explained through colonial theory. It poses the question of whether we do not possess the free will to generate our own conception or if we ceremonially exist.

For too long, we have carried the burden of history written by others and the absurd drama that is staged around our individuality. Here, we are faced with two extreme situations: either we adopt the victim mentality and join the chorus without understanding the lyrics, or we rule it out and reach out for the universal principle. Being colonised is not a repository of righteousness nor excuses for perpetual stagnation and what may appear as dependency complex. Whilst colonisation has inflicted us with deep wounds, such wounds should not become the endless crutch upon which we rest our humanity and the definition of our personhood. History as painful as it may cannot become a permanent alibi for our inaction rather than action.

I want my countrymen to stand up with their shoulders straight and come out from the fixation on our past, that is the reckless encounter between the European and the African Man. The European man now, to say he is delusional is in itself a compliment. He himself has learnt to live on his emotions by abolishing the God who fashioned him in pursuit of ephemeral and vainglory. But one must not adopt such a behaviour, and this delusion, now manifesting itself as primarily a collective neurosis of the European man, must not dictate the future of the rest of humanity. This neurosis, driven by a deep-seated indifference and need to maintain control over the narrative of progress, reason and civilisation, has culminated in an unreflected imposition of a worldview that alienates both European man and the global communities he seeks to influence. Not even the moral law, which should serve as the foundation of his society, has been spared from distortion. As a result, societies with vastly different social fabrics, histories and values demanding not primarily violence but human behaviour from others are coerced into conforming to a totalitarian framework, leading to cultural dislocation and exacerbation of existential crisis. The danger arising from such coercion is that we all lose our capacity to think and act, becoming mere bios—existing in names only without truly living. In this diminished state, the failure to bear the weight of our individuality equates to relinquishing our humanity.

The actions and conduct of every human being, including how societies choose to manage their affairs, are, of course, a matter of private possession. In that private domain, whatever one does is not in the public domain and attracts no consequences for the other. What matters to one holds no significance for the other[17]. However, when society begins to condition people to adopt a certain mode of indoctrination in both the private and public realm to the extent that they can barely function, then our humanity is threatened and the responsibility which each and every one of us must bear is also magnified. But this is not where we must dwell extensively on this matter. We shall return to it in due course. For now, if we must move forward, we must conduct an examination of conscience and stop relegating our mistakes to the helpless infant in us.

What is evil is evil, and no justification can alter its essence to tranquilise our feelings. The existence of evil such as our determination to hurt one another is not the design of any colonial ancestors nor the Creator of the world, but the reckless abuse of our free will and the corruption of our moral sense. It stems from our deliberate choices to stray from the principles which are good in themselves to principles that merely satisfy our selfish desires and ambitions. Anyone can pervert his free will and use his fellow man as a means to an end. We, as beings capable of reason and responsibility, are accountable for this moral decay.

The argument that things would have been different if we had not met is flawed because it is not in our design to know what would have been but what is in the present and the past.

We cannot know the future or any probable event of time. Those things do not exist except in the present. In this respect, Augustine writes that when we make predictions about the future, we do so as if the subject of prediction is already present in our minds[18]. Thus, we must resolutely turn our attention to the present and abandon the futile practice of using the past as a convenient excuse to evade our current responsibilities—responsibility we owe to ourselves.

On the second day, after breakfast, the bell rang, and we gathered in the chapel to continue with the rest of the programme. Things about the seminary were explained to us, including the rules and regulations. We also got introduced to the prefects and the specific functions they take care of. During the orientation week, we were assigned tentative functions, which we had to take care of every morning after Holy Mass.

The function is like one's parish and has to be cared for as one would for his parish. Some boys were assigned the sacristy, library, priests' apartments, and other prestigious functions in the seminary. I was assigned an outdoor function, a small path known as the rector's path. For me, it was exciting, although it was one of the delicate functions in the seminary then. I could be expelled anytime if I did not do it.

Nevertheless, I gave it my all. The discipline I achieved through that was constructive. Now that I am older, I liken it to a notion of responsibility every individual must assume for a course he is pursuing. How one carries out such minor responsibilities affects how he would take care of greater responsibilities like caring for a parish.

Of course, one gets supervised and faces the consequences if not fulfilled. For me, it was a matter of being honest and sincere in the absence of authority. Until the end of the orientation week, we had different programmes and exposure, including games, as we would in a regular school activity.

When the old students arrived one week later, things began to change, and the euphoria of learning gradually kicked in. Coming to the chapel late and sleeping during morning prayers or Holy Mass was frowned upon and had consequences. After the Holy Mass, one must hurry to his parish and care for it diligently. Once the bell goes, you must leave your completed or uncompleted parish and rush to the refectory.

Depending on how friendly the time is, you have approximately twenty to thirty minutes to take breakfast, collect your study materials and go to the classroom. Breakfast was not celebrated in the seminary. Lunch and supper are different. Immediately after sharing the food, you must eat and proceed to the next activity.

Be it as it may, one could still be delayed due to one thing or the other. One of which was the hierarchy in the refectory. If you are a junior student, you are responsible for bringing the food, plates, and cutleries. The seniors are responsible for sharing the food, which is taken according to hierarchy. As a junior, you only take a plate of food if your senior has taken one, and he must have the most significant portion.

The same applies to cutleries. Some seniors are very lenient and would allow their juniors to take a plate of food before they do. Otherwise, it is a punishable offence; you will stand up in the middle of the refectory until the meal ends. You will be jeered at but not paraded and chanted at. Cursed, but no lumps will be thrown at you and whipped with no whip and elaboration of pain.

Whilst others leave the refectory, you will be meant to carry the coolers to the kitchen. I remember one time I made a mistake and had to bring the coolers to the kitchen. That day, I regretted ever coming to seminary. The humiliation was profound. But I remembered I was there for a purpose. Also, I watched what others did and started to do mine. Most importantly, to avoid being entangled with this menace in the early hours before the lecture, it is better to break one's fast during the lecture break. Some even do not eat until lunch. It was conducive, and I always had some groceries as a substitute.

Now, as the bishop's coming approaches, the preparation of our investiture also draws near. The fields were trimmed, and the chapel was decorated. The journey of a thousand miles is about to begin. One of my greatest moments was the debate between my class, JSS3 and SS1. It was an opportunity for me to show my intellectual giftedness.

I have participated in several public discussions, but that was exceptional. Out of the hundred marks, we scored ninety-seven, with me cutting the highest in eloquence. Our seniors could not even beat us by a reasonable margin. They were shamed for it.

Later, one of the prefects approached me. We chatted about where I come from, my school and my state of origin. He encouraged me to move forward and never relent. I was clothed as a seminarian by the local ordinary of blessed memory. The joy was uncontrollable for my family and me. I have made it so far. I am now a seminarian. Like Simeon, I sang the *Nunc dimittis*, thanksgiving God for the height. Little did I know I was also thanking him for the storm he would send me.

After the investiture, we stayed for a few more weeks and left for the Christmas holiday. My life has entirely changed. Now, I attend morning Mass, and instead of wearing flip-ups to the banquet, I wear sandals, maintaining the seminary tradition. My socialisation also had some modifications. Although I rarely cursed before entering the seminary, I tended to abandon them altogether.

Instead of cursing, I now say, "God bless you," in response to annoying utterances. This went on repeatedly with all its challenges. It evokes a sort of identity crisis, especially within the family—no one tells you how to handle it. On the one hand, I was still the last born everybody used to know. The kind and tall, gentle boy that my peers used to know. On the other hand, if anything irritated me, I had to claim that everything was alright to continue to receive reverence because priests and seminarians in Nigeria are revered for their angelic figures and criticised for being human.

With admission into the minor seminary, the expectation of families and the entire public is heightened. It is no wonder some seminarians prefer not to show themselves to the public unless they have been anointed and vested with stole and chasuble. The expectation is much. Sometimes, it is irrational. Even when one has fulfilled them, one sees himself lying down, putting his face on the ground in deep contrition for the ones he thinks he missed. No one remembers he is a mortal, a man who is merely a breath.

Besides people's expectations, we seem to take the laws of the Vatican unscrutinised. We accept the letters of the law and dispense with its spirit. The seminary, as a mother, does not believe that her offspring can be reasonable outside her uterus. Seminarians are also monitored by the air they breathe and the water they drink over the holiday. Particularly in the senior seminary, one faces a series of punishments for what he did outside the seminary.

Thus, it becomes de facto difficult for one to be himself. It is difficult to complain; then one could be seen as a weakling in the office. On the other hand, the psychological aspect of the formation system, which should help one process the effects of such pressure, did not exist for one's good but was a handy instrument to eliminate candidates. We always assume that psychological issues are incompatible with religious life. We use them to justify the exclusion of good men from the religious profession whilst breeding people who would never serve God even if the devil bids them to—and we expect them to be shepherds of souls that they do not know.

During the Christmas break, I also received financial support from people to help me prepare for the second term. However, it turned out that I would not be returning for the second term. Right after the Christmas break, before the resumption day, my mother received a text message that my dormitory was ablaze. Not all properties could be saved. Parents and guardians should, therefore, come and check what has been saved and what is to be bought for the seminarian. Immediately we read the message, neither she nor I could sleep well. Throughout the night, I was saying my rosary, "Lord, let me not be shamed. May my properties be among the ones that were saved."

The following morning, we hurried over our breakfast and boarded public transport to the school. The journey was approximately two hours to the school junction. Then we took a bike to go to the seminary. On reaching the gate, we spoke to the gateman, who allowed us to enter. We met other parents and seminarians who came for the same reason.

Everybody was anxious. I was, too. I was thinking about my life and the next step if things go sideways. I could not think of anything else other than what my fate would be. After some moments, one of the prefects walked us down to the dormitory.

Everywhere was covered in ashes, woods, blocks and bed springs; all were different from black. The roof of the building was open. Before us, some parts of the building also fell. It was a terrible fire that claimed many properties but not life. When we requested to be shown where the saved properties were kept, they directed us to the refectory.

My mother and I went there, but unfortunately, not a single pin of mine was picked. The only property that survived was my box, with which I travelled home for a holiday. Other items like my cupboard, spring bed, mattress, pillow, tentpoles, and everything I left in school before the Christmas holiday were consumed by fire.

I was emotionally devastated. My first big step in life was confronted with this tectonic fall. It would have been consolable if some items like my spring bed, mattress and cupboard were saved. Other things could be acquired little by little. But no—they all turned to ashes. What a pity!

Right after the visit, when we went back home, my family could not understand what had happened, particularly my mother; she started having doubts about my vocation. It could be a sign that this is not my calling. For her, God has ruthlessly slayed and shamed her.

Being in that situation, I did not expect her to be happy. On the contrary, it was her sweat that was consumed by fire. God seemed to have betrayed me! I made the choice of going to the seminary—a choice that no one in my family has ever attempted. I agreed to repeat a class not because I was not intellectually gifted but because I saw that it was the sacrifice I had to make for the future. I chastised myself; I bore the disparagement for the sake of the kingdom of God.

Apparently, the kingdom of God has devasted me. How could it be that not a single property of mine was saved? Why must I be the one whose eyes must well up in tears? Why must every journey be marked with a crucible? At that, I was already inflamed in agony and pain, but I did not get a response either. Later, I told her that this could be a test. God is testing me to know if I can bear it. I knew I would suffer because of my decision, although I did not know how much I would have to suffer.

Whatever the case, I am not giving up, provided you do not give up on me. Given that, we started deliberating on the following steps: I had two options: first, buy new properties and return to the seminary. In any case, my resumption date could be postponed. Second, I forget about seminary for a moment and continue my studies elsewhere, probably my alma mater or any other school, whilst enquiring how to rejoin the vocation. Buying a new property was worthless since I was studying for a class that I had already finished. Therefore, I decided to start my senior secondary school immediately and rejoin the seminary later in September.

When schools resumed, I got registered in a private school where I did my senior secondary level one (SS1). It was a mixed school, and the students were really wild in their approach. During this time, I hid my identity so as not to be randomly questioned. I acted as though I was in the world but not of the world. This was necessary to avoid preferential treatment or unpleasant experiences and properly integrate into the school.

I went to the school and learned much—namely, how to be both human and holy, intertwining everyday conversation with the Divine. I discovered that I could talk to a woman without fear of unintended consequences and converse with a fellow man without questioning my masculinity or risking reprimand. These seemingly ordinary moments became extraordinary glimpses of holiness, deepening my appreciation for the priesthood. Such experiences reminded me of the inherent goodness in human nature, captured in the extraordinary words of the Collect: *Deus, qui humánæ substántiæ dignitátem mirabíliter condidísti*—'O God, who wondrously created the dignity of human nature'—and *mirabílius reformásti*—'and more wondrously restored it.' If God Himself condescended to partake in human nature, it affirms not man's disorder but his potential for participation in the Divine nature.

At the same time, I found commonalities between the Catholic faith and Pentecostalism, as many students were Pentecostal, and our worship often reflected their traditions. For instance, the hymns we sang during morning assemblies became acts of shared worship, uniting us in purpose and spirit.

Occasionally, after devotion, one experiences a great silence among the students. Some would prefer not to talk until the end of the learning session. It appears as if they have undergone an alteration in their level of consciousness.

Teachers will often laugh at well-known verbose whenever they come to the classroom to teach, but in the final analysis, we will be shocked at their non-responsiveness.

People who managed to learn about my identity as a seminarian were rather intrigued and had many questions regarding my departure and potential return. I was probed into the reasons behind my decision and questions regarding the Catholic faith. But as the story was more complex to break into manageable pieces of information, I offered a simple yet resolute response that I would be returning in September of the academic year. With that, there was an understanding that my stay was only meant to be short. It also happened that one of my teachers, my parishioner, was planning to join the seminary in the near future.

The prospect of our paths converging within the seminary and in the parish was met with so much joy and great encouragement. Our thoughts inevitably turned to the contributions we could offer to the mission ahead. There was a shared commitment to service and spiritual growth given to our different experiences. We saw the opportunity to learn from one another, challenge and inspire each other, and be the type of priest we want to be. In all, my two feet in no distance time were no longer to be in a location where such conversations could be deeply held.

I would be leaving them to a different seminary whilst he went to another seminary. During the time I was in the senior seminary, we moved into our own home and thus changed parishes. Until he became a priest, we rarely had time to discuss our aspirations, and there was no time to fulfil them.

For the two terms I studied at the school, I thought maybe that part of our seminary studies should be moved to secular institutions to widen our horizons. It only helps if we undergo intellectual formation by knowing its practical utility among the flock. Most of the time, they are interested in something other than our intellectual sophistication, but instead, a new way of interpreting the same phenomenon in a manner that resonates with their deep frustrations about life. But as it appeared, we were far from it because when we met them, we faced to protect what had been transmitted to us in line with our faith. Yet we rarely believe nor practice them at our own discretion without being forced.

These were just my reflections—and I knew immediately after returning to the seminary I would be presented with a counter-narrative on why things should remain how they are. And it is in our nature to accept it unchallenged due to fear of the unknown. Whatever change one has to make would stay until he becomes a priest, where it is presumed that no one would question his authority. Hence, most of us kept going to acquire leverage.

But I thought that was stupid, too, because making a change is an act of faith, not courage. It is the faith that the alternative is not better in the final analysis. I am unaware of the readership and what it will change as I write this. I write to get hold of the only authority fate has led me to and see what meaning I can extract from it. Thus, one may not see the change he seeks but can find the meaning he is not looking for.

After my SS1, it was agreed that I could return to the seminary if I wanted—and, of course, I wanted to. My mother and I travelled to the new seminary, where I would finish my senior secondary education. When the priest who attended came to the office, I brought up my desire to switch to Chetachukwu to feel connected to myself and the divine. I did not know why I insisted on this, but I think it was because I have been known by this name, and I feel so attached to it because of its meaning. It is the name through which I pray in the most profound sense.

But it struck me as the priest said that only the baptismal name is answered in the seminary. Neither I nor my mother objected. But when we reached home, I took the time to think about this very deeply. Here, I recall one night during my boyhood. As I lay in bed, my body was wracked with chills and sweats. I felt it was my last; with every breath, I could feel the fever coursing through my veins. Waves of nausea and dizziness washed over me. My mother, sitting beside me, was worried and overwhelmed. I could see her fear as her face hovered above me.

She asked for a bowl of water with a small towel. My immediate sister went to the kitchen and brought it to her. Without a word, she soaked the towel in the cool water. As she wrung out the excess liquid, her hands moved with practised efficiency befitting of a good mother.

With the damp towel cradled in her hands, she turned to me, "This will help bring down your fever, Chetachukwu," she said softly. She placed the cool towel on my forehead. The contrast between the coolness of the water and the warmth of my fevered skin was both jarring and comforting. I could experience a gradual return to my normal body temperature. I could barely eat, so she concocted an oral drip for me to drink, a simple mixture: water, salt, and sugar.

Taking a tentative sip, I was greeted by a taste both familiar and comforting. I felt some relief after about forty-five minutes, and so did the rest of the members of the family. They had dinner, and we all retired to bed. I slept next to my mother. Around one o'clock before daybreak, the fever surged forth. It started as a subtle prickling at the back of my neck. Soon, it grew into an all-consuming blaze. As I lay there in bed, bathed in the dim light of the room, I could feel the world around me fading into nothingness. My skin burned with a feverish heat, and my head throbbed with an ache.

Immediately, my mother resumed placing a damped towel on my head. Accordingly, her voice rose in prayer; I found myself drifting into a state of quiet contemplation. With each whispered plea to Lord Jesus Christ, I could not help but wonder if it was not indeed Him who had sent this sickness upon me. Part of me wanted to believe that there was a greater purpose behind my fever, that perhaps it was a test of faith sent by the divine hand of Lord Jesus Christ Himself. But another part of me fails to reconcile the idea of a loving Lord Jesus Christ inflicting such fever.

Perhaps my sin, which I deserved. But I tell you, I was very little to talk about my sins as the source of my sickness. Another problem was my family's economic status. Indeed, if there were enough money, my mother would not be here experimenting nurse but would actually take me to the hospital to receive treatment. In all these, her main worry was who would make the contribution.

After some hours of keeping her awake, I managed to fall asleep and slept till daybreak. Around 6:00 am, when I woke up, she was already in a meeting with my father about a way to take me to the hospital. She knows one children's doctor, Dr Orji. A friend of hers had recommended the doctor to her, and he was very good. My father reached out to the table where he usually kept his money and gave some naira notes.

My mother accepted the money. I nodded also in gratitude Around 7:30, he rode his bike and left for his shop. My siblings were hurrying to leave for their respective businesses, so I also, in the hazy blur of feverish delirium, made it to the bathroom. Warm water has already been prepared in a bucket for me.

Within five minutes, I was done and out of the bathroom to get ready for a doctor's visit. She herself got ready but required more time. First, she had to inform her neighbours at the market that she would not be coming as I was very sick. Then she ate, and we left for the hospital.

When we arrived at the hospital, the room was filled with many patients. My mother and I went to the hospital's reception desk. The receptionist, a middle-aged woman, welcomed us. She had a wonderful demeanour and swiftly guided us through the process of purchasing a hospital card.

My personal information was collected. My mother provided details such as name, date of birth, address, and contact information. Then, we were directed to the waiting room until we were called to see the doctor.

Shortly after, a nurse told us it was our turn to see the doctor. I was afraid to climb the stairs, so my mother back carried me. As we entered the room, Dr Orji greeted us with a warm smile–an old, fair, tall man with grey hair. Chetachukwu, he called me, looking at my file with his eyes widening with a sudden realisation. My mother, in a small chat, explained to him what the name meant, and he responded with some kind of affirmation that it carries strength and resilience. The words and experience sank. Amongst all my doctor's appointments, this is the one that I and everyone in my family remember vividly. Moments later, we were ushered into the laboratory, where my blood sample was taken, and a test was conducted. I was injected and given a drip while lying on the bed. Gradually, I felt a surge of strength returning to me. It was as if the very act of calling my name, combined with the doctor's expertise, had worked together to keep me alive. In the following moments, I slept peacefully, though my bed was drenched in sweat. By the time we left the hospital to go home, I could stand on my own feet and walk unaided. I took this experience to heart, as it showed me how deeply the name we answer to can affect us.

In this situation, the questions that lingered were: Should I really change my name? This name had always reflected my identity; I have seen it had a deeper meaning than I had realised. It wasn't just a label—it was a reflection of who I was, my journey, and the person I was becoming. Being called *Chetachukwu* felt more significant than I had ever understood. It connected me to my heritage, my culture, and the strength within me. However, I gave it all up, following the priest's suggestion. In September 2011, I returned to the seminary for the final two years of my senior secondary education.

Coming into the seminary, the frontal view is of the grave of the seminary pioneer, with a chapel right in front of it. From the frontal view, one can freely walk through the various paths on both the left and right sides. The side areas include classrooms, hostels, the refectory, and lavatories, arranged in such a way that you can move from place to place with minimal barriers. There are also two football pitches, as well as volleyball and basketball courts. As usual, the fields were overgrown, waiting to be trimmed. There is also a domestic quarter for some of the staff at the seminary, and a new chapel is still under construction for major events. Since it was a senior class, the others and I were assigned to our respective hostels. On this occasion, I met my schoolmate from the previous seminary, who became a very good friend. We had so much to discuss: the fire, loss, and why I did not return. This time, orientation week was familiar to me. Everything was the same, including the going lectures and the living conditions. Customarily, we were introduced to the seminary, the centre of the formation system, which is the chapel and the rules and regulations. We took time to study it—although it was done at each rector's conference. The feeding was similar, but the food here was quite out of touch. To feed well means eating special, that is, the food meant for those who have hepatitis. I ate that a lot after recovering from hepatitis. It was the only specially cooked food and that of the prefects. Somewhat feeding for over four hundred seminarians remains a challenge, too. It is in-between quenching hunger and staying alive.

At the end of the cooking and after sharing the food, we recreate the food on our various tables by surreptitiously adding red oil and noodle spices to make the food tastier. Then we can eat and proceed to the next activity. Sometime in October, I had my investiture and once again clothed as a seminarian.

Unlike the previous seminary, I held a relatively prestigious function. I worked as a timekeeper for two academic years and one term in the sacristy. Life as a senior was bearable, but it came with many challenges, especially for someone with a different worldview. One of my devastating shocks was how we divided ourselves into ‚superior' and ‚inferior' races and how friendship is construed as an unholy rapport. This was no different from my previous seminary experience. The reasoning of which is to uphold authority and prevent unhealthy friendships; however, has its unintended consequences.

The reasoning, particularly the obsessive effort to prevent same-sex attraction, was nothing short of delusional. It has created an atmosphere of suspicion, where trust was eroded, and genuine relationships became tainted. Even after leaving the seminary, the damage lingers. Instead of being formed, we become deformed. We—those of us who went through it—are left haunted by the division and mistrust that were instilled in us. This lingering suspicion has become almost instinctual, shaping how we interact with others and forcing us to question the simplest gestures. Sometimes, we use it as a defense mechanism to suppress our unconscious feelings and shield ourselves from vulnerability. By holding onto that suspicion, we avoid confronting deeper emotions—fear of rejection, fear of intimacy, or even fear of being misunderstood. It's easier to distrust than to allow ourselves to be open, to risk being hurt. Over time, this defense mechanism becomes ingrained, so automatic that we no longer recognise it as a protective layer of our personality but as a fundamental part of who we are.

Being a new place, it is common to find people to befriend, people with the same hobby styles, an intellectual partner, or in the case of the seminary, a prayer partner. It was my imagination of a healthy school lifestyle, and I consider it paramount for the seminary formation. In contrast, I encountered a social climate that made us suspicious of each other. There was a substantial social distance; the formators and the students lived in two antithetical worlds. The formators tend to see themselves as the superior race, whilst the students are the inferior race. Within the inferior race was yet another different stratum, with the prefects at the pinnacle of the hierarchy and constantly at war with the senior students who feel they should decide what happens in their strata.

For the new intakes, our own strata degenerated after the rules and regulations were read to us haphazardly, forbidding personal friendships in the seminary and emphasising self-centred life. We suddenly became antithetical to one another to fit into the existing norm. What happens next is that we develop a superiority complex. We become bullies and carry such attitudes to the presbytery to dominate our curates and the people of God. As parish priests, we do not pay our curates' monthly stipends, but we celebrate all the masses to take hold of the offerings. The laities whom we are meant to serve become our servants. They tolerate our friction and allow our sense of entitlement. They bear our emotional abuse and curses laid upon them.

Immediately after the regular school session began, most of us became likeable to gain preferential treatment and those who could not manage joined the bullies. The bullies will steal your cereals, use your water and bucket, wear your clothes, and still hit you for it. They will steal your money and invite you to eat the item bought with it. They have access to food storage and are out to starve an entire table. Cell phones are not allowed in the seminary; thus, when such an item is stolen, you do not utter it because of the fear of expulsion.

Reporting a stolen item in the seminary is almost inconceivable. One also does not want to report his brother and be the reason for his termination from his vocation. In such cases, the whole class might exonerate the offender and gang up against the person who reported the case. It is a fraternity, and no matter what, we try to protect each other. I did not comment to avoid such occurrences when my money went missing.

Similarly, reporting the individual was not an option when another stole my phone. Actually, I did not want him to leave either—at least not from me. Added to my confusion is the seminary belief that you are susceptible to expulsion once someone leaves the seminary because of you. This is the norm—a religious belief, for that matter.

One may object and call it superstition. However, the difference between superstition and factuality is that, here (the latter), someone is willing to plot a piece of evidence against the other to make that happen. This is even more dominant in the senior seminary, where the auxiliaries use their fellow seminarians to settle friction between them and the formators. No soul will utter a word against the formator or the auxiliary.

Instead of resolving conflicts, we see them as an opportunity to gain influence and power. One sees conflict everywhere but wherever. Therein, protection is not foreseen, although it is available to specific individuals. It is a battle of survival of the fittest. To defend oneself was nothing but a sin.

I remember a case of someone who was in his second year of theology but left the seminary because of a minor misunderstanding with the second auxiliary. The fact that he (the auxiliary) told him that he would write a report that would expel him from the seminary and still did is preposterous. When the bishop read his school report and what the second auxiliary had written at the reunion, he showed concern at first. Yet, the candidate never returned to the seminary after several fruitless enquiries and months of waiting in the abyss. The bullying that a handful of men perpetrate against their fellow men when a seminarian visits them for apostolic work is unimaginable.

Some would coerce a seminarian to choose between his apostolic work report and the fundraising typically done for him at the end of his apostolate. They do these knowing full, albeit the money is vital for the seminarian to take care of his living expenses. Of course, he would choose the report because he wants to remain in the seminary. Cassio, in Shakespeare's *Othello*, captured precisely that we put an enemy in the mouth of our fellow men to steal away their brains—that we, with joy, pleasure and revel of applause, have transformed ourselves into monsters.[19]

In every respect, one is torn between a written document and his desire for the priesthood. Being a priest becomes a matter of who has the best report. The paper, therefore, becomes a certificate of wholeness; without it, no one could act *in persona Christus*.

There have also been cases where seminarians were expelled for choosing to observe Lent instead of paying for it. Here, they were compelled to pay a certain amount of money, a thousand and five above and not below that. Some individuals appointed by the rector collect the money. Each seminarian was judged by what he pays, which has so much weight on his report assessment form, such as uncharitable, stingy, and so on. Yet, the money generated neither improves their feeding nor their general well-being.

Instead, the total amount is announced; those who paid more than the flat rate were praised for their effort, whilst those who paid less, their money was returned to them to make it up to a substantial amount in order not to jeopardise their vocation. Despite the imposition of a mandatory offertory, one was still, as a matter of fact, compelled to pay another levy for a Lenten observance whilst threatening him with his vocation. It raises the question of whether one is paying for his sins to be purged out or remitting his vocation. One thing is clear: either one is serving mammon or is serving God. This precarious nature of forming candidates for the priesthood makes me wonder if it is not true that power is the underpinning of human motivation. As it appears, power is intricately woven into the fabric of a community that is supposed to be characterised by brotherly love, shaping our decisions and actions. By critically examining the situation, one uncovers the sad but striking reality that the endgame is nothing but total domination.

Total domination strives to organise our indefinite plurality in such a way that suppresses the autonomy of the individual and critical thought. We often forget to think what we do. Our lives are more about conformism rather than action predicated on the Christian values we tend to purport. It is rooted in our moral superiority and inability to tell ourselves the hardcore truth about our shortcomings. Because of this attitude, the essence of the priestly vocation is barely seen in us. Although we have various ways to assess our functionality, we do not confront the deeper moral and spiritual truths. Instead, as Sheen puts it, we, insist "on the dignity of our priesthood by quickly reprimanding those who show us disrespect[20]."

I reckon on one of the occasions where I challenged a prefect in a friendly conversation on this moral superiority, I asked him, "Why is it that in the seminary, we tend to correct in others what we have failed to correct in us." He answered by telling me that I should not follow the bad guys and that my worldview would change once I progressed in the seminary. I insisted on saying that my worldview on this matter would not change but would only expand, "if I continue with this way, I might end up serving in the village," he concluded. Well, following the bad guys means pushing the boundaries and challenging what is abnormal but appears normal. It means speaking out on what ought to be—and who knows, I may have ended up serving in the village where I would be feeding from hand to mouth if I were a priest. It goes without saying that some priests serving in remote areas are there because they questioned priests in higher positions or the bishop himself and vice versa. To belong means to conform and not ask difficult questions, to fit into the mould rather than challenge it.

For the rest of my stay in the minor seminary and throughout the senior seminary, I kept all my provocative thoughts to myself. It takes a great deal of mental struggle to achieve that. But it is to know the mental struggle than lose oneself to entirely conformity.

In 2013, I finished the minor seminary and went for the perfecting exam, an entrance examination, to prepare for the major seminary. By then, most of us have parted ways. Many took the exam, as well as those who did not pass through the minor seminary. As it happened, I was among the successful candidates. On the day of the reunion with the bishop, we all assembled at our minor seminary to hear our fate.

The reunion lasted for three days, and on the last day, our names were pasted on the notice board. As it happened, I was successful and was placed in charge of the cathedral. It was a function that I least expected. It gives me the impression that my life is somehow tied to something significant so sacred and sublime—a life with divine architecture. It was tough initially with all the verbal abuse and the public disgrace.

In the long run, I mastered it and could complete my task without thinking about what anyone would say. At the end of my pastoral year, I went for our yearly reunion with the bishop and was promoted to the spiritual year seminary.

Life in the spiritual year was unpleasant. We had to source funds and food items in order to survive. We visited many parishes soliciting donations to improve our living conditions and erect some infrastructure. Many faithful, out of their magnanimity, gave us huge sums and stocked our pantry with food and supplies. However, in the final analysis, the living conditions did not change significantly. We still ate the watery beans and rice mixed with red oil and salt. Sometimes, the cook, in her generosity, brought ingredients from home to make the food tasty. We had difficulties getting water as the area itself was drought and high, and digging a borehole was almost impossible.

Most of the time, we used rainwater contained in a drain well. As for drinking water, we had an understanding with a company that supplied us with bags of sachet water. We stored enough to take us through the month each time they came. Later, we constructed a borehole with many GP tanks, and the company also supplied us with water to use in the showers in the rooms. However, the idea of the showers did not work as envisioned, although the GP tanks did as they were necessary for storing water in case the drain well dries up.

One month later, we had our investiture and became vested in the immaculate white cassock and the surplice that hung from the shoulder to the knee. By this singular act, we became senior seminarians. It was a big ceremony. Our friends and families were invited to celebrate with us. My family came, including one member of my Block Rosary Crusade. Seeing me in that cassock was all they could ask for.

Of course, it does not mean the journey has ended, but it does mean I was making progress. From that, I was endowed with the privilege to pontificate at Mass. I can now show myself to the public that I am on a mission to preach the gospel. But I did not show myself anyway; even as we travelled to the village for Christmas vacation, I never wore my cassock at the village parish. I did not want a premature epiphany.

The village community will start counting the years to ordination for obvious reasons. They will monitor and start referring to one's mom as the priest's mother. Of course, they are the ones to organise one's ordination; sometimes, they are the ones who will take the seminarian down. Consequently, it was imperative to have no premature epiphany so that if I eventually left, I would have fewer questions to answer the public.

Notwithstanding, I pontificated, particularly during the Easter vigil, where I recited the *exsultet*. It was a great honour that I stood in front of the congregation with my joyful tone and a strong voice proclaiming the resurrection of the Lord. The ancient words felt alive within as I proclaim them. I felt like I was already in the ministry, and my spirit was lifted high.

It was a rare opportunity for a spiritual year seminarian, and I was glad to have had it. Apart from that, it was the only time I got to wear my cassock in the parish as a spiritual year seminarian. Other times, were in the senior seminary and during my two-times-six weeks of apostolic work.

With Easter being over, we all returned to wrap up the spiritual year phase. This time, it was more challenging than expected. The manual labour was much as the seminary must be tidied up before vacation. The report assessment will be done to determine if one continues in the line of the formation. Even if one has wasted throughout the semester, he must be forthright this last phase as anything could spare him or expel him.

The rector was very good at threatening and did that without mincing words. So, we were very serious about this last phase in all four areas of the seminary formation. We took our function seriously and tried to perform extra judicious activities like cleaning the chapel and tidying up the compound. The lecture was also taken seriously. It was sometimes dull and unelevated. The focus was on being spiritual rather than being academically formed. One could take his siesta whilst the class is going on. It was convenient once one filled his body with so many carbohydrates in the morning. The living conditions were not any better, but we managed it till we left the seminary. When we left, thereabout in July, it was a significant relief that this phase was over. Apparently, we were going to proceed to the senior seminary and begin our philosophical studies.

However, we were confronted with an unprecedented psychological evaluation, which I will take my time to discuss with you. It was unusual because the psychological assessment is neither strictly a prerequisite to joining the major seminary nor joining the minor seminary. It is not conducted except when there is a need to cut the number of seminarians in the diocese. It is conventional knowledge among seminarians, and one that became evident after my class and the cohort behind us had the evaluation. During this time, every seminarian appears to put up a demeanour that represses their complexes because seminarians will definitely be withdrawn as a result of things revealed during the evaluation. This raises the question of why it was conducted in my cohort and in whose interest. Furthermore, it brings to limelight the question of whether we consider psychology as a tool that will benefit the individual seminarian or if we consider it an instrument to cut candidates for the priestly vocation.

In the previous paragraphs, I have hinted at the Church's hostility towards psychology or, in archaic terms, the scientific study of the soul. For whatever reason, this rift exists so that the individual does not confuse psychoanalysis with confession, we need to be sincere when it comes to psychology and the priestly vocation. If we so much believe that God speaks to us directly on the one hand and in the truth of the doctrines and dogmas, we should not tremble of the use of psychological science to unravel individual complexes to make him a shepherd for his flock. If we so much trust in the competency of psychological science, we must have nothing to fear to use it to affirm the attitudes of the mind in unconsciousness. Or is everything in deep contradiction? I understand not the prejudice against psychology and the vocation to the priesthood. People whose vocation has been shattered because of this rift are crying in the wilderness, looking for someone to comfort them.

I do not speak for them! This must be clarified. We must speak for ourselves because only he who suffers knows where it hurts most. It would be unfair to assume such a role and generalise that all or even former seminarians who have passed through the process and were withdrawn because of it or all who left the seminary harbour feelings of anger and resentment. However, the anger and annoyance that fills a magnitude of our utterances, the rage with which we tell the story, and the denial that goes along are worthy of probe. As a matter of fact, one can be doing well, but the revealing of his mental attitude towards one particular *Erlebnis* asks something of probe. Perhaps, instead of focusing on the elimination of vocation, we should focus on what God wants, and that is to equip seminarians for life.

All in all, the test was carried out, and that was the end of my spiritual year formation. When the time for the reunion came, I went to the reunion and was successful. We were split into two among the two provincial seminaries. The seminary I went to was very small compared to the others, which had dozens of seminarians. It is situated near the forest, where seminarians go to fetch firewood.

The compound was bushy when we arrived in October 2015, thus more manual labour for the seminarians and those who will default the seminary regulations. There is an uncompleted hostel building meant to accommodate more seminarians. The formators live with the seminarians in their hostel. As a result, they could hear our moments of ecstasy and depression, and we theirs.

Most of the time, theirs was louder than ours as we could only run mad in the refectory. Actually, a lot of people misbehave in the hostel, but it could only be the functionaries when they want to exercise their authority or the philosopher kings, those in fourth-year philosophy when they think that the first years have not fetched drinking for the room or swept the room.

The chapel is another place where our inadequacies played out. Apart from praying, all manners of misbehaviour and misgivings were displayed. It is the place where we know when our formators are friendly and when they are in enmity. It shows itself during the sign of peace, as those in enmity will never exchange signs of peace.

During the homily, the offended person or the one that caused the mayhem will use the other for the homily. As their disciples as we were, we would sing their praises at the end of the Mass. Not doing or doing it for the wrong person had consequences, too.

The academic block is isolated, almost in the forest. It is unsafe to do prep there—the refectory substitute. The good thing about it was that, if you had your function there, you would rarely come to class late. After we arrived, we were welcomed by our diocesans, and we were given orientation. That is the good and bad thing about the major seminary; you will be guided by your brethren as well as betrayed by them. Although we have *primus inter pares, the first among equal*, who oversees the diocesan affairs in the seminary, nothing prevents someone from reporting to a priest or seminarian he knows best and using him as a bargain. When such a thing happens, the affected person finds it difficult to ascribe his innocence. In a similar vein, one's diocesan priest could also report or save him. The seminary has eyes all over it, and one does not know who is watching him.

The schedule is the same as that of the minor seminary, but more freedom is given. We have autoformation where we engage in no group activity except class and games. Prayer is done in private and in the refectory. The feeding in the major seminary is improved than in the minor seminary. Still, the hierarchy is maintained, as in the minor seminary. However, it is brutal as a philosopher king could send you on manual labour because you failed to provide him with cutleries or took the food before him.

The first years are tasked with all the labour—bringing the food, clearing the dishes, and taking away the coolers. A single mistake can make one regret ever coming to the seminary. In a tone of mockery, you'll be called *Nwa One*—a term that literally means "first year" but carries a disparaging weight, akin to being labeled a jerk or an outcast. As punishment, you'll be assigned the most menial tasks. But first, you'll endure the humiliation of standing in the refectory, in full view of everyone, until the meal is over. Only then will you be ordered to carry away the general pot.

Not doing that could merit further consequences, which the prima knows how to resolve among themselves. If that is with the auxiliary, be sure that it will be written on your report that he is indifferent to communal life and the Church's hierarchy. For that, the seminary suggests that he does not continue with the seminary vocation in the interest of the Holy Mother Church.

Apart from that, during the autoformation, you are on your own, albeit must follow and respond to the bell accordingly. Again, we also go for a walk on Wednesdays. However, we must return before six o'clock in the evening. This is also the time people go and engage in private business. Obviously, some seminarians do not return at 6:00 pm. We must not go for night prep. Instead, we do private study in our rooms or in the refectory.

When the lecture period began, I was thrilled to delve into philosophy, starting with Plato's dialogues, one of the key texts introduced to us on the very first day. We also explored Aristotle, which only deepened my excitement. The joy of studying philosophy consumed me entirely. Beyond my knack for grasping complex concepts, it was a truly distinctive discipline that expanded my perspective in profound ways.

Philosophy instilled in me a disciplined way of thinking and opened my mind to profound questions about human existence, such as the meaning of life and our purpose. As my first post-secondary subject, I was captivated by every aspect of it, especially Plato's *Allegory of the Cave*, Kant's *Critique of Pure Reason*, and the intriguing Gettier problem. These explorations deeply fascinated me and shaped my intellectual curiosity.

While my first year involved little classical philosophy, the second year delved deeper into fundamental philosophical questions. We explored the anthropological question—*Was ist der Mensch?* (What is the human being?), the epistemological question of justified true belief, the ethical question of right and wrong, the psychological question of behaviour, and the metaphysical question of God's existence. I cherished every moment of studying these topics, especially those concerning God, human existence, and behaviour, which consumed my thoughts and kept me engaged far beyond the classroom.

The same year, I began writing—creative explorations that blended my fear and imagination. It was a way to play with words and discover my poetic side, though life seemed to take my words more seriously than I intended. One line I wrote stood out: *"I was left in oblivion; Unprecedented became my closest companion."* At the time, I couldn't have imagined how prophetic those words would be. By the end of that year, I found myself truly in oblivion, with chaos and uncertainty as my companions. I bled metaphorically, floundering in a storm I had not foreseen.

On that sunny Thursday afternoon, 18 August 2017, right after the reunion, people came rushing to me, "Ernest, what did you do?"

"Ernest, this must be a mistake; people who worked for the bishop are not withdrawn from the seminary."

I was thrown off guard. I did not understand what was going on. Then, I was asked to go and check the notice board. On reaching the board, it has been written, stamped, and signed. I am withdrawn.

I would not be going back to the seminary. I did not cry, talk, or do anything at that moment. My heart was not beating faster; looking at my name, I smiled and turned around, which is quite unusual for anybody in that situation. But somehow, I had a strange feeling right before the names were pasted on the notice board—a sense of the beginning of an end.

I did not understand what that meant until I went to the board. Immediately, I called my mother and informed her to get the house in disarray so that before I came back, everywhere would be a bit calm. Still, I need to know what I did; I need to find out what happened. I called the vocational director, but he was not around. When he came back, I went to see him; he said he did not know I should see the bishop.

Like someone being pressed to break a confessional seal, I pushed him to tell me that since he was the vocational director, he blatantly refused that I should go and see the bishop; he would attend to me since I worked with him. Since the bishop was not around, I left for home to face my family.

Immediately I reached home, I was faced with many question marks to which I had no answer. My mother was confused, and so were my siblings. It was not so much a problem for my father; he got along quite easily, and he saw the future. I must utter this phrase. I told them I still needed to find out what went and if it could be clarified.

Of course, I will ask the bishop, but I tried to dispose of their minds of the worst. I will not ask the bishop to take me back. That is the least I can do. In as much as I was never consulted on my matter, the decision was taken behind my back, and I saw no need to have a diplomatic conversation about accepting me. I was, and I will not be the last.

One is accepted with open arms but kicked out like a dog. Even so, a dog is not treated with so much disrespect. Two weeks later, I spoke with the bishop, who told me he would consult with the vocational director to know what happened. After their meeting, I called the vocational director to enquire about the outcome of the meeting, yet there was no answer to my question. He said he could not say anything and hung up the call. Immediately, I broke down in tears and wept bitterly.

My purpose of weeping was not because I did not know what I did wrong; I was crying because it dawned on me the heavy cross I would have to carry for my sins and the sins of others. I wept because of the stigma that would follow me. I wept because I had spent my whole life protecting this precious egg, and now it has cracked. I wept because, indeed, it was over. There was no one else I could run to.

I had no godfather who could speak on my behalf. To God, I asked: What is the meaning of my life? What have I done wrong? What is it that I did that you cannot forgive? Am I worse than David or the ones who go from bed to the altar? Am I worse than the one who had indirectly adopted a child for his betrothed? What about the stained bedsheets that I had to wash? What about the baby's milk I was asked to buy with the offertory collection? What about those times I deposited offertory in an account that does not belong to the Church? How could they go about their business as if it does not matter? This is wrong and otherwise, and you know it, Lord. Look at me and treat me personally. Look at me and tell me that you are done with me. Look at me and say I am not worthy of being your servant. I am not perfect, but at least I know my frailties, and you know it even before I open my mouth to say them.

I could not help asking God to weigh whatever sin I committed on the same scale as David. I could not help but reflect on things I occasionally saw—things a seminarian would be expelled for, but his beloved was committing unperturbed. The lack of shame and carelessness in handling most of our dirty laundry is even more disturbing. Hiding under the shadow of the superior, no harm could ever come to us because it would always be dismissed as a vengeful attempt at character assassination. What is needed is a huge sum of money, such as throwing a birthday or jubilee party, and everybody will be fine.

However, a little mistake made by the seminarian will never go unpunished. This is men being hostile to men, I thought to myself. At some point, I was angry with myself for participating in most of the rivals and illicit acts. Here, I do ask forgiveness to God, his angels and saints. Given Nigeria's economic situation, it is a life most parishioners could never afford. Here is another man living the best of it without any sense of sacredness. Sometimes, I had to pretend to be comfortable with the misbehaving, although I was not.

All these came to my mind that maybe this man up high was punishing me for my sins; perhaps he was trying to smear me for the things I refused to object to. When was the last time I went to confession? What could I have done differently? What would my people do if I was sent home because of what I said or whom I reported? Too many questions, yet no answer.

Then begins to talk to me, my other personality, to try to exonerate me from the shame. They have conspired against me. Ah! They got me! All these people do not want me to become a priest. Finally, they have done it. I am now a laughing scorn to the gods.

I should have taken my reputation with me when fire consumed my dormitory. Instead, I continued. Now, I have failed woefully. I should have seen this coming. I was foolish enough to continue, only to be stabbed prematurely.

My dream has been forcefully taken. A dream once held closely dear. Now, shattered and gone. I have lost the very thing I saw as meaningful. My father was right. I should have listened and gone to the university. Everything has now blurred. The world is a maze full of unsolved puzzles. That is the thing. I make tough choices, and I now have to bear the consequences.

But I did not make the choices like that. I thought about it thoroughly and allowed the desire to manifest. Well, how would I have known? You tell me. I was walking the path other people before I had walked. Like every other path, it was deep, steady, and warm. My dream was clear. But the path was not. Whose fault is it, mine or the path?

Seeing nothing coming out of my enquiry, I accepted my fate and decided to move on. I encouraged my family to do the same: "I would like to take my destiny by my hands; it is not in the bishop's hands but rather mine. My name is Chetachukwu. Thus, God will not forsake me if I call upon him," I said to them.

To some degree, my dad was happy that I was determined to move on, although he did not know what the outcome might be. He questioned me several times about my plans, but I told him that I would be fine and that he would get the details when I was done. The goal was to move and study abroad, but broadcasting it was not part of the plan. Now, I carry out my dreams with utmost diligence. I kept everything to myself whilst working closely with my siblings. Thus far, it was the most crucial cycle to keep close.

I had already lost friends: classmates, fellow seminarians, and priests I had served so well. Except for a numbered few, five in total, with one priest who, in his poverty, remains supportive, others left without notice. In turn, I dismissed the rest without notice. For once, I focused on myself and dealt with myself mercilessly.

One night, my eldest sister, came to me and asked me, "Now, what next?"

I told her I was not going back to the seminary but was also not staying in the country. I wanted to go to England and study, where I would not have to learn a second language and quickly find myself. It is a country that I thought about right from childhood and perhaps the dream of most young Nigerian in my situation—to leave home, to reinvent oneself in a place where the opportunities seemed endless, and the weight of expectations was lighter. They have a symbol that binds them as one: the monarchy and I spent my childhood learning about Queen Elizabeth II. To some degree, going there would not be far from home. However, due to the fortune it would cost, the plan was cancelled.

Another alternative was Australia because most of my diocesan priests work and study there. Going there would not come with so many difficulties due to the collaboration. I knew some priests I could turn to if I got off a rocky start. But that also costs a fortune that I could not afford.

Already, it was difficult to reach the conclusion of sponsoring me. For my family, I could easily register at the affiliated institution and continue my philosophical studies. Or I could look for a congregation and continue with the seminary formation. But I refused, at least not immediately. I wanted to leave home and be myself.

I did not want to be in a position where everyone would check my standards to know whether I had made it. I wanted a monastic life to understand what had gone wrong, to unlearn. So, I knew what I wanted, but convincing my brother, who was to sponsor me, was the problem. I needed a spokesperson, and my eldest sister was able to stand in.

She has been overseeing my education, and convinced him to sponsor me. Now that I am being sponsored, I would not want to make a choice that would also warrant the withdrawal of the sponsorship. Thus, I decided to apply to schools in North America.

I got an offer from a university in Alberta. I started preparing myself to fulfil the strictest immigration requirements. I paid half the tuition and fulfilled other conditions. Eventually, I was denied the visa to proceed. That was yet another blow within a short period.

It was a shock to my family, especially to my mother. She could not understand it. I was beginning to look like a failure to her. I quarrelled with her over it because I could not tolerate it. The least I needed was someone painting me as irresponsible.

But I also understood the pain, the anxiety of not knowing what would happen next if I remained home doing nothing. She always thought I might end up badly. But as Christ said to his mother when she was worried over the wedding wine, I said to mine, "Mother, my time has not yet come, for my fate is different."

By providence, I reached out to a friend who also passed through the same situation. Like me, he did not return to the seminary but started from the scratch. When I told him my story, it resonated with him in many respects, and he encouraged me to push further even if I failed. He encouraged me not to reapply for the visa as it might cost me more time at home. Instead, I should look elsewhere for programmes related to what I was studying before.

Once I have finished the programme, then I can study my desired subject as time is still on my side. I enthusiastically took the suggestions as long as they did not entail any unnecessary time consumption. Over the course of time, he diligently scouted out potential schools for me, with one of them being in Germany. It struck me as peculiar, for Germany had not been a country I had aspired to visit; it had not been a childhood dream of mine.

Despite learning about World War II in school, I felt reluctant towards the idea of going there. In particular, I lacked the disposition or motivation to learn a second language, which added to my reluctance towards the prospect of going to Germany. However, everything shifted after experiencing a particular dream.

In the dim light of early morning before the day breaks, I found myself in the midst of a dream. The details were fuzzy, darkened by the ephemeral nature of my sleep. But one image stood clear to me: I found myself in a language classroom. The room was suffused with a dim light. As I looked around, I realised I was surrounded by faces from different nations, each one eager to master this language.

The pronunciation was different from what I was used to and unpleasantly hard. The grammar had a strict word order and often changed based on what one wanted to say. "It is German," someone whispered in my ear, and I immediately woke up. I did not understand what that meant. I was neither happy nor sad, so I brought the matter to my spiritual director for interpretation.

However, before I presented the dream, he told me that he could not see any headway in other choices I had made except Germany. I was shocked because I was already brimming with excitement that it would turn out differently. I was not eager for the dream to be confirmed, but I had no option but to tell him after he made that statement. We prayed, and he encouraged me to start my application. Within a few days of submitting my application, I got an offer to study in Germany, but others were denied.

It was a moment of joy for my whole family, especially my immediate sister, Kelechi. She said, "Cheta, do not forget me when you are there."

"Of course, I will not. Let's hope that everything works well," I said to her. The anxiety of not getting an offer was relaxed a bit.

Somehow, I knew that would be my last trial, and the visa would be granted. I began the process of gathering my documents and submitting my visa application. Now, I must open a block account to prove that I can sustain myself for at least one year. A total of €8,640 was required. I spoke to my brother, who was sponsoring me. Ungrudgingly, he gave me the money. There was not even a word to pay him back.

In order to prove that I had a good standing character with my school, I reached out to the vocational director to write me a referral. He told me instead to write the letter myself and bring it to him for stamping and signing. But I could not write it. Given the way I left them, it was challenging for me to formulate wordings that would actually describe what I wanted. So I reached out to a priest-friend who wrote the letter and sent it to me via email.

I forwarded the letter to the secretary, who printed it out and gave it to him to sign. After signing the letter, he called the secretary to come and collect it. I picked it up from her and left. There was no exchange of pleasantries, but what pleasantries were we to exchange when, now, I am dirty? On the other hand, the level of social distancing between the seminarians and the priests in Nigeria could add to that. Such distance finds its expansion when one leaves with all looking at him like the lost sheep. But if my memory is not failing me, it is the lost sheep that was most important to Christ, and he hung it on his shoulder when he found it.

Actually, I am baffled by how I have managed to bear this crucible and still have the mental capacity to pen it down. I never rebelled despite all the things I went through and saw whilst there. When I lost my money in the minor seminary, I told my parents that I needed a replacement. I do not recall discussing the details and intricacies of my experience with any of them. I did it for them to protect their innocence and imagination of the priestly formation.

More than that is my determination to bear every trial moment as if it were my last. Nietzsche said, *"He who has a why to live can almost bear anyhow."* But of course, my conviction is put to the test, and I sometimes wonder if it is actually right and necessary to be tested all the time, worst still when people who are close to one are the instrument for the test. And then I wonder if we also sometimes ask ourselves whether God is using us to test the other. Or whether the devil is using us to punish the other. Because the test sometimes seems too much, and I fail to put in place what God wants from me in each instance.

Being a seminarian in Nigeria and, far worse, an ex-seminarian is a story that goes along that line. Always one is tested, and always, one does not know the right action to take. There are things which should be a little easier, given our shared humanity, but they are not. Nothing is being done for one except it benefits the Church, and then I ask myself: What is the Church without those young men? Supposedly, they were allowed to leave the seminary and pursue a career of their own interest with so much support; what would the Church look like? But the same could be said of the seminarians, too, given our willingness to sacrifice our brothers for our gain.

Relatively, the ex-seminarians behave differently because now they have a common identity and have tested life and its crucible. In some instances, one could also say that they have a common enemy: the rector, the vocational director, the bishop, or the priest who humiliated them during their apostolic work or even the auxiliary who suggested that they be expelled. These figures, once revered, have become symbols of disappointment and betrayal, and their actions leave lasting scars on the psyche of those affected. Whether we could continue to live that way remains an open question. A house without a solid foundation cannot stand.

In the weeks to come, I applied for my visa to study in Germany. Within a few days, I got my interview date, and it became clear that things would work as planned. Interestingly, I began to learn the German language. I was able to master some vocabulary before I arrived in Germany. I continued with the pace, which helped improve my conversation.

When the date for my interview was reached, I went for the interview without any stress. The first question was if I spoke German, and with a smile, I whispered no over the telephone, but I was in the learning. The interviewer then moved to specific questions about my school and German culture. The interview lasted approximately ten minutes. He took my passport and told me I should expect their response in the coming weeks.

On 2 October that year, my passport arrived at the post office close to my residence, and I was contacted over the phone to come to pick it up. I got onto a bike and rushed to the post office. When I reached there, I was given a white paper to sign. Afterwards, I was handed over the envelope by customer care. I opened it, and lo and behold, the sticker was pasted. With jubilation, I called my mother and everyone else in my family. Then, I went to my spiritual director to give God what he had graciously given me despite my unworthiness. He prayed for me and sent me forth.

My flight ticket was booked for the same day. I left home on 3 October, and on 4 October, I arrived in Germany to pursue the German dream. Now, I can rewrite my story, I said to myself.

When I left the seminary, I was disoriented; it was like a rejection from the world. It was like I was not enough for God to consider me His servant. In the meantime came the tribulations… In my case, it was profound because I held the priesthood so immensely that I never thought I could lose it. Ultimately, when I did, life grew complicated.

I spent one year at home with my family, reading (primarily psychological books) and writing and praying to heaven to change the fate that beset me. The tempest came from many angles, people I know and do not know. I did not see a need for those challenges, except now that I have written this. I attempted and failed woefully in matters I know how to handle. I was tested beyond what I knew. Each of my breaths was a trail, and each step I made to catch up was a struggle. There was a pile of crises waiting to overtake me.

The way it was for me, I felt akin to a mother who had lost her newborn child to cancer, unable to comprehend the presence of God's love during such a heart-breaking ordeal. The emotional toll was utterly profound, as it involved separating from something which has been a significant part of my life. I was left hollowed out and raw; it was as though every fibre of my being had been stretched to its breaking point, then slowly unravelled in the wake of such profound loss. My pain was relentless, so much that I could feel it from my soul. I felt my loss, every part of it, and it was very excruciating.

This was the only ideal I had known through ages past, and I was very devasted to see that it was all an illusion. But perhaps it was not, for in bringing together my conflicting emotions, I learnt an invaluable lesson, which is that God moves and works in mysterious ways. He cares and is always there; I can run to Him for help.

Looking back, I see these lessons not as things I have achieved by my own merit. They were not things I could have grasped intellectually or through someone else's teaching. As painful as they were, they had to be lived and they had to be experienced firsthand in the rawness of life. These realisations were not handed down to me in moments of peace and clarity; they came through times of confusion and hardship. Ultimately, they came as, in spite of everything, I continued to go to Him and say before Him the words of Psalm 139:1-7:

Lord, I lie open to your scrutiny; you know me; you know when I sit down and when I rise. You understand my thoughts from afar. You sift through my travels and rest, with all my ways you are familiar. Even before a word is on my tongue, Lord you know it all. Behind and before, you encircle me and raise your hand upon me. Such knowledge is too wonderful for me, far too lofty for me to reach. Where can I go from your spirit? From your presence, where can I flee?[21]

The truth is that, in the secret of my heart, no one understands this situation better than Him. There is no place I could have gone to if not to Him. If I chose to bury myself in darkness and night surrounded me, no dark place would hide me that morning would not see me. No refugee would keep me beyond Him. He is the light and will always break through, exposing the shadows that would protect me. Consequently, no matter how far I turned away from Him or how deeply I buried myself in fear and shame, I could not outturn the grace that sought me. At this point, I would like to delve deeper with the reader to unpack the intricacies of my realisation with utmost clarity and intensity and perhaps conclude this chapter.

Here, I return to the hostile prejudice and acrimony towards psychological science in relation to the point I addressed hitherto. Despite its spiritual focus, the Nigerian seminary, if not the Church as a universal institution, seemed to resist engaging deeply with the psychological needs of young men aspiring for the vocation to the priesthood. There is a pervasive mythological narrative that emotional vulnerability and investigating the complexities of the human psyche are secondary, even suspect in the formation of priests. The emphasis is often placed on spiritual discipline, obedience and theological knowledge, as though these alone are sufficient to cultivate a deep, authentic relationship with God and the people of God. But this is understandable, as no person, most especially men aspiring to be priests, a sacred mission, would like his mind to be excavated and mask removed by some scientific theory that sexuality is the core of individual psychological makeup. For seminarians and priests, this can feel like a threat to life, mainly, when celibacy, chastity and spiritual purity are the ultimate ideals. It does not matter what Jung and Maslow say; this is a danger zone. Even as one acknowledges the need for psychological guidance, our religious notoriousness tends to prioritise spirituality more, viewing it as indispensable to our journey towards priesthood and devout life, often to our own peril.

Indeed, spiritual direction cannot be replaced with psychological counselling. By the same token, one cannot replace psychological counselling with spiritual direction. Both are different dimensional approaches, although they work closely for the best of the person who seeks them. The essence of spiritual direction is to help the individual come to terms with his salvation through Jesus Christ in thanksgiving to God. In the same breadth, the essence of psychological counselling is to maintain his psychic stability.

There is no doubt that the Church's practices and sacred music can help maintain the stability of the individual psyche when he sings *Credo in unum Deum, Agnus Dei* or *Sanctus Sanctus*. They possess an unparalleled ability to soothe the restless mind by imbuing it with a sense of tranquillity that transcends mundane worries. Yet, it does not give an opinion on how the individual should proceed with his vocation in his own interest. It follows, therefore, that there should be a balance in forming candidates for the priesthood. However, in the practical realm of seminary formation in Nigeria, the priests and bishops often display more hostility than even the pontiff who promulgated the Vatican II Council.

The spiritual dimension is the *sine qua non*, and to risk it is to risk one's vocation. In the end, we find ourselves churning out priests who are utterly incapable of embodying the grace and humility that lie at the core of their calling. More extreme, we produce priests who fail to understand the human condition because they themselves are bereaved and detached from the real complexities of what it means to be human, confined to their narrow window of doctrinal interpretation and theological dogma. Most often, these interpretations are self-constructed *theologica prisma* and poorly reflect the universal human experience.

I recall a case between Viktor Frankl and a Carmelite sister suffering from depression in his book *The Will to Meaning: Foundations and Applications of Logotherapy*. The case goes: A Carmelite nun experienced depression, which was found to have physical causes. She was hospitalised in the Neurology Department of Poliklinik Hospital. Before a specific medication alleviated her depression, it worsened due to psychological trauma. A Catholic priest suggested to her that if she were a true Carmelite sister, she would have overcome the depression long ago.

This remark, of course, was unfounded and only exacerbated her condition, adding a psychological component to her already existing somatic depression. However, Frankl was able to help the Carmelite sister overcome the effects of the traumatic experience, thus alleviating her depression about being depressed. The priest had conveyed to her that a Carmelite sister should not experience depression. In contrast, Frankl suggested to her that perhaps a Carmelite sister could handle depression in such a commendable manner as she had.

Reflecting on the case and how the Carmelite sister managed the depression, Frankl writes:

> I shall never forget those lines in her diary in which she described the stand she took towards the depression:
> "The depression is my steady companion. It weighs my soul down. Where are my ideals, where is the greatness, beauty and goodness to which I once committed myself? There is nothing but the boredom, and I am caught in it. I am living as if I were thrown into a vacuum. For there are times at which even the experience of pain is inaccessible to me. And even God is silent. I then wish to die. As soon as possible. And if I did not possess the belief that I am not the master over my life, I would have taken it. By my belief, however, suffering is turned into a gift. People who think that life

must be successful are like a man who in the face of a construction site cannot understand that the workers dig out the ground if they wish to build up a cathedral. God builds up a cathedral in each soul. In my soul he is about to dig out the basis. What I have to do is just to keep still whenever I am hit by His shovel. I think this is more than a case report. It is a *document humain*, Frankl concludes.[22]"

It is absolutely unjustifiable to claim that an individual grappling with mental illness or, say, personal weakness and afflictions is unfit for religious life or the calling to the priesthood. Such a grotesque depiction of the priestly vocation as an exclusive pursuit for only the mentally sound and fit is diametrically opposed to the teachings of Christ who is both priest and victim. What about Paul and David, with all their personal afflictions and weaknesses? What about persons with disability? Does that mean they are incomplete till some fitness certificate attests to their completeness?

May I also remind us that it is in direct contradiction with the Apostolic Exhortation, *Pastores Dabo Vobis*, which states that a priest is called from among the people of God. Or perhaps calling from the people of God means selecting those whose robes are spotless.

It suffices to say that the gift of vocation is restricted to individuals who are genetically and otherwise free from the human condition. This is practically nonsense; for once, I am convinced that unless we have blemished ourselves, we would not know what it means to be human, to talk more like a priest. Then, we would not be interested in the salvation of souls but in indoctrination along the lines that suit our particular worldview.

Recently, a seminarian was withdrawn from the seminary for having a psychiatric condition. Before his final exam, he was beset with malaria, eventually costing him his vocation. He was admitted for one week to the hospital and was receiving treatment. When he was discharged, the doctor gave him a report stating his diagnosis. As a follow-up, the seminary requested that he submit a medical report, which he promptly did. A month later, he anticipated a response from the rector, but none came. Instead, he was instructed to undergo a psychological evaluation to assess his mental stability before returning to the seminary. Complying with the request, he began consultations with a psychiatrist who, after several sessions, diagnosed him with an emotional disorder. The psychiatrist's report was subsequently forwarded to the rector.

Eventually, a decision was reached. On that Sunday morning, he and his parents were summoned by the vocational director, who informed them that he could not continue with his formation, citing concerns that his illness might recur. Some might argue that the Church spared him further emotional suffering by withdrawing him from the seminary. Such a perspective might be commendable—if only this had been the sole reason for their decision and if there had been a genuine effort to monitor his health and consider the possibility of his return once he recovered. Instead, he was left without guidance or support, abandoned like a lamb without a shepherd, with no clear path forward or reassurance of care from the institution he had served.

This certificate always determines the seminarian's fate rather than what he has to offer the Church. This lack of empathy from us the bearers of the light and keepers of the faith raises a question of what gospel one preaches and what faith one professes. Why must anyone beset with such a condition be abandoned? What about granting the individual the dignity of time and inviting them to return when they have regained their strength? Is expulsion truly the only resolution? If it were so, Christ would have abandoned all the sick he encountered because they were not worthy to enter the kingdom of God. The man possessed by a demon in the Gospel of Mark 5:1-20 would have been abandoned, too.

In my own case, as mentioned prior, we underwent a psychological evaluation as stipulated by the local ordinary at the end of our spiritual year. This was conducted by a reverend sister, whose work, as we were told, is prominent. The bishop and vocational director told us to seize that opportunity to discuss whatever had been bothering us in the seminary, personal challenges, for nothing we discussed with the sister would be used against us. The essence was to help us in our formation to the priesthood.

Whilst others were sceptical about the bishop and his vocation director and how our fate would be decided after the evaluation, I saw an opportunity to have a humane conversation about my difficulties in the formation system, family matters, and the demons I have been wrestling with personally. My intention was to engage in these discussions to seek guidance on how to move forward in my vocation. When the report came out, I felt slightly uncomfortable after reading it. As if the sister noticed, she asked if I felt comfortable with the information and if she could change it the way I wanted before submitting it to the bishop. "No," I vehemently said. I continued, "Although a majority of the things here are not true, you cannot change the fact that I am intelligent." Two years later, I was withdrawn from the seminary without reason. For some, it was the report. But if so, could we not make the case for deception and violation of the confessional seal? What is the problem here, the use of psychology or our proclivity to betray and kill by using psychology? And lastly, shall we not put on our sackcloth in deep contrition? I felt deceived, as if the truth had been veiled from me, leaving me disoriented and distrustful. I felt exploited, my trust taken advantage of, leaving me feeling used. For the first time in my life, I wished I had been deceitful, as that would have saved my integrity.

But, the corollary is that embracing my assessment without any alteration has remained my reason to live. It has made my faith stronger and given me the clarity needed to tell this story. If I went back in time, I would keep what I discussed with the reverend Sister. No one goes to the confession and, after confessing his sins, asks the priest to change his penance. What happened to me, no matter how fatal it was, gave me a reason to pray and say to God, O Lord, you have probed me, and you know me. I cannot imagine my life without the events that have unfolded, for even if I could, I realise they have shaped me into who I am today and what course I have chosen to dedicate my life to.

After the evaluation, I came to the realisation that it was not the sister who listened to me; it was God, hidden in the person of an evaluator. My discussion with the sister was with God, who searches the mind and heart. Thenceforth, I could feel His mercy and appreciate how much He has been in my life from the day I was conceived. Thenceforth, I could feel real intimacy with God. I could hear him say to me, you are mine; today, I have begotten you.

If He challenges me with suffering, it is not because he wants me to suffer. He himself is suffering on the cross with me. He wants me to discover hidden truths about myself. He does not make promises and fail; instead of failing, he keeps time to his side until he fulfils his promise. What he does, no one can undo, and what he writes, no one can rewrite. He writes in crooked lines, doing what is inconceivable. He is the only person that can think without disclosing his mind.

Indeed, not everyone possesses the spiritual strength to sustain the mystery of God. Hence, in an outward form of religion where all the emphasis lies on what is mundane, everything is possible because once we leave out the inward principle to satisfy the soul, we come to the realisation that God as we speak and understand Him is rather archaic and backward, for verily we see no impression of this reality in our life.

I also do not assert full knowledge of God; I only investigate my mind in relation to how I have experienced Him in my low moments. Thus, the meaning of my reflection remains to share this experience and how it has shaped my understanding of the presence of Him in my life. I pray He opens our eyes to the things of His Spirit so that we may discern His knowledge with the wisdom that He has. I am often asked about how I managed to survive this ordeal and remain a Catholic. The truth is that I cannot unequivocally answer to this question. Being a Catholic is not what I chose to become but who I am. This goes beyond mere affiliation or personal preferences of faith. Instead, it speaks to the core of who I am; my values and my worldviews are shaped by my faith.

Catholicism is not a label I adopt; it is the banner I wear, a fundamental aspect of my being that informs how I perceive and interact with my place in the world. It is ingrained in my upbringing, heritage, and spiritual journey. On the other hand, my faith is my cross to bear. It carries with it the weight of my responsibility, sacrifice, and challenges. Just as Jesus carried his cross, my faith involves moments of struggle, doubt, and pain. Until I am able to bear that perfectly well, I shall not leave it in search of another faith.

I had certain impediments that prevented me from advancing on the path His Majesty had called me for. I had plenty of friends whose friendships were there to help me fall. It worked perfectly well the majority of the time. But when the time came to pull myself together, I realised I was entirely alone. If the experience I have related to you now is what it takes His Majesty to remind me how wicked I am to Him and incomplete without His love and mercy, then I am most grateful to His Majesty for the cross He was pleased to send me and the grace to bear it. By carrying this cross and stumbling many times, He has granted me experience and learning, which others may need twenty or even forty years to achieve. On this note, I cannot hopelessly complain but praise Him for the grace he has bestowed on me despite my unworthiness. For however dire the situation is, He always has something to teach me if I pay attention. Accordingly, I forgive whatever human element sought to disrupt the Divine work to purge my soul from iniquities. I entreat you, Lord, in your mercy, for your love, I beg this of you to forgive our inadequacy, for I have now a clearer knowledge of what you demanded from me, of what I am to you and by your help, may I never go back to who I was.

***

Every individual must decide for himself what the centre and circumference of his life are. This includes recognising one's core values, passions, and aspirations that shape his personal identity and purpose. It involves a deep and honest introspection to determine what truly matters and prioritise it. To the best of my knowledge, each of us is not our own, and one day, we must all answer to our Creator and the precious gift of life he has given us. If He is before us now to eventually account for how we have treated our neighbour, the gift of His vocation, and the opportunities He has placed in our lives, how might we reflect on our actions and attitudes to ensure we have lived following His will and the love we are called to show? If we could take a moment and truly grasp the weight of this accountability, how different would our lives be? Would we be more intentional in our words, kinder in our actions, and more generous with our time? Would we pursue our vocations with greater passion and care, recognising them as sacred responsibilities entrusted to us, not us by our own design, rather than mere personal ambitions? If we could see the impact of our choices on others and on the world, how might that change the way we live each day?

There is a significant difference between who one thinks he is and what one actually is. The former, as we have learnt from Augustine[23], refers to the image and perception we hold about ourselves—how we believe we present ourselves to the world shaped by our experiences, desires and beliefs. Here, one may say the brief answer, "I am a Man" because one perceives himself as a body and soul. In contrast, the latter delves beyond the image we hold about ourselves to the core of our identity, our self-awareness, and the inner workings of the mind and the spirit. Here, due to a lack of knowledge, one may reply with the same answer as in the first, but one cannot give such an answer without floundering in chaos about the superiority of what is inward. The inner man knows this and senses by the virtue of his mind that the true essence of what he is cannot be reduced to fleeting impressions. Therefore, he will always reach out to the world beyond him for authenticity.

In spite of this, the distinctions between who one thinks he is and what one actually is could become irrelevant in one instance. Quite different is a priest whose identity and calling are rooted in the understanding that gives meaning to both questions. As a priest, his identity is fundamentally grounded in his relationship with God and his mission among the people of God. Through his ordination, he sees himself not in terms of personal ego or worldly identity but as a servant of Christ. His sense of self is not based on personal achievement, societal validation, or ego-driven concerns but rather on His vocation to serve and embody Christ's teachings. In this context, the question of "who one thinks he is" becomes subordinated to the larger, more significant reality of being a representative of God's will.

If one must be a priest, one must not only aim to become a priest but also embody the priesthood. He must be the sacrifice and the sacrificer—the victim and the victimhood. When he acts *in persona Christi*, the gap between "what I think I am" and "what I actually am" must be bridged by the grace of his ordination. A priest's identity is transformed through the sacrament of Holy Orders, so his actions in sacred roles are no longer his own but Christ's. In this way, the priest's self-perception as an individual becomes less significant than his sacramental function as a representative of Christ. This is very essential to know as far as the priesthood is concerned, and as far as the redemption of work God must continue'. The Lamb of God is sacrificed, yes, we all know, but the priest is the person of an instrument who re-enacts this mystery and dispenses the grace imbued in the celebration. Aspiring to become this person means embodying a role transcending mere ritual one performs to becoming the thing for the ritual. By offering the sacrifice of the Mass that the faithful bring to the altar, he offers himself in *persona Christi* whilst the congregation does the same by lifting up their hearts to God. Through the words of consecration that bring about the transformation of material substance, removing imperfect particles and bringing it to perfect nature, the priest makes Divine nourishment of the soul, the food of angels and of life. He is a man, but in that state, he is not. And neither does the efficacy of the sacrament depend on his weakness, *ex opere operato.*

Although this may be a hard pill to swallow, the efficacy of the sacrament is found even in the filthiest place. In the same breath, neither does the efficacy of the sacrament being celebrated depend on the loathsome filth of the recipient once there is a good disposition to receive the sacrament, *ex opere operantis.* What the priest does is the same work of redemption which Christ accomplished on the cross upon mankind despite their sinful nature. The blessings received from the sacrament depend largely on the work of the recipient, his faith and love of God with which the sacrament is employed or a prayer of indulgence or a corporal work of mercy is performed.

It goes back to the story in Genesis, chapters 1 and 2. According to the first account, when God created man, He made Him His sapiential framework. Man is not an observant but a participator in the work of creation. He is the summary of existence.

In the second account, we experience man in his unique form, a microcosm of the universe playing a more active role as a procreator and uniting heaven and earth through the power of language. Here, I reckon the work of Pageau, his book *The Language of Creation*. The position of man amongst all created things is symbolic because it distinguishes humans from animals in a cosmological sense.[24] The same tool that God used to create the universe was the same tool that man used to give meaning to God's created works and maintain order in creation. In Psalm 8, we see David reflecting on this divine work and the power bestowed on man differently from other creatures as he echoes, "When I see your heavens, the work of your fingers, the moon and stars that you set in place—what is man that you are mindful of him?" In *Hamlet*, we see Shakespeare reaching the same but one step further conclusion as David, *"What a piece of work is a man! How Noble in reason! How infinite in faculty! In form and moving how express and admirable! In Action, how like an Angel in apprehension, how like a God! The beauty of the world, the paragon of animals—and yet, to me, what is this quintessence of dust? Man delights not me—nor woman neither, though by your smiling you seem to say so."*

There is absolutely no justification for the torment of such unsettling inquiries; if not, in man, one finds the beauty of everything God has created. He is a unifying agent between heaven and earth—a bridge between the spiritual and corporeal world.[25] This role summarises the impetus of his existence even in the face of his frequent lapses of memory. Our ancestors served the same purpose as we read from the story of Abraham and Sarah. As Christ is from the lineage of Abraham, this role became more explicit through which we see God choosing to partake in human nature.

Christ (the logos of the father), although he was God, stepped out from the invisible Godhead and assumed the visible manifestation of God like a man to free him from the slavery of sin and restore him to his original innocence. In his death, he experienced the plight of mankind; he knows his pain, his weakness and suffering and even the death that terrifies him; he knows man more than he knows himself—and he felt the proclivity of man to run away from suffering, *"Father if you are willing take this cup away from me; still not my will but yours be done"* (Luke 22:42). He took them all up to the cross whilst, in turn, bringing freedom to man.

Being a priest amplifies that in the most profound sense. As a priest acting in the person of Christ, one continues God's work by sanctifying the imperfect substances and making them holy. Celebrating the Holy Mass, the priest draws meaning from heaven to earth and raises matter to heaven. It is the very form of ritual that is built into a pattern, follows a pattern, and dispenses its grace in patterns.

The ritual informs, illuminates, and connects the pattern inherent in the world and the meaning it embodies in the creation of the universe. This expresses the most profound sublime truth of the Holy Mass, its narrative and meaning.

The work of a priest is way more profound than our desire for dignity and authority and political relevance. It is way deeper than creating a hostile environment to facilitate the expulsion of seminarians, through which the very inspiring gift of a vocation is tampered with. It is about embracing the stigmata of becoming both the victim and the embodiment of victimhood. Fulton J. Sheen captured this essence in his profound wisdom when he wrote a book titled *The Priest Is Not His Own*. In this declaration, he underscores the sacred truth that a priest's identity is not solely defined by personal perception or ambitions but by a profound commitment to serve others, often at the cost of one's own comfort and safety. But sometimes, we do not see it either because we tend to live by what we desire instead of living by what God desires of us. Or because we do not possess the spiritual strength of Augustine and Aquinas to sustain the paradox of priestly vocation. Or because we possess it but do not want to implement it. Or we want to implement it but are worried about the craziness of the modern world. Or we do not want to do anything about that. Or there lingers a fear that by doing so, we may uncover facets of ourselves that we are unaware of or reluctant to confront. There is so much insecurity, but where is it coming from? How can we make others feel secure if we ourselves are insecure?

A German deacon once made an unpleasant impression on me that he feels nothing about the Mass. I said, well, how would you if all we do at Mass is to buttress the manifesto of our political leanings?

When we observe figures like that German deacon, we must ask ourselves: Is this detachment a product of disillusionment or a defense mechanism against the chaos? If the essence of our rituals has become a mere echo of our political convictions, what do we present to the modern world that has not already been presented to them? In my corner of the world, I see this tension manifest daily. Clericalism and not service to the poor now serves as a deity that demands worship at the altar of success and recognition. It has crept into the very fabric of our religious houses, distorting our priorities and leading us to question what truly matters. But there is a reason for this: because in the seminary, we are formed to perceive each other as rivals rather than as brothers. We are exulted to live as brothers, *Ecce quam bonum et quam jucundum habitare fratres in unum!*—"Behold, how good and how pleasant it is for brethren to dwell together in unity!", but at the same time, we employ the same brother to act against his brother. There is no justification in expecting magic to happen, for as the Latin says, *Nemo dat quod non habet*—no one gives what he does not possess. If we are devoid of genuine love and truth, how can we expect to create a community that thrives on these virtues? We cannot offer what we have not first embraced ourselves.

When it comes to the seminary formation, we must also understand that every individual is unique and novel. He is novel in that his holiness and being human are not transferrable—they are not inherited from the parents.[26] Being human, as Jasper says, is a 'decisive' being: the individual decides what he becomes in the next moment. As a decisive exercise, he opposes the dogmas and doctrines when he feels they endanger his authentic self and intention. Thenceforth, the essence of seminary formation is to bring out the best in the individual aspiring to serve God—not to stifle their motivation or dim their inner light. True formation is about cultivating their unique gifts and deepening their connection to God while preserving the passion and zeal that led them to the calling. It seems plausible to say that we have failed in our capacity to fulfil this mission entrusted to us by Christ. We expel the people we feel are charismatic leaving them deeply wounded whilst keeping those we can drive with collars.

In many instances, before I resolved to write this book, I have watched those who left the seminary—often due to our cruelty and weaknesses—lead successful lives. They become lawyers, doctors, artists, and businessmen—triumphant by all worldly standards. On the other hand, some experience deep suffering to the breaking point from the wounds we have unanimously inflicted on them. They struggle to make ends meet. Whilst my focus is not primarily on those who bore our pain, it is essential to consider the successful individuals for a moment, especially the anomalous nature of their experience. Despite their accomplishments, I have observed that they remain fixated on their first love: the vocation they once pursued with all their heart.

This leads me to the disturbing question of why the call lingers persistently in their hearts, even when they seem to have left it behind. My answer to this may be regarded as a subjective science, but I strongly believe that vocation does not end with expulsion, and there are two ways to understand this drawing from our exposition hitherto. The individual is not primarily driven by pleasure but by deep desires for meaning, purpose, and belonging. When someone enters the seminary, he does so not merely out of duty or external expectation but because he believes he is answering a call that resonates within the deepest recesses of his soul. This call, which can be understood as self-transcendent motivation, cannot be easily be dispensed with. Consciously or not, it shapes one's sense of self, providing structure to one's identity and purpose in life.

In a similar vein, when he leaves the seminary, especially under the painful circumstances most of us do, he may shed the visible trappings of religious life, but he cannot so easily escape the inner world shaped by his vocation. The seminary forms not only our intellect but also our spirit. The vows of chastity, poverty, and obedience are not codes of conduct that can be dusted out from the shelves whenever we need them; they are practices that reorient one's entire being towards God, who made him. This reorientation is profound and lasting. Consequently, even when he re-enters the world, those who have undergone this deep transformation often experience an internal dissonance between who they are and the life they are now leading. In this disparity, the pursuit of life toward God weighs more than the pursuit of worldly pleasure.

On the reverse, one may view it as a fixation on the past, but that would be a reductionist way of thinking about a phenomenon so complex as vocation. The call that initially drove the individual to the seminary does not vanish because it is tied to something much deeper than mere experience or habit. It is bound to the core of his being, to his understanding of what is sacred and meaningful. Therefore, this lingering call is not a simple longing for a lost past but an ongoing pull towards an unmet union. More broadly, it seems more accurate to say it is God's way of shaming what we know about the nature of our vocation to the priesthood.

In the hardness of our hearts and the rigidity of our minds, we are often too focused on preserving the old ways, disregarding the nature of this calling that lies beyond our understanding. We frequently approach this vocation as if it is something that can be easily defined, controlled, or dismissed—thinking it is solely a matter of choice or circumstance. We believe that expelling or withdrawing a seminarian is the ultimate means of preserving the vocation, as though we could simply erase the divine pull by severing the external purpose. In our limited human wisdom, we assume that closing a door can shut out the deeper truths it signifies. But the deeper truth is that vocation in itself is not born of itself; it is not something we possess by will—it possesses us, drawing us into a relationship that transcends our understanding and will. Seen in this light, the persistence of the call, even after it appears abandoned, is proof that we are but gatekeepers of this vocation. Now, whether the vocation of a seminarian after their dismissal or withdrawal aligns with man's original vocation as God's work is a question that remains open. Ultimately, we cannot fully discern where man's original vocation as God's creature ends and where his vocation to the priesthood begins. The priesthood is not an isolated vocation but a participation in the divine plan for humanity. In the act of answering the call to the priesthood, a seminarian is not simply choosing a career or a path of service. He is, in a profound sense, aligning himself with the larger narrative of God's creation and redemption, and it is within this context that the priestly vocation finds its meaning.

It follows, therefore, that through this process, we can discern the true nature of Divine calling. Fulton J. Sheen often articulated vocation as more than just a profession; it is a love affair—an intimate relationship with God. To be called by God is to be drawn into a divine romance, where the soul becomes united to its ultimate Beloved. In this sense, the call to priesthood or religious life is more than mere career aspirations; it becomes a covenant, a binding relationship between the soul and God. As Augustine wrote, our soul can never find rest until it rests in Him. When a person enters the seminary, they respond to this divine call, offering their entire being to pursue a higher love, God. The vows he takes function as a form of spiritual marriage—a dedication of oneself to the service of God and His Church. Just as in a human relationship, when this bond is broken, it leaves a scar—an ache that does not quickly fade. In the Bible, we read that God's call is irrevocable: "For the gifts and the calling of God are irrevocable" (Rom 11:29). Once God has seduced a soul as in Jeremiah 20, placed His hand on a soul, that soul is forever marked. Even if a person walks away or succeeds in other realms, the divine imprint remains.

This is why I am skeptical about some of our brothers who lead a different life when they leave the seminary under any circumstance. I am aware away that leaving the seminary can feel like freedom from the allegory of the cave. But perhaps we may think about that worldview more critically. Is it truly liberation, or is it merely an exchange of one set of constraints for another, more insidious kind—more responsibility? While it may seem like a newfound freedom, the deeper truth is that what we perceive as an escape from the shadows may, in fact, be a step away from the light of Divine purpose. That call is still echoing in our hearts, reminding us that true freedom is not found in wordlessness but in the first love, the fulfilment of a higher purpose.

Leaving the seminary is not the end of one's vocation because God is not finished with you unless one willingly exempt yourself. Leaving the seminary is the process of individuation. It is a process of breaking away from the vicious cycle of perplexity and anguish of self-constructed prison. It is a process of becoming an individual set apart for the mission that only God Himself assigns.

Being docile about what life will send your way is a prerequisite to knowing what life has in store for you. Leaving the seminary is a process of becoming human and divine in a world that is simultaneously full of angels and demons. Not that you were not in the seminary and not that one cannot be in the seminary, but that you become this in a different way accompanied by the ever-loving Father, God, the eternal Thou in Buberian terms. Leaving the seminary is a process of becoming one with heaven and earth. It is an opportunity to look at the world unconventionally.

Whilst you suffer to regain your stand, it will not last for long and He is already suffering with you on the cross. Frankl could prove that "if there is any meaning at all in life, then there is meaning in suffering. Suffering is an ineradicable part of life, even fate and death. Without suffering and death, human life cannot be complete."[27]

Frankly, we do not need Frankl to tell us that before we can see the meaning that lurks in inevitable complex situations. Understand that there is a learning happening whilst you are in those moments of crisis. Pay attention, form your action, and you will see the opportunity where the crisis has emerged. Do not wish for it to have happened to someone else instead of you but bear it with the same dedication you would if you were a priest.

See that you are shouldering the responsibility which no other than you can bear ideally. See, it is only a test that God wants to know if you would stand it. He has called you. He is not going back on his words.

See that no man can take away anything you have learnt from you; the good and bad times you had in the seminary, not a single soul would take that away from you. God will never allow suffering greater than you to take you down.

Like Abraham, you are making the ultimate sacrifice, which will shake heaven to do something in your favour. This sacrifice will shake heaven to bless you and the earth to respect you. The sun shall not smite you because you have paid the ultimate debt. Only God can determine what and when to stop you.

Leaving the seminary should be dignified and celebrated by the people who love us and have been there from the beginning. It should be seen as an extension of the call. Do not be afraid because of the promise we have made to our families and how our families have presented themselves to the public, because of the covenant our parents had made to God before our conception, as in the days of Samuel or the uncertainties of starting a new life.

We all should be frightened of the alternative that, however much we try to hide in the uterus of such an established system as the seminary, the more significant challenge lies in pastoral work and outside the uterus. I also suppose that if every time exists in the mind of God, He again is aware that at this point in our life, we will leave the seminary either of our volition, as a result of our inadequacy or human wickedness. He is aware because even before we approach the chapel to speak to Him, He knows, and whilst we speak, He listens. He knew us before He formed us in our mother's womb, as Jeremiah said, and right before we were born, He dedicated us and appointed us for various tasks (Jer 1:5). Thus, if we leave the formation, it is evident that He has deemed us worthy of another mission.

The mission God assigns to His sons and daughters will only be made manifest by Him. It is something that requires our attention and trust. It will take time to accomplish, but as He said in the book of Habakkuk 2:1-5, He will not disappoint if it delays. One will lose many friends; I lost the very people I cared for and loved. Actually, for this mission, you do not need them to survive. Alone with none but thee, God must be one's prayer. You do not have to worry though the earth should rock, for as He said in the book of Isaiah 43:1-3:

But now, thus, says the Lord, who created you, Jacob and formed you, Israel. Do not fear I have redeemed you; I have called you by name; you are mine. When you pass through waters, I will be with you; through the rivers, you shall not be swept away. When you walk through fire, you shall not be burnt nor flames consume you.

And Isaiah. 41:10-13

Do not fear I am with you; do not be anxious: I am your God. I will strengthen you, I will help you. I will uphold you with my victorious hand. Yes, all shall be put to shame and disgrace who vent their anger against you; Those shall be as nothing and perish who offer resistance. You shall seek but not find those who strive against you; They shall be as nothing at all who do battle with you. For I am the Lord, your God who grasps your right hand. It is I who say to you, do not fear, I will help you.

Once we trust in this truth, God's victorious hand will uphold us, and those who abandon us will fade into nothingness.

May all we do be, for Christ's sake, who makes the priesthood.

IV
Stings of the Past, Loss of Inward Grace

Moving away from the familiar shores of my past was not just good but transformative and profoundly enriching. On many occasions, I found myself in situations where I discovered new horizons, opportunities, and versions of myself I knew existed but was not buoyant to explore. Doors were opened, adventure was, and endless possibilities were, including the privilege to think without being coerced. Here, things are structured with meticulous attention to detail and a clear sense of purpose. The organisation extends to every facet of life, including transportation.

Bus and train connections are meticulously planned and integrated seamlessly into our daily routines. Timetables are synchronised, routes are optimised, and information is readily accessible, ensuring smooth transitions between destinations. In Hermannsburg where I lived, life was not just affordable; it was remarkably so. The cost of living was modest, allowing a student like me to enjoy a comfortable lifestyle without the burden of excessive expenses. Individuals were not always immediately approachable, but it did not detract from the overall beauty of the city.

As I studied at a small international university, forming friendships was manageable in its intimate setting. The close-knit community fostered an environment where frequent interactions and connections were easily made. Whether it was through shared classes, sports activities, or casual encounters in cafes, there was always an opportunity to meet.

There was undeniable freeness among students and professors. Things were unlike the typical German university, where the chasm between the scholars and their mentors was deep and dreadful. Some of my fondest memories were formed during late-night study sessions in the library, campfires and spontaneous adventures exploring the surrounding countryside. One could undertake hiking through picturesque landscapes. We regularly toured through the forests.

It was also our means of meeting local people. Our lecture attendance was modest in size. As such, the intimacy of our classroom studies was really felt. With fewer students, we had the opportunity for more personalised attention from our tutors. Although there was a lack of larger institutions' appliances, it offered a unique and enriching academic experience. It was also theology, so it was *déjà vu Erlebniss* for me. Whilst there, I took that advantage to cultivate what would guide me in the coming years.

One of the memories that has remained vivid in my mind is the visit to Bergen Belsen. The details of my feelings do not come to my mind, but I was angry and frightened at the same time. As I walked through the grounds of the site, I could not shake off the weight it bears, the suffering of those men, women and children who were consumed by the horrors of man. The tour guide was benevolent in explaining the history so that it came to life before our eyes. '*Nie wieder*', we all said strongly in different ways, denouncing past atrocities.

The declaration was not mere words; it became a commitment for me and the lens through which I viewed my life in Germany, the political landscape and religious activities. As someone who comes from a country that was once torn apart by civil war, I felt very ashamed, standing in sombre reflection upon our collective failure to deeply acknowledge what has happened in the past and how deeply this is polarising modern Nigeria. The historical narrative remains conspicuously absent from our educational curriculum, a profound omission that despicably echoes the lack of ideals and consciousness among the political elites. Its tempo is not stable, which reflects a broader disregard for truth and intellectual integrity. The leaders, swayed by convenience and political expediency, perpetuate a sanitised version of history, enabling them to curry favour from the forces that put them in power[28].

One learns about the World Wars and discusses them intelligibly, but a similar narrative is bleeding in our hearts and longing to be made sense of. No regard for this horrible past that holds us together, for which the effect is the perpetual cycle of ignorance and disengagement between the past, present and future. Unlike the Igbos, who bear the indelible scars of the conflict and have tied their suffering and resilience into the very fabric of their memory, the rest of the nation has yet to attain this profound level of consciousness. *Egal egal* is almost the mentality of an average person. Yet, this pervasive indifference does not stem from the thoughtful action of a developed psyche but reflects a deeper societal malaise.

Perhaps, as the compelling narrative has been, the Igbos are rebellions; thenceforth, matters concerning them may divide the country and bring further conflicts as to say that peace after the civil war has been laid on a genuine foundation. Then, the moral and political philosophers might ask me if the peace and identity of a nation could be founded on a false narrative about who they really are and where that would lead them. We have not undertaken the essential inward gaze, the critical introspection that one often witnesses among Germans, young and old alike.

Be cautious in suggesting that I equate a developed country with an 'underdeveloped' one. Often, these are nothing but egregious ways to escape the critical severity of the problem. The exigency of my statement stems from practical reason, which is essential for deriving good actions[29]. Since practical reason is the basis for deriving good actions, my assessments and, if you may, comparisons are grounded in a profound understanding of the practical realities each place faces. One must acknowledge that things are not perfect in this part of the world.

The current political and religious landscape has failed to acknowledge the hard-earned lessons of history. The consciousness of avoiding past mistakes is ever-present in the fabrics of the young and the old one encounters, yet it is alarmingly absent in the actions and rhetoric of those in power. It is as though the memories left for us by those who endured the suffering are ignored, drowned out by the clamour of political self-service. One sees that despite solemn pledges, we still face actions that uncomfortably mirror the past in every form and shape. The insights from history are ignored, eclipsed by narrow vision and short-term desideratum.

There is, consequently, no effect, no difficulty in proclaiming that we regret the past. The maxim must be: if I must pay tribute to the past, I must openly confess in my actions that the past is horrible and believe that in the present, there is a kind of path that I would thread which is inconsistent with the idea of humanity as an end in itself. And if I by myself take that path simply to escape the duty I owe humanity, I risk using another person as a means to an end. Aside from the familiar presence of hatred for the *Other*, what I am unleashing includes deviating from the religious principles of *infinite dignitatis* in matters concerning the individual on which the law guiding this nation is predicated and avoiding substituting what is Godly with sheer political abracadabra. The political, above all, must be subjected to what is religious.

It is a categorical imperative, a duty for all men according to which the state must govern itself. The preamble of the Grundgesetzt summarises: *Im Bewußtsein seiner Verantwortung vor Gott und den Menschen, von dem Willen beseelt, als gleichberechtigtes Glied in einem vereinten Europa dem Frieden der Welt zu dienen, hat sich das Deutsche Volk kraft seiner verfassungsgebenden Gewalt dieses Grundgesetz gegeben.*

By implication, what is political must align with what is Godly—underscoring the infinite responsibility of governance to reflect divine moral imperatives and uphold a mode of being that transcends human laws. It is not hypothetical; thus, the objective is to be guided by a higher sense of dignity and respect for the human person, ensuring that pursuing power does not close down on the fundamental values of humanity and faith. It places governance on a binding sacred contract involving the governor (God), the governed (Man), and the governance process (actions and intentions). The triadic relationship elevates the act of governing to a divine mandate, wherein the political and spiritual realms converge to uphold the common good. The governor, as divine authority, imparts guidelines and principles; the governed, as human participants, engage with these principles through their actions and decisions; and the governance process, as a pillar of security and order, ensures that these interactions are regulated and guided by the highest moral standards.

One may immediately object: One may say that God does not belong in the law that governs man and must, without further contemplation, be immediately removed. However, such objection does not come from the soul that knows not God, but from the soul that knows and believes that not only man but the state that rules him must be subject to the governorship of God and where the rational inclinations of man cannot get him further, God must make the decision[30]. But he will not accept it so as to escape the misery of having to justify his action to humanity, thereby risking the good for humanity in order to preserve himself. One thing is for sure: if he is not conscious of the fact that God should be there, he will not do anything to prevent God from being mentioned there. Consequently, one should outright reject any kind of conception that is not guided by higher principles but by mundane characteristics.

As Jung opines that *just as man, a social being, cannot, in the long run, exist without a tie to the community,*[31] so also, I add, the state will never find its justification for existence anywhere except in the extramundane principles capable of relativising its overpowering influence. Thenceforth, the state has a responsibility to govern its subject in a way that adheres to moral principles that surpass human inclinations and temporal concerns. This responsibility entails that the state must govern not only with its power but in accordance with a superior principle that directs human conduct towards preserving equilibrium between its power and the ethical values that promote the welfare and dignity of its subjects.

This responsibility goes beyond politics to religion, the place of sacred, demanding an unalloyed adherence to imperatives that produce and foster an authentic search for truth. For Christians, this means praising the risen Christ through what we do to prove love and the oneness of our belief. It necessitates a resolute rejection of the merciless craving for division, embodying a moral imperativeness of duty that binds us to a higher good. For if we are unable to manifest our faith in deeds, and reject any first impulse that tears our common belief, then we fail not only ourselves but also the very essence of our faith. Alas, in heaven, the judgment of God will not be the Catholics vs the Lutherans nor the Protestants vs the Orthodox, but rather the righteous vs the unrighteous. It will be the ultimate measure of our adherence to the divine commands, our manifestation of faith through deeds, and our commitment to the love that Christ embodied (see James 2:14-26). I imagine that earthly divisions will dissolve in this heavenly tribunal, and we are left with nothing but what we have achieved in our spiritual journey.

To understand how this applies to the conduct of human affairs and why it is necessary, then, without doubt, the only option is to delve into personal intricacies and the matter with things as I observed them. This would be rocky, but I promise to return to things as they were. At some point at school, my education was threatened due to financial instability. With limited knowledge of the language and few job opportunities in my small city, I myself was at a crossroads to forfeit my education. So many things came into play, especially how it would affect my stay.

Thus, I decided to seek scholarships and contacted many foundations, but proficiency in the language was decisive, except for one organisation. For them, language was not a factor; one could still be supported to learn the language, but my religious affiliation was. It turns out that they have no mandate to support Catholic Christians. In another instance, my application was accepted, but after the review process, I did not hear back from the board. I only learnt the reason at a later stage. And, of course, they are not mandated as well to support Catholic Christians.

For whatever reason, such demands are made, I could not comprehend the rationale behind it, especially considering my genuine need for financial assistance and commitment to my studies. I could not wrap my mind around it. I assumed that I was free in this country to practice my religion as I deemed fit. On the contrary, the realisation that being a Catholic could hinder my access to opportunities shook me as unbelievable. Worst still, it was a Christian organisation. That fact alone drove me to insanity.

As I understood it, there are reasons why things are as such. One could think of the legal framework, the funder's interest, but most importantly, the doctrinal and dogmatic rift between Catholicism and Protestantism in times past that caused the Reformation. One could feel it even when they gather for the so-called *Ökumenischer Gottesdient*—the constant scrutiny to highlight every flaw within the Catholic Church. This theological tension, which was not just a pivotal event in ecclesiastical history, but also a global phenomenon, continues to impact people's lives today. The fight between Catholicism and Protestantism shapes religious practices and influences cultural, social, and political landscapes in Germany. This has left a lasting imprint on individual identities, communal life, and societal structures where the Catholics are seen as reactionary and the Protestants more progressive, modern and up-to-date with the dynamics of society.

Furthermore, Catholics are viewed as backwards as rigid and authoritarian, whilst Protestants are seen as champions of democratic values, personal liberty, and social progress despite their own historical and contemporary challenges. In a broader context, the Reformation greatly impacts governance and public life.

But it is also not apparent that all those things the Lutherans do, taking the soul out of the liturgy, is the perfect practice of Christianity. Indeed, I appreciate the beautiful emphasis on the direct relationship between man and God, free from established authority and ritualistic formalities. In contrast, the highest relationship with God is the *Imitatio Christi*, and the procedure has been carved out by Thomas A. Kempis and St Ignatius of Loyola in his *Spiritual Exercises*. Once this *imitatio Christi* becomes *imitatio mundi*, the supreme paradox of Christian values is watered down; the soul becomes null and void; our actions become a mere artefact with no inward grace.

After the rejection, I could not secure funds immediately to return to school. I thought of quitting, taking a break or vocational training to raise funds. Indeed, such treatment also created nostalgia, and I tried finding my way back to the seminary. Eventually, I started looking for universities to study Catholic Theology. But this nostalgia came with a mixed feeling of mistrust and was very fickle as the Catholic liturgy, as I have experienced it here, came to bore me.

Whilst the Protestants are pointing out the flaws of the Catholics, there is pressure for the Catholics to align more closely with Protestant norms, which is often most evident in theological contexts. The pressure manifests in various forms, including adaptation of liturgy, ecclesiastical reforms, and shifts in theological emphasis. There was so much emphasis on what Rome should do rather than what we should do as followers of Christ. Homilies and sermons were full of anger and bitterness about what was wrong with the Church. One could imagine a Sunday homily where the congregation should be filled with so much grace from the Ambo. Instead, the homily is read in a measured tone to speak about moving the church forward. The intensity of this pressure is starkly evident in heated debates over sexuality and priestly celibacy. Added to it was the existing tension between the German Catholic Church and Rome, with their mission to reform the Church. The good thing then, which is also the beauty of the Catholic faith, was that even though I could not understand everything, I could still follow the liturgy and obtain the grace that God dispenses through the priest.

Naturally, one might desire more engagement with the liturgy than just sitting on the pews, nodding and smiling, but I did not consider this so much of a problem. I wanted to say something, for in many capacities, I have been confronted with this anger and bitterness on a personal level. Still, I was engulfed by fear of saying what had already been considered taboo even before I conceived it. All too often, it was about the German Catholic Church against the whole Church because the German Catholic Church was not morally bankrupt like the rest of the Church. The result is a dangerous dichotomy that fosters an 'us versus them' mentality, risking the Church's unity and the teachings of Christ. "That they may be one, as you, Father, are in me and I in you, that they may also be one in us, that the world may believe that you sent me," prayed Christ in (John. 17:21), but such divisions as we have them today perpetuate a schism that corrodes the essence of Christian fellowship. The imperative we seek is fault lines, drawing divisive boundaries between the people of God motivated by pride and a distorted sense of righteousness.

Fundamentally, we have reached a point in the Church and perhaps the Catholic Church at large where the question of sexuality by reputable theologians deprives one of the inward grace of an outward sign. When we celebrate the Mass, we do not celebrate it because we are convinced and mandated by Christ, the priest, to do it, but we do it with so much indignation as if we seek to defy Him. Our hearts burn not with devotion but with resentment and anger that our feeling is not valued, in such a way that every word uttered seems like a silent protest against the very idea of His sacrifice. Our thoughts stray from the divine mystery to the carnal; the holiest of rituals is reduced to a mere stage for our own lustful inclinations. This ruthless focus on sexuality has become a stumbling block, obscuring the path to spiritual nourishment.

As one might still stumble on this issue, I will now restrict myself to the Church. Worthy of mention is that I speak here not as a theologian myself but as a layperson who was seduced by the immense beauty of the Eucharist and believes in the mission of the Church to guide individuals in search of the meaning of life instead of exacerbating the hunger for meaning. In this respect, one may find certain errors in my conceptions. It is left for the theologians and others reading this to take note and separate the wheat out of the chaff.

It is not that the question of human sexuality and its attachments is not important in the human person, but it must be discussed with carefulness and be conceived in two folds instead of just one. "To the man, the world is twofold,"[32] Buber says. Per this twofold attitude towards the world, whatever concerns man must be seen in two ways: spiritually and physically. But primarily the spiritual, for without understanding it, one observes some fragmentations in the formulations the individual makes about himself. For this reason, we must highlight the spiritual and the physical.

Sexuality is a Divine gift to sustain the existence of man and all other created things. It is the means of bonding and fulfilling God's command "to be fruitful and multiply, fill the earth and subdue it." In Genesis chapter 2:24, "Therefore a man shall leave his father and his mother and cling to his wife, and the two of them become one body." This mandate is that through this process, man would be able to bring to life another individual like him in God's image and likeness. Thus, sexuality becomes a microcosmic union of heaven and earth[33].

The institution of sexuality represents the dual pattern from which reality is modelled. The coming together of two distinct types to bring about a new world constitutes, in part, how the universe grows itself. Once the male and the feminine parts unite, the higher principle of being descends to the lower principle of being, and meaning is brought to being.

Essentially, this is a representation of higher intimacy of love, something stronger than the desires of the flesh, which only sees the individual as a biological animal, a means to satisfy one's irascible appetite, a mere *res*. In this profound respect, which we talk about, it is not about the giving but the giving and the receiving of love, love in its sublimity nourished and expressed in the encounter between two distinct individuals. Love, therefore, is the primordial and positive driving force towards their growth as distinct individuals and maturity as persons whilst maintaining the source of each person's[34] vocation and each person as the precious source of its realisation.[35] In actual effect, sexuality is the calling of man to love, a form of love incarnated in the body that bears the mark of a person's masculinity and femininity.[36]

In other words, the expression of love should not only be in a spiritual or emotional sense but also in a physical sense, having bodily form. Hence, human sexuality is a unified whole in which the physical action conveys a deeper emotional and spiritual connection. Therefore, the meaning of sexuality goes beyond the biological make-up and its utility to satisfy the concupiscence to mean, as described by the Church's document, the "intimate nucleus of the (human) person."[37]

Therefore, human sexuality cannot only be understood in the light of biological and, most notoriously, political nuances but of divine revelation: "Sexuality characterises man and woman not only on the physical level but also on the psychological and spiritual, making its mark on each of their expressions."[38] The Church highlights such diversity, connected to the harmony between the sexes, enables complete alignment with the Divine plan based on the unique purpose that each individual is destined for.[39] In another context, the document writes that human sexuality is not something purely biological; rather, it concerns the innermost core of the individual.

In other words, sexuality is not just a physical or biological characteristic but a profound aspect of human identity and vocation. As a vocation, it is meant to be integrated within the whole person, respecting the dignity and purpose bestowed by the Creator. This understanding calls for recognising the sacredness of human sexuality and its role in expressing love, generating life and participating in God's creative work.

In light of the challenges posed by human sexuality in the modern world, it is imperative to engage with sexuality not only on the basis of how we feel but with wisdom and fidelity to God. The desire dominating the search for sexual expression is, as Augustine puts it, 'to love and to be loved'.[40] It is a genuine human desire which, if no restraint is put on it, by this, I mean creating a shore to confine its strong waves; this desire will defile the individual's soul. For when the hellish fire the senses ignite burns, every part of the human body is moved towards satisfying the proportion and nature of the desires.

These desires have only one function: expressing themselves regardless of where the individual is and his circumstances. Thus, it happens that even at the Mass and in moments of deep supplication to God, the senses can commune to stir up images and motions of impurity to distract the agent and make him prey to the devil. John of the Cross explains in *The Dark Night of the Soul* the devil uses such images and motions to disquiet the soul, wheretofore the individual would want to give up prayer altogether because he thinks such motions occur whenever he wants a quiet moment with God, which is true since the devil attacks him more during those alone moments than at other times, so that he may give up spiritual exercises entirely.[41]

Such things as complex as human sexuality must be deeply understood before making a ludicrous claim of its nature and inculcating our self-fashioned tyrant values in the young. It is not even in our place to educate them about human sexuality, especially when the parents and guardians are physically and morally capable. The fact that politics in itself has captured sexuality and the rest of us are deeply ingrained in it points to, on the one hand, an aberration, a distortion of priority and a spiritual disintegration in the affairs of the human condition. The individual longs for salvation, which society is not healthy enough to provide. Instead, such longing is exacerbated by creating more distortions in his mental health.

On the other hand, it brings to the limelight the inner struggle within the individual to create a harmonious balance between his selfhood and sexuality and the failure of theologians as doctors of divinity and psychiatrists and psychologists as doctors of the soul to help him map out a modality by which he would determine his own existence.

Politically, he is promised legal freedom and protection from enemies to actualise his fantasy. In contrast, what is happening in him exceeds what political elements can manage, yet they will not admit it! Education was supposed to give him the tools necessary to navigate the complexity of being. But even the education process is shredded of any form of meaning, and his own human heritage is denied of him. Subjectively, he is taught to think: I am what my sexuality is and can be attracted to any person or thing. I am free to explore myself and engage in the 'jungle of erotic adventures'. I must free myself from the modes of being imposed by tradition. Every emotion has a predicate of value and must be declared to the public so that they would notice and acknowledge my innermost struggle. By so doing, I can determine my existence without any external judgment or limitations placed upon me by culture and religion.

But the corollary is this ruthless pursuit of self-definition and liberation from traditional constraints often culminates in a paradoxical enslavement. The deeper aspiration for absolute autonomy devolves into a fragmented identity, perpetually oscillating between ephemeral desires and the profound, unmet yearnings of the soul. In the quest to articulate and indulge every transient emotion and impulse, the individual forfeits a coherent sense of self, becoming untethered in a vast expanse of moral relativism and subjectivity. Additionally, disclosing his innermost struggles in the hope of gaining validation from an external audience ironically subjects him to the judgments and societal expectations he strives to elude. In essence, he becomes ensnared in a cyclical dynamic wherein the quest for emancipation through sexuality and self-expression engenders a deeper entanglement with the very forces of societal and internal disarray he sought to overcome.

Indeed, such subjective identification appears to carry in it a sense of self-consciousness and self-assertion of individuality, which I like to think symbolically resonates with God's self-designation and determination as *Ego sum qui sum,* "I am who I am" in Exodus 3:14. By declaring 'I AM', God shifts the attention away from what the Israelites and Moses would expect that He would say of Himself to what He truly is: eternal being with neither beginning nor end. He shows us His superiority to the material and temporal condition of created existence, the ruler of all things that exist, corporeal and incorporeal.[42] He did not want to limit Himself beyond what man can conceive of Him, for he knew that once He gave a name to Moses, the Israelites would seek to confirm if it was indeed the God they knew.

Thus, He did not only give Moses a name but also told him about His nature, 'I AM', thereby maintaining His eternality and immutability. However, knowing full well that it might be difficult for one who does not possess the spiritual strength to grasp His absolute nature, He spoke further to Moses in verse 15, saying, "*Dominus, Deus partum verborum, Deus Abraham, Deus Isaac et Deus Lacob, misfit me ad Vos; hoc nomen mihi Est in aeternum, et hoc memorial Meum in generationer et generationer*," that man may focus on His deep significance and meaning to him instead of the deep exploration of His own self-perception and identity.

Verily, understanding God as an absolute Being in this conception is rather a stumbling block. Augustine reasons that it makes sense to think that God "mercifully accommodated his grace to humanity by revealing his name in these [temporal] terms."[43] He even noted how difficult it was for him to hold a grip on this thought. In his *Confessions*, Augustine recounts in one passage how he was able to understand in spite of his limitations. He writes:

> By the Platonic books, I was admonished to return into myself. With you as my guide I entered into my innermost citadel… When I first came to know you, you raised me up to make me see that what I saw is Being, and that I who saw am not yet Being… and I found myself far from you 'in the region of dissimilarity' and heard as it were your voice from on high: "I am the food of the fully grown; grow and you will feed on me. And you will not change me into you like the food your flesh eats, but you will be changed into me." And you cried from far away: "Now, I am who I am" (Exod. 3:14). I heard in the way one hears within the heart, and all doubt left me.

Thanks to the Platonic books, Augustine was admonished to return to his inner self, whereby he could find God as He truly is. It stands, therefore, to argue that God is ever-present and for man to really discover Him as He truly is, he must be abandoned to Him, and nothing must matter to him except fulfilling God's will. In doing so, He grants the grace that is necessary to penetrate His Being as a spirit, as he promised through the prophet Jeremiah (Jer. 33:2-3). For whilst He adjusted to man's comprehension, He went further to tell Moses and the Israelites, "I am the Lord your God, you shall not have any other gods besides me" (Exod. 20:2; Deut. 5:6), meaning that one could not deal with Him as a familiar being because such familiarity could risk reducing Him to a mere human construct, a hypothesis to be proved, diminishing the reverence that comes with recognising the profundity of His existence. He knew that becoming overly familiar with Him might result in the presumption of his grace and protection without acknowledging our responsibility and the need to be humble and obedient. He wants us to abide in Him, for without Him, we can do nothing (John 15:5). Being in God makes all things new, the old things shall pass away, and the new things will begin as it is written in the Holy Scripture.

Likewise, when looking at the mode of perception of one's own sexual identity as the ultimate mode of being, it makes sense of what the individual tries to cognise about himself. He asserts to himself and others his individuality as something determined not just by things external to him but, most notably, internal, exactly in the same manner God organises His own self-designation. In such an act of understanding, the individual intuits himself as he is affected internally. However, if he considers his capacity to cognise himself, he witnesses a pattern that is far superior to his subjective propositions of self-determination. He witnesses most purely, an inherent and unchanging existence of a person according to the particular representation which is given to him a priori. He is not because of Himself or ourselves, nor as He appears to us, but He is just is. It follows, therefore, that God's self-designation is the foundation and indisputable leverage that every individual should seek to uncover things about himself and dispel all the 'whimsical inconsistencies' resulting from societal moral decadence. This also means not sacrificing one's true self to be slaughtered as a mere biological process. Regardless of the internal war, the true self is neither determined nor lived through socially constructed body parts. The terrible consequence of such is that the mystery of the divine presence in each and every individual that transcends his imperfection becomes utterly fragmented.

If the determination of the true self can occur outside of what God knows man to be and the mode of being that transcends every sphere of a proper conception of being, but merely whatever he says to himself. Then, it is affirmative what Kant opines, that the consciousness of self, in this case, is thus very far from the knowledge of self, especially in situations where one does not fit into his preconceived categories and where a new category for the sake of conception is required to understand the self[44].

God knows the imperfections and struggles of human sexuality since, in order to deliver man from the slavery of sin, He did not abhor the Virgin's womb. He entered the very fabric of human existence, embracing our frailties and limitations. In the mystery of the incarnation, He took on human flesh, sanctified it, and affirmed its goodness despite the distortions introduced by sin. The Virgin's womb became a sacred vessel through which the divine and human nature were united by Jesus Christ. This profound act of love and humility signifies God's intimate understanding of our condition, including our sexual struggles. He knows the genuine struggles to free oneself from desires that overburden the spirit with the necessities of the body in this world.[45] He knows the secret prayers in the silence of the hearts to lift the guilt that shrouds the heart. Whereby, King David devotedly prayed after the prophet Nathan came to him, *"Cor mundum crea in me, Deus, et spiritum rectum innova in visceribus meis."* God understands the plea for spiritual purification and to inebriate the soul with his grace. Yet He may not take the imperfections away because, for some of us, that will even make us prouder.

God's ways are not always to remove the thorns from our flesh but to transform our hearts through them. In His wisdom, He sometimes allows us to struggle with our imperfections to cultivate humility, dependence on His grace, and a deeper understanding of His love. These struggles can become opportunities for spiritual growth, drawing us closer to Him and profoundly shaping our character. Paul speaks to this in his own experience of a 'thorn in the flesh', which he pleaded with God to remove.

In response, God says, "My grace is sufficient for you, for my power is made perfect in weakness" (2 Cor. 12:9). Paul's acceptance of this truth led him to say, "Therefore I will boast all the more gladly of my weaknesses, so that the power of Christ may rest upon me" (2 Cor. 12:9-10). Thus, in our own lives, the ongoing presence of imperfections and struggles can serve as a reminder of our need for God's grace. Our weaknesses are not because the God who created us is weak but because of the absence of God—the grace and illumination of hope that we are not alone and the understanding that our senses can only be meaningful by living beyond our senses. When we embrace our weaknesses and bring them to God, we empty ourselves out upon Him to His transformative power, a power that can work through us in ways that reveal His glory and love.

It is an error to elevate sexuality above God by the theologians and to think of it as the most important aspect of the individual's life—feeding on it rather than feeding the individual's soul. When it happens that those we seem to be protecting are abandoning our teachings and proceeding elsewhere to find God, and with quite another temperament contradicting the doctrines and rituals of our teachings, we must ask ourselves what it is that is pushing them. In my view, it lies in the apprehension of God, as He is. For once, the individual understands that we are not God! And that his carnal pleasure is only working against his true self, and there is nothing like being one's own enemy. He learns that even though he cannot understand the origin of his conflictual desires, it is not the sole expression of his wholeness.

Thus, he proceeds with great humility, thinking not only of his own life and having little satisfaction within himself, but he also considers others to be far better than himself and, in the words of John of the Cross, "usually have a holy envy of them and eagerness to serve God as those people do."[46] He learns that projecting his sexuality onto others is only a flight from the magnitude of what is calling him from the inside and how little he has done to manifest it. Ultimately, he realises that the only way to find peace is to turn to the inside, forsaking the gift of this miserable world and thus shall find rest in God.

What I am unfolding here does not make one immune to this coaster of emotions. No human being is immune to these desires of the flesh, but how we handle it is different. The point is that with the grace of God, we can rise in full conviction that we are more than our natural inclinations. Only by looking up to God will one overcome his inadequacies. We cannot repress our Godly instinct to worship sexuality and expect the rest of our being to grow. This is a dangerous illusion, as we may be embarrassed to discover that we are spiritually stunted. Human sexuality is a gift from God—not God in itself—a transformative process of life through which our identities, connections, and sense of self are profoundly intertwined. This intricate interplay shapes our experiences and relationships in mysterious and profound ways.

As a transformative process, Jung, in his essay on *Psychic Energy,* writes that sexuality is a vital force that drives individual development and self-realisation. Jung began by discussing how physical events are understood and then deeply related to sexuality. He describes the mechanistic and energic standpoints of physical as *sine qua non* to understanding sexuality. The mechanistic explains life's events regarding cause with unchanging substance following fixed rules. The energic viewpoint, on the other hand, focuses on the essence, the reason behind the event and traces its effect back to the cause on the assumption that there must be an underlying energy capable of explaining the changes in phenomena and that it maintains itself constant throughout which would in turn lead to entropy, a state of general equilibrium.

According to Jung, the human psyche operates on a fundamental energy which, in some way or other, is connected with physical processes. This energy is not necessarily sexual but a generalised life energy that drives the psychological process of man. To understand this is to take the psyche as a closed system in its own right and not as a mere mechanical process. Thus, for Jung, the instincts of sex, hunger and aggression, are expressions of this psychic energy. For him, sexuality, on the other hand, is not a mere instinctuality but an indispensable creative power that serves as both the fundamental source of individual existence and a profoundly significant element in our psychological experience.

We could call sexuality, as Jung suggested, the 'spokesman of the instincts', which is why, from a spiritual standpoint, sex is the primary adversary because, with sexuality, the spirit sees a contender that is closely equal and also related to itself. Sexuality holds within itself a claim over the spirit's essence during processes such as procreation, pregnancy, birth and childhood. It cannot be eliminated because where then would the spirit find its expression if not the creative acts of sexuality?

Sexuality must be conceived in symbolic terms and not necessarily in carnal terms as it embodies deeper psychological dimensions that transcend mere physicality. The one-sided interpretation now from theologians of the Church reflects a fragmentation of ideals and a poor understanding of human nature. It seems that we are under a spell not to see beyond lest we uncover our deep-seated ignorance. Worst, everyone is forced to accept it as some sort of a dogmatic constitution, and those who do not accept it are regarded as the bad guys and must be deprived of their social security. Even reaching this point in our civilisation requires seriously examining our collective conscience.

Indeed, the exigency of our times implores a profound examination of conscience as our collective consciousness oozes a decay in our collective ideal. We stand at the precipice of moral bankruptcy, teetering perilously on the edge of moral oblivion. As stewards of reason and custodians of the word of God, we must soon enough cast off the shackles of intellectual dictatorship and moral relativism. We must resolutely speak against the tyranny of orthodoxy, and the epistemic barriers that confine our collective consciousness to the confines of moral obliquity.

As for the individual, one must be very careful in selling himself cheaply to a childish appetite for conformity. One's life is not anchored on his sexuality, and there is no need to make others believe otherwise. Truly, those coaster of emotions as we know it are very disturbing and can cause colossal damage. But we also know that they are fickle and will pass away once they cannot achieve their aim. What is required of one is to acknowledge his self-worth, mainly who he is and take responsibility for his being.

Whereupon one thinks that the responsibility is too much to take, one must not put himself in danger but only take what he can bear by the grace given him. To understand oneself, this includes the issues posed by one's sexuality; one must first return to the fundamental facts of his being irrespective of the authority which has made it possible for him to deviate from those fundamental facts. He must purify his mind unto God and depend only on God as if man does not exist. His imperfect body must be converted into the first matter, purifying all infirmities and yet containing in itself all necessary things.[47] This also includes the willingness to say no to certain theologians and their allies who pose themselves as having God's mandate here on earth yet cannot speak the name of God unashamed.

Indeed, I did not intend to go this far, but the matter is so important that one must dedicate his time to it. If the Church is on the right track, society will have a certain level of decorum. The stakes could not be higher because the trajectory of the Church is inexorably linked with the very fabric of society itself. If the Church, as the moral compass of civilisation, steers true upon the tempest of human affairs, then there is hope, however faint, that society may be imbued with a semblance of such decorum. Through the Church's moral authority, the bedrock principles of a just society and virtue are promulgated.

But once that moral authority is eroded and all we are left with is division and discord, the consequences are dire, namely a fractured society. One may disagree with me, but perhaps we should return to our basic law and read the wisdom of the old in-between lines with no indignation or wilful blindness to use the other as a means to an end. Our forebears drafted these principles as a temporary solution to their time and a timeless guide to governance. The bedrock of our society, encapsulated in these laws, offers a profound understanding of human nature, societal needs, and the balance of power.

Consider the profound interpretations of human dignity, liberty, justice, and equality that are articulated in this basic law. These principles were crafted at a time when the struggle for survival and freedom was excruciatingly high, and as a result, they possess a depth and weight that is noticeably absent in modern legislation, which is often influenced by fleeting trends and immediate pressures. In search of progress and modernity, if we do not overlook them, we focus on their technical ambiguities in order to discard them as if they were a malady handed down to us. Thus, it becomes de facto difficult for someone to take you seriously if all you do is only pay lip service to these principles whilst allowing your actions to be dictated by the events of the past, whims of fashionable trends and political expediency.

These are my observations; thus, whilst I had my horrible experiences, I did not quiver because I knew if I followed the principles in the spirit our forebearers have laid them and not as man would try to amend its formulations to please his dark proclivity, I would eat my cake and have it, too. These men dedicated their lives to the pursuit of truth and the establishment of moral principles to guide our actions. On this note, despite the current, I hold on to their teachings and principles as a beacon of hope and guidance.

Despite what my nationality says, I hold on to the enduring values they espoused and the doggedness they displayed. What matters most to me is what I can learn from them and how this can help me achieve my own view of things not how you define them by modern twisted standard. With such an attitude, I resolved that there was no need to focus on the denial of the scholarship but to work towards my goal.

Considering the long summer holiday, I chose to enrol in an intensive language course, foregoing work and income for the duration. The classes demanded my full attention, leaving no room for other pursuits. After the semester, I moved to Göttingen to stay with a friend and study the language at the A2 level. I attempted to work during this period, applying for various positions and securing a factory job through a recruitment agency. However, after a two-day trial, my grammatical errors and accent led to my dismissal.

Subsequent job applications proved unsuccessful, prompting me to abandon job hunting and focus entirely on mastering the language. I started the course in August and by the end of the course in September, I could write a letter and hold some conversations. My grasp of verb structures improved, making me feel ready for the job market. However, as much as I wanted to continue my studies, I had to return to school as it reopened.

That same month, I was awarded a scholarship, making my return for the second year possible. Upon my return, I could converse in German with the locals and better understand German music. My classmates were enthusiastic, and my professors were convinced I would excel. Later that month, I applied for a position as a care helper in a home for persons with disabilities. The manager, a friendly and welcoming Russian woman, conducted the interview in fluent English.

She explained everything about the foundation and its work. She invited me for a trial without asking many questions and encouraged me to return if I wanted the job. During the trial, a worker-oriented me to the job, explaining the clients' observance and the staff's responsibilities. Initially, the work seemed tedious and overwhelming. However, it was the best work experience I have ever had. The lessons I learnt there profoundly changed my perspective on human nature and reinforced my passion for a career in counselling.

After the trial, I returned to the manager and expressed my desire to take the job. She invited me back, detailing the necessary documents to finalise the contract. Things progressed swiftly, and soon, I began working there. My work proceeded smoothly, giving me ample opportunities to improve my language skills through constant communication with clients and colleagues. During the following summer holiday, I took another intensive course and went a step ahead of what I had acquired before.

My language proficiency improved significantly with consistent practice, and I became more easily understood. I worked with the care home for a year. When it was time for my internship, I decided to transfer to their location in Hamburg, partly to secure myself financially. I relocated to Hamburg to begin my internship in the autumn of that year.

Living in Hamburg presented its own complexities. I rented a room in a shared flat with a widower in his early 60s, who insisted on communal living to an extreme degree. Despite bringing my own belongings, he desired shared use of towels, flannels, bedsheets, and even meals. The washing machine has to be used once and the laundry has to be done together. Whilst I appreciated communal living to an extent, I also declared my need for independence, particularly in matters of personal space and culinary autonomy. As tensions arose over differing lifestyles and expectations, I attempted to accommodate his desires out of a sense of guilt and empathy for his circumstances. Yet I reminded myself that I was not responsible for his situation and maintained my need for personal agency.

Despite efforts to find a compromise, our living situation remained fraught with tension and misunderstanding. His insistence on control and my desire for autonomy clashed repeatedly, creating a volatile atmosphere. In hindsight, it became clear that our living arrangement was unsustainable. One day, I purchased a pizza to satiate my hunger, only for my flatmate to scrutinise its contents, specifically checking for pork. Despite my prior explanation of my dietary rules, he felt compelled to police my food choices, questioning my adherence to tradition when the pizza contained pork. The intrusion into my personal choices left me incredulous and frustrated, prompting me to seek alternative dining options. As tensions escalated, it became evident that our cohabitation had reached its breaking point. His desire for a partnership, whatever that entails, did not match with my need for autonomy, leading me to seek a new living arrangement without flatmate.

Surprisingly, the conflict soured evident in his removal of Divine Mercy sticker on my door. Realising the untenability of our living situation, I resolved to find my own space, free from the constraints of our mismatched personalities and unstable emotions. I could not help but draw parallels to Ivan Ilyich's plight, finding myself ensnared in a relationship fraught with disillusionment and discord. However, unlike Ivan's tragic fate, I knew this man not from Adam, but this flat has made our paths cross. All this time, I couldn't help but think that individuals like him should not be allowed to live alone, especially not with younger people. His attitude does not only highlight a generational gap but a fundamental clash in lifestyle and expectations that made coexistence impossible. It was not simply about his habit; it was about his desire to impose himself on me—the overbearing need for control and the intrusion into my choices. Somehow, I think something deep might be going on in his life, which can only be compensated by exercising influence over others. How can I live with someone who imposes stringent rules without respect for boundaries? To some extent, I suspect he was trying to escape his individuality, immersing himself in my own life. Could it be that my presence evokes an image of helplessness and in need of care?

The individual in question lost his wife one or two years before I moved in. This sheds light on his overcompensating behaviour. We must do everything not out of contingency but out of necessity. He assumes my world, and I his world. In his fantasy, I might be a surrogate for his lost companionship, interpreting my independence as challenging his sense of connection. It was clear that he needed companionship of a different nature, perhaps more akin to a caregiver or a peer with similar habits and preferences rather than a younger, independent individual like myself.

Abruptly, more unpleasant situations arose. He disconnected the internet, fully aware of the impact it would have on me. The move hit hard, leaving me reliant on the limited mobile data, which quickly depleted with minimal use. Frustrated and needing solution, I decided to confront him. On that Sunday, we convened a meeting to address our issues.

He accused me of not contributing financially, specifically regarding the internet. He asserted that if I wanted to continue using it, I would need to start paying. He also mentioned that he had installed the internet because of me, and with my departure, it made sense to disconnect and return it. The conversation crystallised for me the growing animosity and reinforced the necessity of finding a new place. This latest act of spitefulness was the final straw—the impossibility of continuing to share the same space.

Then, he began complaining about my music and singing, something he previously had no issues with. This was particularly annoying given that every week, he invited friends over to play loud folk songs, laugh, and shout at each other with wild abandon. The air would be thick with the scent of alcohol and cigarette smoke, their words slurred, and their behaviour boisterous. Despite the disruption, I accepted this situation in good faith.

Finally, he resorted to verbal assaults, calling me '*Arschloch*' and other vulgar names. He began banging on my door whenever I was in my room making calls, reading or praying. I was afraid that one day this man would do the unthinkable. In that moment of deep frustration, I confronted him, declaring, "You are a devil, and heaven has given me the power to overcome you. Like Michael, I will crush your head, and not even your skull will be identifiable by archaeologists." Being determined to leave, I cancelled my lease, but he initially refused to accept it, citing insufficient notice.

I submitted another notice, which he begrudgingly accepted. After a relentless search, I found an apartment that suited my needs and began moving my belongings out gradually. On the last day, he approached me with an apology, fearing I would bear a grudge against him. I told him, "Although I did not appreciate your behaviour, I hold no grudge against you." With that, I left, relieved to move on from the toxic environment and start anew finally.

After moving and settling into my new apartment, I had the opportunity to reflect on everything that had transpired. I wondered why my life had swung between moments of ecstasy and periods of complete suffering. Now, I had the apartment I wanted, but the consequence was incurring debts from buying furniture and essentials. My student job did not provide enough income to cover these expenses. Previously, I had everything I needed, including television, in my old apartment, and my only financial concerns were food and miscellaneous expenses.

I found myself in a precarious situation, questioning why things had unfolded this way. Was it because I had left the seminary? Was there an unseen force at work rewriting my story? I thought perhaps my past was still haunting me for not becoming a priest. The thought weighed heavily on my conscience, often resurfacing shame and the stigma that one would never make it once he left the seminary. Consequently, the trials I now faced now seemed like a form of penance reminding me of the commitment I had abandoned.

Each obstacle, each moment of that experience, felt like a punitive measure to cleanse me from the initiation that accorded me the privilege and grace of my past decision as if the universe itself were holding me accountable for straying from destiny. The weight of this perceived penance was immense, pressing down on me with a force that was both spiritual and emotional. It was as if my soul was being tested, my resilience and faith constantly challenged by the shadows of my former vocation. And I did not know what to do with it. The sense of guilt was pervasive, seeping into every aspect of my thought and filled with remorse. I questioned my worth, wondering if the man was a tool for divine retribution to correct me for my departure from the seminary.

Yet, as I pondered these thoughts simultaneously, I began to understand that life's challenges were not punishments for my choices but rather opportunities for growth and self-actualisation. Each obstacle tested my resolution and faith and was not a mere catalyst for punishment. My journey away from the Church to secular society led me to new experiences and lessons that shaped my character and expanded my understanding of the world. I realised that every path in life, whether chosen or forsaken, contributes to one's story. The seminary had imparted valuable lessons that continued influencing my decisions and interactions with the external world.

The discipline and spiritual insights gained there were not lost; they were integrated into my daily life, guiding me through turbulent times even though I was unaware of it. Each person's journey is unique, filled with both triumphs and trials. What mattered most was how I responded to these challenges with faith, gratitude, and an open heart. Reflecting on the kindness of those around me, I saw the hand of providence at work. Their support reminded me that alone I would not have done.

Through that, I found the strength and courage to move on. Additionally, I realised that everything I had prayed for was manifesting, albeit unexpectedly. If I had prayed for strength, God provided it by placing me in situations requiring strength. If I had prayed for wisdom, He provided me wisdom by placing me in circumstances where that wisdom manifested. These prayers are already answered; the strength and wisdom are somewhere latent, and these situations are simply an avenue for one to see and prove it to himself.

It would be stupid to think that every difficult moment in our lives tests our capabilities. But it is even the stupidest thing to think that there is nothing to learn from these situations because the universal human feeling is that suffering is bad and must be wiped away from the world. But as Kant writes: *If a man can will at least health, how often has not the discomfort of the body restrained him from excesses into which perfect health would have led him?*[48] Thus, in a bid to escape discomfort, we might overlook the intrinsic value of the experiences that come with it. This duality implies that whilst suffering is inherently unpleasant and should not be glorified, it nonetheless has a role in the broader spectrum of human experience. We often develop a deeper understanding of who we are and the world around us by enduring and reflecting on our challenges.

The realisations were both humbling and reinvigorating. My personal trust in the divine plan was challenged, even when it led me down unexpected paths. It reminded me that God's ways are not always predictable, but they are always purposeful. Each trial and challenge must be seen as an opportunity for me to prove my faith in God's plan, and God is not always proving Himself to me by performing miracles. This is what will lead one to a newfound sense of peace and purpose in a world rife with so many ambiguities.

The question should not always be what God can prove to us but what we can actually prove to God. And indeed, one has a lot more to prove to God. Our lives are not mere tests of God's existence or benevolence; they are tests of our own character, integrity, and devotion. Each day presents us with opportunities to demonstrate our faith, love, and commitment to His will. It is not enough to passively await signs or miracles; we must actively engage with the Divine, striving to live lives worthy of His grace and approval.

In every action and every decision, we have the chance to show God that we are worthy of His blessings. It is a daunting task, to be sure, but one that is filled with meaning. For in proving ourselves to God, we deepen our relationship with Him and fulfil our true potential as human beings. By so doing, we will no longer be held down by the strings of the past but liberated by the potential of our future. Our actions, our choices, and our devotion to God will serve as the guiding force propelling us forward. Once we submit to no other than God, we become vessels of His love, channels of His grace, and instruments of His will in the world.

The imperative of this is categorical. For Christians, it is one that will transform our divisive inclinations. In submission to God's will, we find common ground, a shared purpose that binds us in a way our worldly affiliations and ideological cacophonies cannot and will not. The unity is not merely a superficial inclusion that finds its full expression under the mighty bureaucratic intervention, but a profound integration of our mind, body, and soul to always act in the present towards a singular divine mission. The mission is to embody truth, kindness, and love, reflecting the nature of God in our interactions and the conduct of human affairs. It is a mission to act under the same condition that we will that our maxim would become a universal law.

For it is not enough to proclaim the Creed, "I believe in God," one must also embody and live it. I believe in God is not just a creed but also a commitment. It is a commitment to act as conduits through which God's favour flows into the world instead of distortions and suffering from the devil. Our actions, inspired by His Spirit, illuminate what is dark in the world, bringing hope to justify the ways of God to men[49]. Therefore, we become agents of change asserting the Eternal Providence, not devil incarnates asserting eternal destruction.

This submission is not a passive act but an active process of surrendering our ego and personal grandiose. It necessitates a perpetual reorientation towards a higher good, the transcendent who is the source of authority and purpose. It requires a *kenosis*, self-emptying, where one divests himself of self-serving purpose to make room for God. Only through this process can we bring back what our childish rational appetite for modernity has deprived us of, for the true meaning of what we seek (whatever that is) comes not from asserting our will against the Divine but from aligning ourselves with God's will. As we move forward, we must acknowledge that much work must be done. Our past has been metamorphosed into a thing of value that shapes our human relationships. The patterns of current affairs no longer serve our growth. Everybody wants to protect his own interests. For the Yoruba man in Nigeria, the Igbo man is his problem. And for the Igbo man, the Yoruba man is his. Each sees his brother not just as a different tribe but as an obstacle, a figure of past conflicts and competing ambitions. Somewhere else, the farmer perceives the herder as a threat to his existence, whilst the herder perceives the farmer as his. None of them will concede to the existence of a unifying essence that binds them together. For the Protestant man in Germany, the Catholic man is his problem, and for the Catholic man, the Protestant is his, and the problem extends beyond individuals, feeding into a collective resentment that shape our private and public life. Everyone is bitter and resentful because of things that have long since lost their relevance in the present. And I ask: Have we not got a better thing to do, for God's sake, than to scrutinise the other based on a history made before he was born? How can we judge someone we have not met before based on prejudice we harbour against his religious affiliation? Are we not trapped in cognitive distortion of our own making?

Yet, we pride ourselves on being civilised and enlightened. We parade our advances in knowledge and innovation. But what does it really mean to be knowledgeable? Is it measured solely by our capacity to acquire and analyse data, or does it also encompass our ability to feel? Can we even call ourselves enlightened if we continue to live in the shadow of inherited biases? For all our achievements, we still stumble over the most fundamental human challenge: to see others not as labels or symbols of past conflicts but as individuals with their own complex experiences and aspirations. We have created all these beautiful technologies to facilitate human communication, yet we still labour profusely to bridge the small distance of prejudice and ignorance.

I have not the right to tell others how they should conduct themselves. As I said before, life here is different from the rhythms and comfort of home. My misfortune, which anyone may hold against me, is having to leave home for a place so different in their way of life. But even so, I perceive no difference in our humanity. In actual effect, we still today facilitate the dehumanisation of the Other either through rational means or emotional responses. But while it may be true that our cultures and way of life may vary widely, at our core, I see no difference. I have no right to confine myself to "retroactive reparation[50]." As a man, all I am asking man is to be human.

V
Adrift in Us vs Them

What do we really want to achieve with race? The black man, what do you want with race? What importance does it have to be 'black' or 'white'? Why cling to these hues whilst neglecting the spectrum beyond?

What madness drives us to fixate on mere shades of skin? Is not the soul's worth beyond such petty distinctions? Shall we not seek a realm where all are seen for their true essence, unbound by the chains of colour? Must we not ask ourselves: What is the true measure of a person? Should not character, virtue, and intellect take precedence over pigmentation?

Until I left my homeland, I never thought of myself as black and in need of salvation from the rest of humanity. Perhaps it was because I did not have a complexion that could be categorically likened to the colour black, nor did I have black features in nature that could stain a white garment. Suddenly, I found myself in a world where I had to demand from my fellow man the perception of me and myself rather than the perception of my colour. One duty I am left with, which weighs heavily on me, is only to renounce myself through fashionable choices and sacrifice my individuality on the altar of trending utopia. Thus, instead of joining in what appears to be a market of identity, I have kept myself busy trying to understand myself as 'black' and why everyone would want to save me.

What do they really want with my identity? Previously, my identity was shaped by a confluence of beautiful traditions, histories, and social structures, none of which reduced me to a mere colour. I was an individual among individuals, a unique being created in the image of God with a rich cultural heritage interwoven through my existence and evidence in the languages I speak. However, things are different now as I have encountered men in a society that inscribes an identity foreign to how I see myself. The gaze of others, laden with historical prejudices, atrocities and constructed binaries, all seeking to encapsulate me within the system of their preconceived notions about who I am. Suddenly, I am black, not through a self-affirmation of identity but through an imposition of a racialised lens that saw me only in opposition to whiteness.

With this transformation, a new mode of being and perception is forced upon me, where my individuality is subsumed under the weight of a collective black identity given by the dominant white culture. Sometimes, if they do not know what to call me, they will call me a person of colour. Then I wonder if I am a person of colour, what is white? How can I be addressed in a manner that only perpetuates a dichotomy devoid of meaning? What other unspoken norm, positioning of whiteness as the default and everything else as 'other', lies behind that term?

I grapple with the realisation that, henceforth, I am not only a person defined by a rich Igbo culture but also by the external world, those who know me truly and those who are out to aggrandise themselves by my story. I cannot exist as myself; I am now a representative of blackness, burdened with the stereotypes, prejudices, and expectations that accompany this categorisation. I must confront the duality of my existence: the essence of who I am and the appearance of who I am perceived to be based on the accommodation of mass standards. It is like being trapped within the double consciousness of seeing oneself through the eyes of the oppressor. The internal conflict becomes a battleground where the authenticity of my identity clashes with the imposed narratives of society, particularly that I am delicate and need to be saved.

On one hand, the essence of my being is rooted in my lived experiences and personal aspirations. This part defied the simplistic categorisations imposed upon me, transcending the limitations of racial labels to encompass the full complexity of my humanity. On the other hand, there is the appearance of who I am, shaped by the prevailing stereotypes, biases, and prejudices of others. In the eyes of others, I am a set of predetermined attributes stripped of my individuality and agency. This external perception threatens to overshadow my true self, confining me within the myopic system of societal expectations.

Already, this self has been deeply wounded by the crisis it had suffered at the hands of a system that supposed to support. Here he is, trying to put his life in order and being disturbed by those who do not know his story and do not want to know except in a sense that enriches their folly. They are only interested in the colour and not the meaning that the colour embodies. Their casual remarks and insensitivity pierce through the fragile veneer of composure one attempts to maintain.

Thanks to his first encounter with the *Thou,* who has meticulously helped him chronicle his past and wield it as a strength, causing the real self to emerge and offloading the burden he has most heavily bore. Once again, everything made sense, and he was ready to achieve his dream. He felt very much alive, and internally, he started functioning to the best of his ability. There was work to be done in most of the endeavours he set out to pursue, especially writing. Those require time but would be made manifest at the appointed time.

With this clarity, he thought he could move on to the next phase of his life—being a disciple of Socrates. However, life here abruptly became toxic as now everybody around him thinks that he is going to die the next minute. A trigger warning is given each time we encounter a literary work of art. One wonders if everyone will have an emotional outburst or if something else is happening in the background. Verily, there were instances where individuals had an emotional outburst, not because they did not possess emotional intelligence but because they had been convinced that they lacked emotional intelligence and could not constructively deal with these complex topics. Then, hurries the tutor helter-skelter to console his infants.

I argue that this conditioning can only stem from a pervasive culture that grossly undermines the human being and the capacity for complex discourse. In its zeal to protect the black man, the contemporary pedagogical system paradoxically undermines the development of critical faculties necessary for grappling with the profound and often uncomfortable truths of our existence. Indeed, one may assume it is well-meant. On the contrary, the misguided approach actually nurtures a form of learned helplessness, wherein blackness is not merely shielded from the vagaries of existence but is actively deprived of the opportunity to cultivate the grit required for meaningful engagement with the moral and existential dimensions of race and identity. Thenceforth, stifling the growth of the individual and his inner desire to engage in a transcendental dialogue.

It denies the soul the crucible through which it must pass to forge a proper understanding of itself and its place in the world, thus thwarting the quest for a genuine and meaningful existence. It becomes a vehement tendency of soft paternalism, where individuals' autonomy and intellectual agency are subordinated to a safeguarding worldview **However, life here abruptly** became toxic as now everybody around him thinks that that ultimately stifles intellectual and emotional growth. The days when the pursuit of knowledge and wisdom was revered and championed by those who sought to expand the horizons of human understanding are long past. In their place, we now find a culture of complacency and intellectual stagnation, where the richness of discourse and the vigour of the spirited debate are replaced by the comfort of unchallenged beliefs in race and the ease of superficial engagements with black identity. People are so liberal and notoriously compassionate that instead of placing emphasis on not only the emotional but also the rational aspect of being, they place exaggerated adoration of race and transient gratifications of racial discourse, neglecting the profound cultivation of the mind and spirit.

And I ask myself: Where do I find myself in all this discourse? Where do I belong? The immediate answer is nowhere because I denounce the same old tricks that were used to wipe out my individuality and traditions. I denounce this collective neurosis of suppressing the black man by the white man and the white man by the black man. Even though I am beset by this madness of having to negotiate my identity in the events of life, I must constantly remind myself that whatever happens, it is not because of my colour but it is because God wills it. If one, by his foolishness, allows himself to be used as an instrument that divides our humanity, may this division be his lot, too. May his hate flee before I come.

I yearn for a return to a time when intellectual rigour and emotional resilience were not just encouraged but were foundational principles. I envision a return to the school of Athens, where the classroom was a crucible for critical thinking, and challenging discourses were not shied away from but engaged openly and thoughtfully with. I long to be taught by the likes of Schiller, Goethe, Jung, Frankl, Dostoyevsky, Tolstoy, Lewis and Arendt—men and women who stood tall. I want Fulton to be there at Mass, not just saying what feels right to my emotions but what will keep my soul alive even after my demise. I long for Shakespeare to entertain me—to teach me the sophistry of words instead of the mundanity of speech, to elevate my thoughts with the eloquence of his verse, and to transport me to the timeless realms of human nature that he masterfully portrays. Can I find these noble men and women whom my mind is recalling as I write this? Or are they but phantoms of an idealised past, shadows cast by the flickering flame of my memory? These paragons of virtue and excellence who saw and navigated the turbulent seas of moral and existential challenges with grace—do they still walk among us, or have they been eclipsed by the tide of time?

Perhaps they exist, not in some distant, unreachable past, but in the hearts and minds of those who dare to dream of a more enlightened present. But how and where do I find them? Because they are the only people who can guide the black man in discovering the old wine in a new skin. Please take me back home to where one is taught to confront uncomfortable truths and grapple with the moral and existential questions such discussions inevitably raise. Take me back home, and my mind will find the rest it deserves.

The home I seek is the one that will foster the Aristotelian concept of eudaimonia, where one flourishes by exercising his virtues in the face of adversity and not by having sex and compassion as his moral banner. It would champion the Socratic method, where questioning and critical dialogue are the means to cultivate understanding and wisdom. It would bring back the Holy Writ as the basis of enquiry—the only book where the beginning and end of the world are apparent.

All of this aberration, the constant pampering, scrutiny and expectation predicated on my complexion, weighs heavily upon me. I cannot bear it because I am peddling between two extreme ideological cacophonies instead of learning. Every interaction is tinged with suspicion; every word I utter is scrutinised for hidden meanings or unconscious biases. It feels like I am under surveillance by Big Brother against offending or betraying the ideals I am expected to uphold. The burden of representation, of being seen as a spokesperson for an entire race, is deadly suffocating and disparaging, threatening to consume the essence of my being.

But this dissatisfaction extends beyond the fixation on the black race to sexuality as well, wherein the two are frequently named as a couple, insinuating a correlation between blackness and sexual preoccupation. This, as it appears, posits being black as inherently synonymous with, or even subordinate to, a heightened state of sexual awareness or activity. Thenceforth, perpetuating a reductive narrative that undermines the complexity of both racial and sexual identity. One also observes the deliberate calibration to shape every discourse around this area. At the heart of this calibration lies the manipulation of language and rhetoric to frame discussions in ways that savour particular agendas.

This manipulation is evident in the selective emphasis placed on certain aspects of identity whilst neglecting others, as well as in framing issues in ways that prioritise the interests of the privileged few over the marginalised many. I consider this a subtle form of totalitarianism, cloaked in the guise of neutrality and objectivity, that serves to uphold the status quo of the mighty ones and perpetuate violence. One only needs to take a class with Solzhenitsyn's *Gulag Archipelago* and Jung's *Undiscovered Self* to grasp the profound nature of our savage instincts.

Here and there, one sees utter depreciation and decay in our capacity to use reason. Nothing makes sense except it is justified by the theory of race and sexuality. Every dot is connected to them, however distinct and distinguished they appear. Instead of examining life situations by finding their unique meaning, we read race into them to suit our self-serving purpose. We define them in a way that aligns with the absolute race and sexual theory. We project narratives that everyone must follow, and those who fail are brought to justice by the almighty State. One who wishes to survive must profess the racial creed and relinquish touch to the inner self. He must believe in the narrative that people like me have no moral faculty or even self-control but only violence. We need help because infants always need contact with their mothers. He must profess the building of prejudice into every interaction and make everyone more aware of race at every cost, at all times and places. He must profess to examine situations for evidence of racism, and it is okay to simplify a hugely controversial issue. He must believe that knowledge is situated culturally and there is nothing like having access to objective truth. He must believe in an endless cycle of reflection.

See, I find it difficult to understand your fixation on race and sexuality, not that within my intellectual capacity, I cannot—but it is utterly depressing to be continually immersed in these ideas as the only way to achieve objective truth! There is no different story; everything always returns to race and sexuality, and there is no escape route. If I wish to escape, I am beaten down by your mob for failing to think in line with the orthodoxy that purports to save me. I am suffocated to forego my experience and accept the group's madness.

Truly, I see it as infantilisation that despite the strange qualities God bestowed on us, you have only come far in your civilisation to impose self-annihilation not only on your people but also on the people of other nations. You do this so meticulously that despite the perceived limitations placed on the black man alongside your descendants by your own colonial atrocities and the black man having fought to rise above these limitations, altogether, we begin step by step to diminish in meaning. The values that make us distinct are the things we must give up. And to be given what? A fickle morality? Simultaneously, you assert your moral superiority, chanting your songs of liberation, proclaiming that all the hatred you project, the wars you wage, the castration and burning of one another, consigning ourselves prematurely to our graves, are purportedly in service of justice for the black man. Yet, beneath this duvet of altruism one discovers the troubling truth of the flight we have taken from ourselves, our own hypocrisy and the insidious perpetuation of injustice. What a grotesque distortion of priority! How dare you! Are you my *Chi*?

Suppose we are fighting for the freedom of the 'black' man; we should at least know the difference between sexuality as a means to an end and the black man as an end in itself. In that case, I think it will be incumbent on us to respect his infinite dignity and take it seriously when he confesses he is under mass intoxication. For it is already racial violence if, for the sake of escaping being conceived as not 'black enough', I withdraw my individuality from all public matters. Artikel 1 of the Grundgesetzt reads: *Die Würde des Menschen ist unantastbar. Sie zu achten und zu schützen ist Verpflichtung aller staatlichen Gewalt.*

This principle of inviolable human dignity must be at the forefront of our efforts, guiding our actions to ensure that the quest for his freedom does not compromise the well-being and humanity of those we aim to liberate. It is inconceivable that we have run so away from ourselves that our ugly behaviours fail to perturb us. But the decay continues to ooze out no matter what. And once we cannot contain the burning sensation of such repression, we project our shadow on every *Ausländer* because they have the most distinct features in the midst of the majority. We perceive them as the locus of the problem and highlight their attitude as what constitutes a parallel society. But upon deeper introspection, we confront the unsettling truth that the root cause of the matter may lie not in the *Ausländer* but in the very framework of our collective values and how much we have beautifully decorated our masks not to reflect what lies behind the façade.

The pernicious narrative that demonises the *Ausländer* is not just a reflection of our deep-seated maladies but a stark manifestation of our existential dread. We project this dread outward onto those who are visibly different, whether black or white, fabricating an external adversary to mask our internal disquiet. This diversionary tactic allows us to avoid confronting the malady of the self and the fact that everything we seem to hold together is crumbling day by day, not by the *Ausländer* but by our ideological babel, which fragments the image of God in us. Consequently, no matter how the *Ausländer* tries to belong, how closely he imitates your customs, and how fluently he speaks your language, he cannot fit in on one thing: the Tower of Babel because there he is meant to be a victim and not the perpetrator, the oppressed and not the oppressor.

Listen, we have a split world. Solzhenitsyn has hinted at this, and I agree with him.[51] This split determines what we hold as valuable: the ability to thrive and fashion a new life is based on this split. It shapes our understanding of what is valuable and delineates the paths available for one to navigate towards a good life. On one side, there exists a vision of autonomy, where individuals are equipped with the tools to forge their destinies and pursue their aspirations freely. This perspective values autonomy, self-determination, and the opportunity for personal growth. Our ideological differences do not play a role because the individual's autonomy is the only valid unit of analysis. And notwithstanding the problematic repercussions thereof, we have succeeded in moulding the individual to think for himself without any guidance from an established authority. On the other hand, lies a landscape marred by legal complexities and bureaucracy. Here, the letters of the law play a crucial role in decision-making. Once they are quoted, there is no further requirement. Whoever is not satisfied must take his matter to God.

Indeed, it is conventional knowledge that I hail from a society where people are gripped by fear, engaging with their government and the judiciary system to exercise their fundamental civil rights stemming from a moral bankruptcy in the legal system. A poor man or woman who went to court might be convicted of a misdemeanour if the accuser is an influential politician in the country. The basic democratic principles are shamelessly trampled upon, resulting in a dearth of judicial fairness and accountability. Either because the principles of democracy as we inherited them are unnatural to our organic system of government or because it is nought but a blatant disregard for civilisation.

In any case, this egregious disregard for fundamental human rights and human dignity has tragically cost the lives of countless young, vibrant Nigerians. The absence of a transparent and impartial legal framework is not just detrimental; it is utterly reprehensible for any society to function without a clear and objective justice system. As commendable as those legal formulations may appear here in Germany, as what man has achieved during his course of civilisation, this, in turn, creates a trap whereby freedom becomes contingent upon one's ability to slay his individuality in favour of mass intoxication. In such dire circumstances, those unable to comply often retreat and withdraw from societal interaction.

This inherent contradiction is recognisable if one can decipher between good and evil. But the persisting blindness resulting from too much politicisation of race and sexuality seems to have taken hold of our maturity actually to confront our responsibility. It allows us to deflect attention from the true sources of decay within our society: our ideological incoherence and profound disconnection from universal principles. The best theory and the most attractive practice are not the ones that make us humans but rather the ones that treat us as racial contingents and sex apparatus.

By critically analysing the situation, it becomes evident that the ideas that treat us as such only condition us to modify our internal organs to the dictates of our construct. But also it is, absurd—and it is even more absurd because not pursuing them means remaining impotent in one's endeavour. There is a decline in the courage to do the right thing or stick to one's conscience. There is a lack of originality in our actions. If one wants to move forward, he must tread cautiously and timidly to avoid offending the gatekeepers. Everyone wants to succeed but in a fashionable way that accommodates the psychosis of mass standards and implicitly denies one his own freedom. We seem not to care about our conscience or the moral implications of our acts. On another note, who would be interested in his conscience if we never pose the moral question at all? We have lost the capacity to reflect—to conduct a general examination of conscience to improve what we give out in the world.

We can no longer afford to sit and ask ourselves, where am I heading to, how have I trespassed, and how have I treated my neighbour today? Everyone wants to speak, but no one wants to listen! We are in a climate where everyone wants the truth but tells lies. We want peace but speak words of hatred. The words encourage no commitment and lay no foundation for higher truth. But we cannot do anything because this is also how we have trained ourselves to be or perhaps what we have allowed ourselves to become. The deal is that we, the men who have been crying for emancipation ever since our encounter with you, go back to the primitive stage. For you, nothing is grave. The words you utter are mere games to satisfy your hero's journey, which is to reduce things and label them. These include even the most complex phenomena of race and sexuality. It also includes our daily language.

The English language has evolved so much that words such as 'critical' no longer mean exercising a careful judgment or judicious evaluation but exercising a careful judgment in a manner that aligns with the race theory. As many limitations, I have with the English language, and despite having claimed it as my own, I cannot even see myself in the language anymore. I see myself estranged, unable to discern my own reflection within its vocabulary. My decades of learning in my homeland devoted to learning the language now seem to mock me with their futility. I cannot even begin to articulate the depths of my despair when confronted with how much I have left my mother tongue to acquire this language. Nor the German language, which is so disarrayed that attempting to speak of it fills me with indignation. This one language my priest lecturers in the seminary praised so well for its clarity now comes to me very distorted. I must live each day in quietness of mind, searching for words to express myself better because I am unsure of how they will be received, of the judgment and perception of other people.

There is an unseen threshold hovering beyond reach, imposing a standard that must not, under any circumstance, be surpassed. I must hold back each time the words surge within me. It is like walking on a tightrope trying to find my way, not knowing if the word I choose will lead me astray. At times, I find myself grappling fiercely with the question of how we can attest to the validity of our own judgment in such a corrupt nature. How can we determine the reality of our own reasoning if all men think alike? Once one opens his mouth to speak, he is seen as evil because he thinks contrariwise. He is the oppressed and must never feel like the oppressor. He is the victim and must never think like the perpetrator. He is the patient and must never think like the doctor. All these must be considered before he opens his mouth so that his words will not be twisted. Then, one may ask if there is any truth in any utterance if one must lose his voice before he speaks. Is there truth in any utterance if one must hide his true self behind his words and project the self that would meet no doubt? Who will be endowed with the wisdom to decide which view to air and which judgment is right or wrong? Who will be conferred the privilege to decipher which research question or theory passes muster? And all these questions we can neither pose nor answer because we are shielding blackness from the vagaries of existence without knowing we are disparaging his effort to become a person and sending him to the bottomless pit of hell.

I do not mean to diminish the efforts and struggles of those who genuinely have fought for a better world. Nor do I intend to romanticise the state of alienation and misunderstanding that has been wittingly or unwittingly imposed on the black man. Rather, I aim to highlight the deep-seated flaws within our thinking of race, which has left the black man and his soul in a perpetual circle of existential despair. My duty here is to unleash the man—to highlight the inherent oppression and subjugation to a continuous process of objectification, where one's identity is reduced to a set of superficial characteristics without a universal imperative. The aim, as Fanon has beautifully demonstrated in *Black Skin, White Masks*, is to otherwise and dehumanise, casting the black man as an eternal outsider, irrespective of his efforts to conform or excel in the dominant culture.

But I do not limit myself to Fanon; neither do I confine my exploration to his worldview alone. We must look beyond such affiliation to the realities of our time, which is that the black man is still not perceived as a human being but an objectified construct. This is done mostly by men who profess to champion the emancipation of the black man from colonial slavery. Thereby reducing his humanity to mere external characteristics and trapping him in an endless cycle of marginalisation and self-forgetfulness. It is a vicious circle where the black man, no matter how ardently he strives to prove his worth, is constantly met with suspicion, prejudice, and systemic barriers imposed by people who claim to harbour altruistic intentions towards him. Especially if you do not conform to their idea of blackness, they raise the bar of inequality and perpetuate the outdated myths of racial hierarchy, all the while cloaked in the rhetoric of benevolence and reform. Here, the black man is both hyper-visible and invisible—scrutinised and yet overlooked. His identity is dissected and appropriated, yet his humanity is persistently denied. He is important, but only as a tool for political aggrandisement.

Gentlemen, we need to return to our foundational courses. We have traded the pursuit of truth for the comfort of consensus, leaving our pupils ill-equipped to challenge prevailing dogmas or think independently. This is a simple failure and a complete breakdown of Western civilisation. The centre can no longer hold, and we cannot do anything about it, for he started the disintegration through an unwarranted invasion.

The time has passed when we experienced proper guidance and mentorship from you, whom we entrust with our conscience. Now, we are left with race and its attachment to sexuality, which has virtually hypnotised every aspect of human affairs. The 'peculiar evil[52]', as John Stuart Mill puts it, is that we rob the entire human race, an entire generation, and posterity of potential truth and cure to a particular epidemic.

I think it is good to be immersed in race and sexual theory, but what practical relevance do they hold for our lives, the lives of my poor parents in the village, or are we merely engaging in a futile exercise of intellectual indulgence? Moreover, what we are being told might only be a tiny speck of the whole truth and, when put into context, will not imply any connection with grounds of natural reality. Truly, I learnt them, but afterwards, I felt even more empty. I say this not with so much satisfaction but with deep regret that strikes me through my breast.

I reckon the first lecture series that dealt with racism, where a lone voice objected to my statement that we must not only look at racism subjectively but also objectively. For her, everything the black person says must be believed without questioning or helping the person discover another approach to life. I wrestled with my feelings and did not know what to make of them. Thus, I felt sick. I felt lonely, for God's sake! This also means withdrawing my interest and becoming a passive participator in public matters. With all the benefits I had received for my education, I had to prove to myself that I was not just wasting them. It was a significant moral burden to bear, one that I would have managed well. I needed to justify to myself the privilege I had been given, however much that what I expected was not what I was getting in return. The other option was to sit tight and see to the end. However, I could not just sit, notwithstanding the stress it has put me through. Thus, I need something to steal my attention away.

Since I have acquired some printed pages, I resolved to read them. Whilst reading, I noticed that any book I laid my hands on confirmed the ideas I had been thinking about. The more I read, the more I gained clarity on some of the conceptions that had kept me busy. It was like serendipity; with every book I encountered, each page turned speaks volumes about the very ideas I had been occupied with. It felt like the universe conspired to align my thoughts with the written words, to affirm my ideas, reassuring me that I was not adrift in madness.

But still, I had to work hard to discern the profound from the superficial and to retain the profound by which term I understood them. In actual effect, I started to write my memories down, including keeping daily diaries. My main goal for doing that was to escape the constant arrant nonsense of this kind of pedagogy.

I wanted to let go of the feeling and finally be free, but I could not. In the long run, things took a different approach after I had this dream.

In this dream, I found myself in a room suffused with a soft, archaic glow. The time went back to antiquity. I remember the room. The furnishings in the room had a distinctive elegance of the mid-century design. There were two swing chairs and a centre table made of a polished wood surface gleaming golden glow. Its lines and geometric shapes spoke of the aesthetic of the era. Nearby was an iron bed and a tent pole erected beside them, where I had just poured my dried clothing and was folding them. Across from me sat a tall, gentle figure in one of the swing chairs. His presence oozes a sense of a life spent pursuing knowledge and understanding. I was busy folding my clothes whilst he engaged me in a talk of shared passion and purpose.

We delved into the depths of our interests and aspirations. At that moment, I told him what I aspired to become. Immediately, he startled, his eyes widening in shock for a fleeting moment before regaining composure. "Is not gonna be easy," he told me, and I suspected out of his own experience. "Is gonna be tough, man," he repeated. "But you must write," he continues, "I encourage you to write daily."

I interrupted by telling him that I write every day at the moment and told him about what I have written so far. And then, as if granting a benediction upon my aspirations, he gave me a gift of unparalleled significance. He revealed to me the gates of possibility and how to use them. There and then, I bowed and promised that I would use them. Raising my head to ask further questions, I found out he had gone. I, too, abruptly snapped into consciousness.

I started scribbling in reaction to the dream, intensely pouring out my frustrations and confusion. Apart from study hours, I dedicated myself to this task, spending staggering hours scribbling to understand if I was the problem or if they were their problem, always coming *en masse* with irrepressible violence. It was both therapeutic and exhausting. With each passing day, the intensity of my engagement with the writing process grew. My headaches, yet I could not tear myself away from the page until I felt I had written it down. In actual respect, there was no other way to understand what was going on except to resurrect what they were trying to suppress, my innocence, and present to them my emancipation from their rebels.

I bring no charge against anyone who holds a different view and who believes that race and sexual theory are more important than our lives. Like you,

I have battled relentlessly with the question of whether there is an alternative approach to matters as such, especially as life goes on and the crucible of fire one had to pass through as a result. It is a very difficult question to answer. In the same breath, I think affirming that everything is meaningless unless viewed in the light of race and sexuality, which narrows down complex events such as racism, is not only a false conclusion but also a deadly mirage. It is self-deprecating and renders the person who believes in it impotent. How far such a worldview can explain contingencies and what—if any—approaches should be undertaken to address them remains unclear. Here, I reckon, in a discussion, I narrated a story about my rough days at work. It was about a lady who thought of me as a servant boy she could handle during my internship. She gives me work to do even when there is clearly nothing. Whilst I am doing that, she is making another list to get me engaged the next minute I am done.

This persisted for so long that I had to put a stop to it. Oddly enough, she does that to everyone, even to the manager. After narrating the story and its ordeals in synchronism with our discussion, as if the use of power was not enough, the experience was immediately narrowed down to racism by the moderator as the underlying motivation for her actions. Needless to say, I did not comment on race talk more of the ism.

On a closer look, I think it is already racism if all I am to the Other is nothing but the shade of two hundred and six bones. I think it is already racism if one cannot see beyond my colour. In this respect, my body is no longer the temple of God but a place where the evidence of colonial enterprise and mass murder is imprinted and reified. It is an instrument to amplify political beliefs and demonstrate their power. It is an instrument that bears witness to the political institutions that colonised my homeland. It is an inscription of truth, which must be accepted by men and women. It is the only truth about who I really am and what my story is and would be. It is the most factual and convincing story of my whole existence.

I acknowledge that there is historical evidence for why race is the most important factor to consider when discussing the conduct of human affairs. The African man is often looked down upon not as a person with reason but only with emotions. He is a person whose feelings and thinking are not separated like the European man. He is someone without conscience but only impulses. He resides bound within the well of his emotions, bound by the whims of affective currents, devoid of the detached independence that grants autonomy of spirit, unlike the Europeans.[53]

His spirituality is demonic. To get married to him is rather to reproduce his kind. We know all these too well, as written in our history, biology, and psychology textbooks. Anyone interested knows where to find them. There is no need to make a list of the prejudices against the African man here. Thus, before disregarding the issue of race, it is imperative to look at the good arguments that point to the dark proclivity of man.

Aside from historical veracity, it is imperative to consider experiences that profoundly reverberate the ills that the race theory is working hard to heal. In this respect, I will consider a rare but complex experience about freedom of movement. In what follows to be a sojourn in a foreign land for the pursuit of an academic degree, I wrote Office 1 in February for an extension of my current status. My caseworker reminded me that my Pass would expire in October. I confirmed this and informed her that I had an appointment for a new Pass in the coming weeks… Consequently, we agreed that the renewal of my status should be postponed until at a later date in February, after my appointment for the new Pass.

After attending the appointment, I showed up as scheduled for the extension of my status. I informed my caseworker that I would be going for two terms abroad under my program and expected my status to be extended until my return, as required. However, my status was only extended until a limited time in October, when my old Pass would expire. Its validity started from the day I received the appointment instead of the day the appointment took place. This was odd, given that extensions usually cover the entire period of one stay abroad.

Moreover, the validity typically begins from the biometric submission date, not the day one receives a notification of the appointment date. According to my caseworker, the decision was influenced by the impending expiration of my old Pass despite having a new Pass. She advised me to return with the letter of agreement and other documents when I mentioned my stay abroad. This was reasonable since I had not yet received confirmation from my host institution.

Conversely, when I gathered the required documents in May and requested another extension appointment, neither my emails nor calls were answered. I sent another email in June and a letter explaining the importance of the extension and my exchange abroad, but I received no response. I waited until July, then applied for the status needed for my studies abroad without extending my current status, which should have been the case. I assumed that obtaining another status where I was going would be difficult without the extension, as the longevity of my status was insufficient to show I could return to my home institution after my studies.

After a month of no response from either office, I contacted the international office of my host institution to inquire about travelling there whilst my application was processed. The response was unsatisfactory, as concerns about aliens are always too complex to manage. Immediately, I reached out to several offices, posing the same question and making it clear that I was an exchange student from so and so country, but even they could not offer a precise answer; they told me it was possible under the General Agreement to stay in the country of my host institution for three months whilst my application was processed. In contrast, office 2 warned that entering before a decision risked denial.

As a result, I decided to start my journey online, hoping that office 2 would facilitate my application. Week after week, I emailed and called to inquire about the status. Each time, I was told my case was pending and that I needed to be assigned a case officer. By way of preparation for this, I cancelled my lease to avoid paying double rent even though I ended up not living in the room I had spent for, and the money was not recovered. The good thing was that I did not have to pay for the room where I was living after cancelling my lease.

Apart from that, the family bore intricacies of fate and was very helpful in dealing with the office there. Unlike in my previous city, where I waited patiently, this time, letters were written, and calls were made to help me achieve success. But the caseworker made it more difficult for me. He said he would work on my application and issue a fiction certificate until he could do the work. I couldn't contain my enthusiasm; one problem was down; I could finally travel again.

Weeks later, I sought an appointment, but he told me he could not work on my file as others were before me. I requested at least the fictional certificate to travel, as he had mentioned earlier. He then scheduled me for 28 October for it. I was overjoyed until abruptly, he cancelled the appointment because he had been fully booked. I was devastated, questioning why my appointment had to be cancelled.

Unable to understand his reasons, I sent him several emails detailing my ordeal. I expressed that I had defied counsel to cancel the process because I believed it wouldn't be dark forever. My family had advised abandoning everything, but I dismissed their advice to pursue my dream. I wondered if I was being naïve and over-ambitious, but I concluded that I was living my life, not someone else's. If this meant enduring crises, so be it.

After sending the email, he reinstated the appointment he had cancelled. I burst into tears and shared the news with family and well-wishers. We felt relieved and resumed our usual activities whilst awaiting a response from office 2. One Sunday morning in August, I received an email from office 2 requesting further documents to prove sufficient funds. I translated and sent the documents few days later.

My lectures continued online. Two months later, office 2 requested another proof of sustenance. This I sent. Two weeks later, my application was rejected on two grounds: It is unclear whether I can have access to my stipend abroad, and it is unclear whether my stipend will affect another stipend.

Nonetheless, I had some weeks to appeal the decision. Here, I didn't inform my family, knowing their likely opinion. After deliberating with my institutions, I decided to appeal. With help from a lecturer knowledgeable in such matters, the appeal was drafted and sent to them on time. Afterwards, I felt exhausted and out of energy for the first time, struggling to keep up with everything that had blown out around me. My will was strong, and my heart true to the course, but I questioned the worth of my desire. As such, I started making plans to return to my home institution, and it was successful. It was initially bizarre, but it improved with time.

A month later, I received two emails: one from the court annulling the decision of office 2 based on my documents and requesting further processing of my case, and another from office 2 to contact their main office for further proceedings. I stopped the proceedings, feeling I had reached my limits. About three months later, I received an email from office 2 rejecting my application because I had chosen not to continue the program. They must have waited until the last minute to assert their full authority over me.

In the common rational knowledge of race, there is only one avenue of understanding this account, which has profound implications for how we might want to proceed with future events. This pathway leads us into the realm of race theory alongside bureaucracy, which are indispensable devices of modern-day political organisation cum operation.[54] Here, the scrutiny and treatment of an individual are predicated upon their status as an *alien, an Ausländer*. The lens through which the state perceives him is that he is an undeveloped bushman, very strange and less evolved than the Europeans. Any regard for his humanity is inconsequential because he is closer to the animal world in the eyes of those who subject him to such treatment.

Due to the presumption that every *Ausländer*, especially a black man, is inherently criminal, he is mentally sick and brings with him infectious diseases everywhere he goes; he must be thoroughly investigated in a state of exception akin to a criminal. This form of scrutiny extends beyond mere observation; the person must be controlled until there is nothing more to be controlled. And if even the mechanism of control proves insufficient, then it becomes necessary to use force and tell him that he is less human. The main aim is total domination of both the body and spirit. There is a desire to own him, although without absolute possession. As a result, bureaucracy is used to perform the tasks that we can actually do for one another[55].

And if he, by any chance, insists on retaining what is left of his humanity after all the ordeals, the dominant individual would have no option but to reconsider his humanity and assert himself as more human and obviously has a Divine mandate to rule over his subject.[56] Consequently, even as there was no need to reject my application but to grant the residence permit immediately based on a court order, more time was purchased so that the application would still be rejected for reasons which, of course, would appear plausible. Only that they were, as they were, a framework to assert the final authority and put the individual category of humans in which he belongs. It is unavoidable to draw this conclusion given that it is only the person who is not an *Ausländer* is availed the luxury of free movement even if they are financially incapacitated.

But it does not follow that when an *Ausländer* acquires dual nationality, that individual, in the spirit of *Amo: Volo ut sis* (I love you, I want you to be),[57] is granted every right and dignity inherent in being human, similar to one whose identity may be "biologically" rooted. This, in part, is because any contact with the *Ausländer* in his all too noticeable difference reminds us of the limitations of human activity—limitations that our political life assumes to resolve .[58] When we meet the *Ausländer*, we are confronted with a "frightening symbol of the fact of difference, as such and individuality as such," indicating realms where change and action are impossible, provoking our destructive impulses.[59] The anxiety surrounding this confrontation, as we grapple with the uncomfortable truths of our limitations and the nature of existence, ultimately manifests as othering and exclusion.

These processes of othering and exclusion are not structures which can be directly perceived; they are not mere situations of facts or rights but are strategies that constitute the immanent validity of the law. Within this framework, an *Ausländer* immediately loses his 'right to rights', and his presence becomes a challenge to society. Thus, wherever he appears, he is seen not as a man among men but as a living indictment of the fragile order upon which our society rests– a symbol of inequality, estrangement and all that must be suppressed to preserve the illusion of unity in plurality. In his neighbourhood and place of work, his deeds are not explained as a necessary consequence of being human but of some alien qualities; he has become, as Arendt puts it, "a specimen of an animal species called man" and must be scrutinised and dissected within the confines of the laboratory that has rendered his anomaly. The more he is observed, the more his humanity is diminished until he is reduced to an abstraction–a symbol of everything that must be excluded to maintain the status quo. In this space, his potential self is stifled, his identity erased, and his right to belong is de facto denied.

This year was indeed a true *annus horribilis*, marked by profound resentment, sorrow, excruciating pain, unprecedented disappointment, and constant uncertainty about the future. I cried myself to sleep all the day and night. I sometimes wonder why certain people find things easy and others do not. Things like moving from one destination to another should have been humane without any recourse to bureaucratic intervention, but they have required far more struggle than expected. The crux of the matter resides in that racism, unlike other forms of societal ills, carries with it a touch of the authenticity of innocence[60].

It masquerades behind veils of ignorance and denial, camouflaging its insidious nature beneath the guise of tradition or cultural norms. Unlike overt forms of discrimination, which are often met with immediate condemnation, racism operates covertly amongst people. Its subtle manifestations can be difficult to detect, cloaked in the rhetoric of due process and legality. It is no wonder that some people believe that there is no objective way of looking at it because, all things considered, we are in a racially hierarchical society, after all. The subtle authenticity of innocence makes racism all the more insidious, as it allows it to persist unchecked, perpetuating harm and suffering under the guise of normalcy.

But that is not all we have to say, and I shall not depart, leaving you adrift like a solitary vessel upon the boundless sea. Instead, I shall stand steadfast and give you a hand that you may walk safely to land if you wish. Amidst these faults, we must exercise scepticism and find a pathway illuminated by the light of self-awareness and agency. The black man, or whatever he is, must look beyond the limitations imposed by this external scrutiny and assert his intrinsic worth. Instead of relying on the dehumanising effects of his status, he must reclaim the narrative and redefine his identity with grace as it pleased his maker to send him these very tough experiences.

One thing is clear: one day, we must all die, and we must account for them and how we dealt with them. Truly, I described an extreme condition that characterised the broader spectrum of human affairs and why race theory was part of what characterised my lessons. It will be nearly impossible to make a counterargument as to why race is not a relevant variable.

Nothing stops the facilitation of my application or at least treating me first and foremost as a human being without resorting to bureaucracy. In contrast, this may be true for all people in my part of the world. However, it may not be of the same magnitude and may be different in context. Thus, an oversimplification of this complexity may not fit into real-world human affairs.

One might boldly assert my naivety and insist that I deserve whatever treatment befalls me. Yet we must confront a harsh reality: behind every decision and action stands a human being bound by the directives imposed upon him by his superiors and the various interests he has to represent. Whilst this should not substitute for institutional reform, I would also be concerned about the actions that I am taking against them and how that, too, might reflect my own inadequacy. If I took a protest, believe me, I would be acting out of fear for the things I cannot fight or control. This, too, would result from fear of what is in me that I cannot behold in the other: hate.

This fear would stop at nothing until it destroyed me. It will start by crippling my belief system to convince me that I am different from the rest of the human species and, in all instances, must be treated as an infant. After that, it will water down my motivation to move forward by changing my perception until I am able to see nothing but darkness and fear itself. Then, it will model my behaviour and turn me into a monster that no other can tolerate—not even myself. It will do everything for me, but it will not remind me that there have been times when I beseeched God for strength, nor the occasions when I humbly submitted to the will of God, "Thy will be done." Implicitly, I fortified myself to confront any challenge that the divine would decree upon my path. As a consequence, the challenge could not have made me weaker but stronger.

I wield no power over how one chooses to interact with the world. Who am I to tell you how to conduct your life when I am dripping in so much imperfection? On the contrary, interaction with reality should not be from one solipsistic and delusive prison where only we know what is going on in that prison. As far as racism is concerned, this is the problem, not that racism does not occur, but rather that the narrative and how we approach it is terribly flawed. Many thoughts on racism are one-dimensional. A one-dimensional aspect of seeing a phenomenon can never advance to an unbroken truth.

In effect, whenever we presuppose that one race is superior to another from any camp whatsoever, we immediately run into trouble justifying our claim. And one of the reasons is that nothing is to be purged in the other person, which is not in us all. Not being a racist does not mean that one is due for canonisation. One harbours prejudice, hatred and vices much worse than racism.

This is not hard because our treatment of one another, even the black man we tend to protect, starkly contrasts with the hollow sweetness of our words. The hypocrisy is glaring: we preach unity and solidarity, yet our actions are characterised by self-interest. The dissonance between our rhetoric and reality is a testament to our failure to embody the principles we so readily espouse. Perhaps I will make it understandable by stating this example: At the end of it all, I faced myriad obstacles in finding someone to guide me through the final battle. People I approached seemed preoccupied with their commitments, leading to many questions about aligning my interests with theirs or sticking with my own.

My idea also felt threatened because not finding a supervisor had many consequences. Thenceforth, I turned to an individual I deemed a reliable ally who had previously proven invaluable in my crisis. This person is a vocal proponent of saving the black man and a stalwart advocate of sexuality. I sought his assistance, anticipating his willingness to work together on my work and learn from him as a tutor. To my initial satisfaction, he agreed to take on the role. However, any relief I felt then was swiftly eclipsed by a mounting sense of apprehension as our first discussion unfolded. It soon became apparent that our ideological disparities ran deeper than my ideas.

On the one hand, he held steadfast beliefs about separating morality from scientific inquiry. In his view, the introduction of moral questioning into the realm of science was not only unwarranted but fundamentally flawed. There is no way to prove them because they are all normative statements. Furthermore, he espoused a viewpoint that regarded religion as a comforting illusion. In contrast, as our meeting went on, it became increasingly evident that our differences extended beyond matters of methodology and my chosen field.

My choice of literature, which I had meticulously selected to complement the thematic scope of my work, was met with disdain and scepticism. Carl Jung and Carl Rogers were all dead white men, and their scientific contributions are inconsequential. For him, my central focus on psychology was misguided, lacking the progressive edge he deemed essential for a black scholarly discourse. In a perplexing turn of events, he suggested that I shift my focus towards anthropology, viewing it as a more suitable avenue for exploring the complexities of human behaviour and societal norms. As if that was not enough, he urged me to delve deeper into trending topics, advocating for a more pronounced scholarship on those of nonconforming affections.

Whilst I recognised the relevance of these themes within the broader context of my work, I struggled with his insistence on prioritising them above all else. It seemed as though he had overlooked the nuanced intricacies of what I proposed to do, reducing its significance to a narrow and predetermined set of parameters. To myself, I ask: What are the underlying motivations behind his fixation on this particular aspect of my project? Why the emphasis on sexuality? What significance does it hold within the context of my scholarship?

It seemed curious, baffling at the same time, that he would single out sexuality as a primary area of interest, especially given the broader thematic scope of my project. I struggled to reconcile his insistence on elevating these topics above all others. Was it a reflection of his personal biases or ideological leanings? Did he view sexuality as a lens through which to gauge the relevance and impact of my study? Or perhaps there existed a deeper rationale rooted in his own scholarly pursuits or professional interests? What about my ideas? What happened to them? I told him that I had an aim, and that was what I would focus on. As part of me already knew what would happen, I objected conscientiously to his imposition. Accordingly, he confirmed my assumption that what he demanded of me was a conversion to some cult where I would supposedly be more useful with all my natural endowments. Thenceforth, he took the work personally as his utterances were more of "I do not agree with the author."

Now, I must concede that my work was not without its flaws; undoubtedly, my passion for the topic may have made me miss important details. I also acknowledge that the field I chose, just like any other field, has its flaws. However, my supervisor's interest was not for me to define my position in this field but to outrightly reject my own scholarship. He has studied geography and all its intricacies. His titles are Master, Doctor, and soon enough, Professor[61]. More than two decades is what he has spent to be able to lead me by the hand. But here I am, a pupil, daft and incorrigible—unable to be led whilst seeking that which can never buy me a good reputation. To argue with him would amount to unintended consequences because the truth is that whatever I say, however truthful it is, would never make an impression on my listeners if I do not follow his theories. His theories are important which I must follow and find my way out of the darkness that has beclouded my sense of reasoning. But of what practical necessity do I rest all my belief and strength in this story if not on a mere satisfaction of one's compulsive impulses? As such, I decided to let things slide, but the impression the experience made on me threw me into a lot of discombobulation.

Obviously, sexuality and the issues surrounding it are very important to him. However, it is not in the scholarly way one may think of it. What I observe is a kind of fetishism—the transformation of sexuality into a form of deity and racial theory into a creed that professes belief in this deity. This ideology, which reduces the black man's identity to race and sexuality and posits the black man must unconditionally discuss them as *the sine qua non* to understand his place in the universe, is, in essence, a dictatorship. This dictatorship, with keen support from the State, has swallowed the religious instinct of its followers. The establishment in which it operates, namely the state, has assumed the role of God.[62]

Moreover, it strikes me as peculiar that individuals who ostensibly feel that they have altruistic intentions towards the black man simultaneously uphold the ideology of race and sexuality yet reject the notion of a Divine entity when the black man's identity, at least in Igbo cosmology, is tied to his *Chi*.[4] This paradox expresses a deeper philosophical inconsistency and a hidden god, *deus*

---

[4] See Chinua Achebe, *Things Fall Apart*.

absconditus, in Jungian terms.[63] On the one hand, they champion equality and justice based on secular humanism. At the same time, they neglect the spiritual element that is often integral to the pursuit of genuine liberation and human dignity. When put into question, this dichotomy raises objections about the concealed god, their ethical framework, the completeness of approach, and their competencies for addressing societal wounds.

Seen through this lens, all notions that race and sexuality are inextricably linked to the black man's identity—and, by extension, to every individual—as the exclusive framework for understanding their experience is religion, and its worshippers are many; educators, priests, psychologists, psychiatrists, doctors and scientists zealously upholding and propagating its doctrines with an uncontested resolution. It permeates social behaviours and structures, dictating everything from personal identity and relationships to foundational policies and cultural norms, leaving no aspect of life untouched by its influence. Like many religions, this belief system presents a comprehensive worldview that enables followers to understand the world, answers profound existential questions, and outlines moral guidelines. It sets forth its own dogmas, commonly regarded as inviolable and not subject to scrutiny. Any deviation or dissent from these dogmas is frequently met with ostracisation.

The fervent devotion to this ideology, often characterised by seriousness and intolerance towards dissent, further parallels religious fervour. Adherents engage in rituals of ideological purity, such as performative acts of solidarity or public displays of allegiance, akin to religious rituals. Moreover, the State's endorsement and enforcement of this belief again mirror the institutional power structures commonly associated with organised religions. The state is the arbiter of truth, morality, and identity, wielding its authority to stifle alternative beliefs and promote adherence to its sanctioned doctrines. It provides a framework for individuals to find meaning and community whilst also perpetuating hierarchies based on perceived adherence to or deviation from these constructed ideals.

As human beings, we often navigate our social and personal lives with almost religious fervour, seeking validation and acceptance within these frameworks. Sexuality, as a form of divine expression, dictates notions of purity, sin, and morality, influencing how individuals view themselves and others. Similarly, racial theory, acting as a creed, dictates social hierarchies and justifies various forms of discrimination and privilege, reinforcing societal power dynamics. In this paradigm, both sexuality and race are not merely aspects of identity as one may purport but are elevated to the status of sacred doctrines. They demand allegiance to a god who can relate to our sexual urges. Those who conform to the dominant interpretations are rewarded with social capital and acceptance, whilst those who diverge face persecution. The dynamic mirrors traditional religious structures where dogma and orthodoxy define community and belonging. If one can understand that, perhaps one can also understand that the intertwining of sexuality and race as quasi-religious tenets reveals the deep-seated need for man to create order and meaning in his life. These constructs offer narratives that explain the world and one's place within it, providing comfort and a sense of purpose. However, they also underscore the potential for exclusion and conflict as different interpretations and practices clash.

This is dangerous to our civilisation because once sexuality becomes a substitute for God, the *kpim* of everything, that God is simultaneously abolished because those two cannot coexist.[64] He cannot be deified because deification means that one can find traces of the actual God, the Supreme Being. Deification implies a singular, supreme entity, and introducing others into this realm does not necessarily dilute the very essence of what it means to be God Himself. There cannot be God and other small gods to whom man pays homage clandestinely. In an actual sense, the endeavour follows the idea of Nietzsche's *Übermensch* to fashion a different kind of God that will align with human values and understanding, one that embodies attributes more fluid and relatable to human experience.

It does not matter if that means imposing our limitations and bias so far as the end justifies the means. We see this in the way people address God as being unmarked by the distinctions of sex. This reimagined deity would bridge the gap between the divine and the mortal man, providing a sense of connection and relevance without compromising the unique sovereignty of the true Supreme Being. In this way, man seeks to create a deity reflecting his ideals, aspirations, and struggles, offering guidance and comfort intimately tied to the human nature.

The result, therefore, is a profound crisis of meaning as the foundational spiritual and moral frameworks that have historically guided human behaviour and provided a sense of ultimate purpose are eroded. With that God abolished, individuals find themselves adrift in a well of relative values and transient desires. The sacredness and transcendence associated with the divine are transferred to the realm of the temporal and corporeal, which, by their nature, are fleeting and often unsatisfactory. This reorientation leads to a sense of profound existential void and disillusionment as the deeper, enduring connections to God are replaced by transient desires of the flesh and societal validations. As if that is not enough, it further destroys our social fabric by altering our collective understanding of morality and ethics. Simultaneously, we become cynical and begin to fight and kill one another in a bid to defend our ideological positions.

In these circumstances, the basis of our shared values becomes more subjective and divisive, potentially leading to moral relativism and cultural fragmentation. Pope Benedict XVI, then Cardinal Josef Ratzinger, on the day before his election as Pope, warned against the 'dictatorship of relativism' *whose desires do not recognise anything as definite and whose ultimate goal consists solely of one's own ego and desires.*[65] He related these shifts back to the warnings of St Paul in his letter to the Ephesians: "So that we may no longer be infants, tossed by waves and swept along by every wind of teaching arising from trickery, from their cunning in the interests of deceitful scheming."

The consequences of such a paradigm shift we can deduce from the current state of human affairs are manifold. On the individual level, one struggles with his identity, experiencing inner turmoil as one seeks fulfilment in what is essentially superficial. On a societal level, we are bereaved of a unifying, transcendent principle, which increases conflict and disunity as competing ideologies vie for dominance without the cohesive force of a universally acknowledged divine principle. In our different capacities, when we did our analysis well, we should be able to tell what level we are at regarding the fragmentation of collective values and the proliferation of disparate belief systems. The manifold consequences are not shared between black and white, left vs right; in the same way, the angel of death knows not black or white, man or woman, animal, or plant.

Thenceforth, to pretend to publicly defend my freedom whilst you punish me in private represents to me the highest form of a hypocritical charade—one that continues the unyielding machinery of colonial subjugation, to suppress a man who would always be considered as your hopeless inferior. It is still the same imperialist character where one man wants to rule man by offering gestures of "protection" and at the same time denying him the chance to his freedom, his individual autonomy. And I, for once, will not withhold this but say to you that it will not be long before you are ensnared in your own web of ruin and sophistry for subjugating a man you did not fashion. All I am calling for is that humanity may finally put an end to the instrumentalisation of man—that we cease reducing each other to mere tools for power. Then, it is racism as I felt it—to be coerced into a box and expected to adhere to a predetermined set of beliefs and interests simply because I matched the demographic features of blackness. It is as if my individuality was being subsumed by a group's collective identity to which I may or may not fully belong. I thought true acceptance and inclusivity extend beyond banal labels, allowing contributions from different thinking patterns, beliefs and interests. If that is not what it means, thenceforth, the subjugation of an individual into doing what his master says is not just mere compliance; it is a deliberate reinforcement of the same system where racism thrived. It does not matter what features I have; once I have the features needed to exert control, I stand the chance of losing my individuality.

It stands, therefore, to argue that there is still racism not because we cannot control our dark proclivities but because our proclivities have assumed some surrogacy for real humanity. This surrogate behaviour manifests in actual marginalisation, our perception of the marginalisation, and our actions towards it. In our various institutions, the perpetuation of racial bias and hierarchies is not just incidental but essential to maintaining the status quo. Seen through these predicaments, one must dare to say that the fight against racism is another face of the banality of evil where individuals and institutions who claim to be fighting for the marginalised sustain the very evil they ought to eliminate. For a true fight against racism, all we need is an examination of conscience and the suppression of these destructive tendencies but also a profound transformation in our collective mindset and cultural values.

One must accept the truth of the matter that the centre can no longer hold and look for an alternative to this viral malady. Whilst we are clamouring for physical traces of racism, the devil is using others who hold such narrative subjectively dear to map out punishment for those who do not and try to attain perfection beyond this ideological war. John of the Cross has it that he accomplishes this by instilling within these souls a profound irritation towards the perceived sins of others, fostering within them a vigilant and restless zeal. Others are made to experience vexation not directed at others but turned inward towards their own imperfections. They exhibit an impatience that is not humility but a fervent desire to transcend their flaws swiftly.[66]

So intense is their longing to attain sanctity that they aspire to become saints overnight. It is on this note that I appear to hold the belief that all those who sing the anti-racist mantra are not solely driven by a genuine desire for social justice;

a deep-seated human longing for heroism and meaning also fuels it. In a world where genuine acts of heroism seem scary, and people are longing for meaning, the racial narrative provides a readily available avenue for an individual to feel heroic and experience stimulation of meaning.

By embracing it, an individual casts himself as the hero, standing up against cultural ills and social injustices. It offers him a sense of purpose and meaning in the chaos we have created to constrain him. In fighting against racism, he finds a cause worth fighting for, a cause that imbued his life with meaning and depth. But little does he know that he only takes a flight from himself. Frankl considers this type of flight 'centrifugal leisure', which does not allow for contemplation and meditation on one's life.[67]

This type of flight is predominant in today's anti-racist narrative in contrast to 'centripetal leisure', which allows for solving problems—primarily confronting them with humility. Due to the former, any idea or book that challenges us to go beyond our irascible desideratum to see life differently beyond the category of white vs black or white vs red must be cancelled. The hardest task is to be upright and steadfast in our dealings with one another, but it is not so hard that there is no way forward. To achieve this, we need a new adventure that does not aim to demonise the other but sees him as an individual—an *imago dei,* first and foremost. There is no balance sheet to be drawn in the game of black vs white, left vs right; for whatever shortcomings I can point out in you, I can also find a corresponding one in me.

We ought to have learnt that from Becker in his groundbreaking work, *On the Denial of Death*. The central thesis put forth by Becker is that human behaviour is largely motivated by an underlying fear of death. This fear takes various forms and leads to the creation of beliefs and ideologies that offer a sense of meaning and immortality. For him, our ideological battles often reflect this deeper existential struggle. Viewed from this perspective, when we engage in debates over issues like black vs white or left vs right, we are not only discussing principles but also seeking validation for our own worldview to alleviate the existential dread that lies beneath.

By acknowledging that our opponents are similarly driven by fundamental anxieties, we can approach whatever it is we are trying to achieve with a greater understanding of what each of us has up our sleeves. This does not diminish detrimental actions or convictions but speaks for a more profound examination of conscience, and self-reflection if you may. If we recognise that our ideological adversaries are confronting the same existential anxieties, we can progress towards a more constructive discussion. Instead of perceiving one another as mere opponents to be vanquished, we can begin to regard each other as fellow humans, each grappling with the task of discovering purpose and stability in an inherently unpredictable world. To begin, we need a new adventure to learn this, and to afford ourselves one, we must risk being lonely.

The events of life are much more complex than they appear, and we cannot package them all in one fancy handy suitcase like race and sexuality. In other words, life is an intricate enigma and must be met with open arms, analytical and critical minds, and not overthinking them in one dimension that brings the conclusion that matches our emotional conviction. I hope the reader can conclude that doing that diminishes the uniqueness of being human and the meaning embedded in our unique situations. I hope the reader can see that in the conduct of human affairs, there are no black or white liberals or conservatives but complex layers of truths so complex that attempting to reduce them to simplistic dichotomies is blatant naivety. This is not a matter of left or right; all these often make us fail to perceive the broader context and complexities. One dimension people of reality Kant says:

> are subject to a malaise which may even turn into moral corruption, a malaise of which the unthinking are ignorant—namely discontent with that providence by which the course of the world as a whole is governed. They feel this sentiment when they contemplate the evils which greatly oppress the human race, with no hope (as it sense) of any improvement. Yet it is of the utmost importance that we should be content with providence, even if the path it has laid out for us on earth is an arduous one. We should be content with it partly in order that we may take courage even in the midst of hardships, and partly in order that should not blame all such evils on fate and fail to notice that we may ourselves be entirely responsible for them, thereby losing the chance to remedy them by improving ourselves.[68]

Kant's expression is not a pious aspiration but points directly to what happens when we choose to cast the other as villain instead of looking inwardly at ourselves. We should not be quick to cast out the evil that lies without leaving the evil that lies within. We have much more work to do to change ourselves than others. There is no alternative to that than to eschew the evil in us. Is that not why we assiduously advocate for one human race, that all came from one man and have sinned, and no one can stand the Ideal judge?

See, evil is not the catastrophe we suffer but an act by humanity.[69] In this way, we all commit racist acts. It may not be clearly racism, but in one way or another, we show hate, jealousy, envy, discrimination, deception, anger, and revenge, and we tell lies. The difference between these levels of human emotions is that racism seems to have acquired moral and political legitimacy. In consequence, we primate what is politically correct over our proclivity to commit the same act since it is most true and certain. But what is true and certain is that we all have these inclinations seethed within us, waiting for the right opportunity to use them. As long as we are fallible, we continually have to undergo a transformation to become the Divine Individual. In other words, we must constantly change into our potential selves. The magnitude of the change is inconsequential but will showcase itself through our challenge. Every challenge in life is new in form and pattern and does not happen twice. We only pass each challenge once.

Each phase is unique and rife with utter complexity. Yet, uncertain as it were, we must live even as the world grows in inhumanity;[70] a little atom of Divine trust will calm the storm. Although our faith and intention might quiver and trust compromised, there is no need to fix the storm but survive it. It is only when one attempts to fix the storm that he discovers in the other's actions the traces of racism. When one rushes to fix things, he fails in his capacity to precisely comprehend the complexity embedded in what he is fixing.

As a result, he grows in perplexity and despair. Therefore, when the events of life take their course, things that you can neither fight nor control, it is best you embrace them and give up control. Focus on the things you can control, and focus on Him, who looks at every other thing. Whilst the tempest rages and it seems overwhelming, God is always there. He walks over the waters, God's glory thunders, the One that has control over the mighty waters, as the psalmist says. He is there between your suffering and your redemption. Dwelling so much on racism and anti-racism creates the illusion that we are saving ourselves when God is the one saving us.

Indeed, moving beyond this level requires not merely dwelling on the unpleasantness of circumstances but rather a fundamental shift in worldview and approach. One must be the change he wants to experience in his situation. He must possess the willingness to relinquish something held subjectively dear in favour of embracing a higher significance. At any given time, one can decide how his story will end. To find oneself in a despairing moment is one thing to overcome is another.

Life can be brutally unfair. But the question for me (perhaps it should be for you) is, what do I do with it? How do I want my story to end? Whether one answers them or not, one must pay keen attention to the direction given to him, the emotions around and within him and most importantly, his inner conviction. Similarly, one must not ruthlessly disregard the institution.

The institutions are not structural buildings. The purpose of establishing them is to give meaning to the values shared. We are the institutions, and if there is anything wrong with them, perhaps something is wrong with us, too. The institutions cannot be effective unless we are effective in our little capacity—unless we eschew evil and integrate our goodness into the totality of life. Where the inner self of man degenerates, there would also be degeneration in his outer projection.

We must admit that there is racism in the world as much as we have to acknowledge that blaming everything on race waters down the effort to find a viable solution. An account of human history is enough to guide us on this path to discovering the truth about the human condition. It should also show us that we should not blame the evil that oppresses us on political power, social inequalities, or the sins of our ancestors. Certainly, this variable ought to be considered. Everything that happens has a material cause.

In the same way, it should, as Kant pinpointed, show us that we have every justification for acknowledging these problems as our own and holding ourselves responsible for all the evils which spring from the misuse of our reason, for we are quite capable of realising that the same way we would recognise it and behave differently which would be to misuse our reason even nature advises us otherwise.[71] Truly, genuine humanness is possible, but only if we tame the evil in us individually. Once we have understood this, racism as evil holds little weight in tipping the balance in our favour when the scales consider the entirety of merits and faults.

VI
The Abolition of God

The questions that concern me and that we must all ask ourselves are: What moves man to make uncanny and ludicrous claims about God? What motivates him to assert seemingly absurd claims regarding who God is? The things about God are too complex to comprehend to sacrifice his understanding of them on the altar of our petty political ideology. By politics, I do not mean the act of policymaking and governance but the political leanings. All too often, these distinctions are inextricably linked that one would not mind committing an error. And it does not matter because, in today's world, the political ideologies have taken over the process and the very truths we hold credible are the oversimplified ones—devoid of any paradox. This is evident in the attitude of some Christians, who withdraw themselves from any paradox that is unique to their faith.

The objective is to dismantle our deeply ingrained symbols, principles, and convictions, which we hold as unchangeable, in pursuit of uniformity and inclusivity of meaning. The objective is to abolish God and assert our independence from external authorities or perceived divine control, and we have succeeded in doing so by assigning God a gender-neutral pronoun! What we have is a trend of worship which is making us morally bankrupt and leaving us spiritually impoverished. We constantly strive to dilute the logical contradictions entrenched in our faith throughout history.

Yet such endeavours are undeniably foolish, then the mysteries as we know them today are not there because some group of dominant men in society stamped them as morally legitimate truths and beliefs. They are there because just as ideas are scattered and dispersed in our memory from the beginning of time, the mysteries and truth about God are imprinted in our hearts from the beginning of time (Jer. 31:33, 2 Cor. 3:3). Any attempt to wash it off would require a hyssop and total dismantling of the individual psychic. But we have yet to succeed psychologically with that, which means we have a considerable distance to traverse.

Things have gone down the spiral since man began to use his reasoning without the guidance of an established authority, which allows him to make petty claims when he cannot sustain the logical contradictions of his faith. Therefore, a task arises to simplify these logical contradictions step by step and elevate them to the order of holiness to increase the likes of those who are spiritually constipating. If achieving inclusivity proves unattainable, then the Christian faith, by its very nature, fails in its mission and should be thoroughly reconsidered or even discontinued. Our comprehension of belief and faith in God remains incomplete unless scrutinised through the political lens, which often distorts the unbroken truth of sacred texts. Consequently, we frequently fail to grasp the spiritual losses we incur, preoccupied as we are with fulfilling irascible desideratum.

To speak of God in gender-neutral terms demonstrates the length of man's strength to sustain the paradox of the faith he professes and how deeply frustrated he is with the things he cannot confine into a system and, at the same time, yearning for their meaning, for it must be overtly admitted that everything his mind cannot define is either incredible or insane. It is not that the things he set his mind to are always beyond the reach of his knowledge, but he occasionally neglects his knowledge of himself and desires to have everything outside make its impression on him. But as A. Kempis writes, foolish is immeasurable the man who attendeth upon other things leaving his soul impoverished. Such an inordinate understanding of God and uncomplex projection of religious phenomena robs the soul of its values so that it becomes incapable of further development through that sheer quality of being empty.[71]

Similarly, it causes the delusion that the cause and solution to the misfortunes he is experiencing lie without and not within—and he no longer stops to ask himself how much of this misfortune and tribulations we have given in. He is so proud of himself that he can hardly conceive of himself as capable of evil. Since he has lost this consciousness of evil, God is abolished to a system, whilst religious rituals become external formalities without any inward grace. In actual effect, man becomes a mere artefact that can be refashioned to reflect these external formalities shaped by him.

In an outward form of Christian religion, where all the emphasis lies on what is physical, everything is possible because once we leave out the inward principle to satisfy the soul, we come to the realisation that the Divine reality we have believed in the past is rather archaic and backward, for verily we see no impression of this reality in our life. It is like Adam and Eve in the Garden of Eden. But unlike our them, we have no shame in our nakedness and are apt to stripe everyone else naked. It is as if it is not happening already with the methods implored to make it appear less brutal. For once, I do not think this epidemic display originated from the outside to the inside but from the inside to the outside, showing the impoverished part of man that the Divine Majesty has not remotely touched.

But God cannot come from Heaven to touch this part of man. This ought to be the duty of theologians to speak life into every man; however, in the Christian community, as Jung rightly observed, these souls are shed "like dry leaves from the great tree and now find themselves 'hanging on' to treatment."[72] The more profound and complete knowledge one thinks the theologians have acquired, the more severely they exhibit spiritual laxity without any qualms. If they could turn to Freud for an explanation of human sexuality instead of Augustine, then it is a stark sign of emptiness and banality—a glaring testament to the hollowness and triviality of our values.

No man with God in him leaves the other impoverished after encountering him. Verily, God is incomprehensible. We can only attain a limited knowledge of God. Still, even with our limited faculties, we possess absolute knowledge about Him that cannot be doubted despite those limitations. Even without the factual knowledge of God, He is clearer than the sky and brighter than the sun.

Here, I reckon the *I and Thou* of Buber. Indeed, the way to comprehend all these facts is not actually straight. It is chaotic and interminable and requires humility and simplicity. The humbler and simpler one is, the more things; indeed, deep things of the world are revealed to him whilst he slumbers. Because he has submitted himself to God, the Light of Understanding, as in Wisdom chapter 9, He reveals Himself to him as in 1 Kings chapter 3:11-15.

The fear of God is the beginning of wisdom, one has read from the opening chapter of the book of Proverbs. Instead of man submitting to God that He may let His light shine upon him so that he may understand how he made things and came to be through Him, what one sees is the desire to profit from that knowledge without any fear of Him. Christian education was meant to help man overcome his faulty expectations and be in a state of the highest union with God. On the contrary, neither Christian education nor education in itself has achieved this core purpose.

Ultimately, the search for meaning has been exacerbated amongst people of different origins. The initial process of learning, where one asks questions in pursuit of the core truth of existence, has been replaced with cascade alienation of unconditional values. This speaks to the second reason why we have succeeded in abolishing God. But I tell you again, there is more to this than the physical eye can actually take through its retina.

Everything is tied to the spiritual because that is where the decay starts in the human life and then evaporates into the physical. We have not done enough in Christianising the soul, to the point that Christ can come in and dwell against the barbaric activities of our modern world. The German Lutheran Church, for instance, may preach the gospel to the heathens, but the question of where God is, which populates their own hearts, has not heard that our God is in the heavens. This is seen in the trending discernment of the gospel to match the expectations of the congregation, followed by its poor interpretation regardless.

There is always this attitude to fix Rome's problem and bring Christ to people in the outward form, thus robbing the soul of its mysteries and leaving it prey to the devil. I say this not as a conspicuous moral judgment but as an observation of someone who has participated in the service, of which everyone is free to square with his own conscience, even though I am afraid we may arrive at the same conclusion.

Faced with these ardent situations, there is nothing to expect from a man who has learnt philosophy and theology than the denial of his faith and to treat God as the object of intellectual scrutiny. In reading the Holy Writ, he does it with a cunning attitude of scrupulous moral investigation of the technical formulations that will constitute a subtle discourse. Not knowing that although God inspires the Scripture, He dances to his folly the moment he begins to read it with a strong impertinence and not, as Kempis recommended, 'devotional and simple'.

I myself cannot entirely grasp the tremendous elements of its writing and structural alignment. Nor can I grasp with my poor little mind the meaning it harbours. But I, too, for my part, prefer the precious gift of humility, knowing full well that an effective way to understand a tiny spec of it is not by my proud-hearted but by falling on my knees as in my Psalm 51. Why would I be so foolish to claim ownership over something I cannot fathom and countless people can understand it better than I do?

On the other hand, if we choose to leave God and treat Him not as a God but as a mere concept or abstract idea, anybody can fashion as he likes; He will always find a way to make Himself known to the next generation. God does not need any mortal help to pass His name on to the next generation. He made it clear that if we fail to praise Him, the stone will cry out (Luke 19:40).

He, whose throne is in the heavens and the earth, His footstool, does whatever He wills. He can command the green grass to bow down in His worship and the elephant to sing His praises. By the very power of spoken words, He does this not by magic. He has also given man such power, but man uses his to speak fallacy and sow discord. And precisely, the fruit of such discord is changing the name of God and watering down the beliefs of the Christian faith. To that, there are some objections to be raised, and they run thus:

First, traditional religious teachings often describe God as a transcendent being, existing beyond the limitations of human understanding, including gender. Similarly, God is immanent, present, and active within creation. Therefore, using gender-specific pronouns may inadvertently anthropomorphise God—buttressing the idea that God is a corporeal being and imposing human characteristics and limitations onto a being that surpasses human categories.

Furthermore, God embodies qualities and virtues that transcend human gender distinctions. For instance, God is often described as embodying both the 'masculine' and 'feminine' attributes—strength and nurturing, justice and mercy. As a consequence, using gender-neutral pronouns aligns with the theological assertion that God's nature is beyond human gender categories, maintaining consistency with the doctrine of God's transcendence.

Indeed, it is true that God is not a corporeal being; He is a transcendent being because if He is a corporeal being, then His corporeality must depend upon some other thing that gives Him animation and that which gives what gives Him animation must also depend upon some other animating power. This can go on to infinity, but we cannot do that because we would not have the first and last animating being, bringing our propositions to no logical conclusion. Therefore, it is necessary to admit that, in fact, there is a first animator who is not animated by any other being. And if this animator calls himself a '*He*', then His He-ness is not caused by another being. Therefore, God is a masculine deity whose masculinity is not caused by any other being.

Second, if God's he-ness is man's flawed thinking and nothing but the projection of Western patriarchy, then there would have been four persons in one

God to validate God as a feminine deity and not even a gender-neutral deity. But considering the truth of general and special revelation, there is no fourth person of the blessed trinity. Therefore, God is neither a feminine deity nor can He be addressed in gender-neutral terms. Hence, God is a masculine deity.

Christian insistence that three is one and two is four is not a relatively new conception but goes back to the symbolic significance of uneven and even numbers. Since the old times, uneven numbers 1, 3, 5 and so on have been associated with masculinity, whilst even numbers 2, 4, 6 and so on with femininity. In the Chinese tradition, uneven/odd numbers are referred to as Yang (male) numbers, whereas even numbers are Yin (female). The number 3 is significant because it points to the three critical stages in a man's life: birth, vocation, and death. Three is associated with the idea that the balance between Yin and Yang can be achieved through the third element for a harmonious whole.

Even in various spiritual traditions, the number 3 symbolises creation, manifestation, and the time continuum—past, present, and future. The number 3 symbolises the nature of existence and the interconnectedness of these temporal dimensions between the past, present and future. In the intervals of time, it is more mysterious because both the past and future exist in one constancy, the present. This holds true for Augustine; when recollecting and telling a story, we look at the images of the story in the present since they are still in memory. When we think out our actions for the future, we premediate our actions in the present, although the action lies in the future. When the action begins to come into effect, it comes into effect in the present, and since then,[73] it is no longer in the future.[74]

What is perhaps apparent at this juncture is that God cannot be a female deity, nor can He be addressed in gender-neutral terms. Even if I dispense with the trinity as my valid unit of analysis and base my argument on the belief in one God, just like the other Abrahamic religious traditions, I still cannot conclude that God is a female deity. The gender-neutral God is divisive and does not bring together different worlds with a history of hating each other.

There can be only one God, indivisible and immutable. The past, present and future are distinct intervals existing in one single constancy, just as the trinity in the Christian tradition is three persons in one. Unless we dispense entirely with the Scripture, it holds a profound symbolic meaning for these numbers, are also used for divination to perpetuate unprecedented suffering, leaving one to seek their material explanation.

The significance of these numerical patterns can be found throughout the pages of the Scripture, illuminating deeper truths and offering insights into the Divine order. The creation of heaven and earth in 6 days plus 1 day of rest signifies completeness in the order of creation, whereas the number 6 means incompleteness. The number 6 represents imperfection, and it is the number of beats mentioned in the Book of Revelation. The number 7 in biblical numerology symbolises perfection, completion, and holiness, 7 days of creation/7 days in a week—culminating in the Sabbath day. It is a reminder of the Divine Order that underlies the foundation and patterns inherent in the universe.

The universe is a creation of pattern, works in pattern and rejuvenates itself in pattern. This pattern is inherent in man, the microcosm of the universe and the impetus of everything God made. Through the same pattern, he mediates between spiritual and corporeal reality. Thus, in African Traditional Religion, when the chief priest wants to perform certain rituals, he stands barefoot on the soil, gazing to the heavens and connecting the power above and below.

This is analogous to the moment of consecration in the Mass, where the priest raises a material substance to heaven and draws meaning to earth, as well as the materialistic explanation of the universe in terms of energy, matter, space, and time. Again, in the Book of Revelation, we have the seven seals, trumpets and bowls signifying the complete plan of God's redemption, judgement, and the fullness of his intervention in human history. And nine, pointing to the nine choirs of angels.

Apart from the religious relevance in investigating the nature of God, psychologically, number 3 is associated with the three aspects of an individual's consciousness—mind, body, and soul—signifying the unity of the Divine Being in the individual and his approximate means of expression. The trinity, Jung opines, is a "decidedly masculine deity of which the androgyny of Christ and the special position and veneration of the Mother of God are not the real equivalent."[75] To explain, the Holy Spirit overshadowing the Blessed Virgin Mary, the higher, spiritual, the masculine descending to the lower, the earthly, the feminine and producing a son—not merely a divine figure detached from humanity, but a unique son who embodies both divine and human qualities does not make the Blessed Virgin Mary a fourth person. Instead, it made her *Redemptoris Mater*.

The drama played out in the redemption story, and its effect is to unite the opposites, human vs spiritual, mortal vs immortal, male vs female and evil versus good. The unification of the opposites started with the first account of creation in Genesis chapter 1:27, where we read that God made man in his own image and likeness and the second account of creation, where we read about the separation of man and woman from man, from Adam's rib. The story of Adam's rib carries what we need to know: Adam was originally androgynous until Eve was separated from him. In this early, asexual generation, man existed in unity with Mother Nature. However, following Eve's separation, man began to distance himself from nature, influenced by the presence of woman. Thus, the sexual differentiation between man and woman in the original myth was understood as a step away from the initial unity or perfection of creation. This interpretation persisted in Semitic culture and, notably, in the first Christian century, where various midrashim and even St Paul distinguish between man created in the image of God and man as male and female.[76]

Paul's concept of the "body of Christ" (e.g., Rom 12:4-5; 1 Cor 1:10; Eph 4:3-4) symbolises a unity that embraces all opposites, harmonising diverse qualities within Christ. Early interpretations saw this as Christ embodying and reconciling world opposites, such as male and female (Gal 3:28), creating a higher unity. Ephesians 1:23 further suggests that Christ integrates and reconciles all opposites into a cohesive whole. While we are not negating the fact that these texts may be subject to multiple interpretations, we cannot deny their leaning towards a theory of unity, which finds its culmination in the birth, death and resurrection of Christ.[77]

The androgyny of Christ represents the mediation of the opposites. However, this mediation is not carried out on a superficial level but on a deeper level of human experience. The oppositions are real-world dynamics, such as light and dark, order and chaos, love and hate, masculine and feminine, and conscious and unconscious. These oppositions are not problems to be discarded but essential elements that drive the growth and integration within the individual. Through this experience, he is opened to the possibility of experiencing God and accepting the message of Christ. Without this experience of the opposites, there is no experience of wholeness, the inner approach and no experience with God and sacred figures. For this purpose, Christianity emphasises sinfulness and original sin to reveal the profound, universal struggle of opposing forces within each individual, at least from an external perspective.[78]

This, in brief, shows that there is always a tension of opposites. Nonetheless, they often illuminate the intricate balance of the order of creation, Divine

Revelation, and human experience. This holds true for the alchemic tradition. Jung observed that regardless of the leanings of the alchemy towards quaternity, there is always a vacillation between three and four which comes out over and over. There are there and four colours. There are always four elements; however, the three of them are grouped together, with the fourth occupying a special position. Four, Jung writes, "signifies the feminine, the motherly, the physical; three the masculine, fatherly, spiritual. Thus, the uncertainty as to three or four amounts to a wavering between the spiritual and the physical—a striking example of how every human truth is a last truth but one."[79]

It would hardly be correct to say that therein lies the crux of the problem, which is the subjugation of women and, thus, responsible for the rift in both the Church and society since it is easy to show how the trinity (three) is masculine deity and four is a feminine deity. God, in His infinite wisdom, has premeditated on this problem; thus, He elevated the Blessed Virgin Mary, pointing to her as the gate of heaven and easy access to the trinity. In the Catholic faith, this dogma is well-defined. It is not an arbitrary invention of faith, as we often think about doctrines and dogmas. The central idea of God in this regard is deeply rooted in the Scripture.

For humanity to have someone they could resort to for maternal protection and comfort, it was essential to have an amiable feminine figure despite the androgyny of Christ. The turning of water into wine at the wedding in Canna establishes this to an incontrovertible degree. God showed us his truth beforehand so that we may easily find our back to Him when the "collective dominants of human life fall into decay"[80] and the unconscious individual process sets in. But due to various prejudices, the critical relevance of the special position accorded to Mary as the Mother of God is not well established in Christianity—and for such prejudices, we are swimming in a whirlpool of swirling vortexes of thoughts.

With that in mind, it must also be said that as much as I admire Jung's understanding of the numerical significance of showing that the He-ness of God is not an arbitrary construct, and having implored my own knowledge of such phenomenon, I must restrain myself from Jung and further assertions that might give the reader the impression that 1) God has a body, and 2) separate entities or divisions within Him. When I highlight the numerical significance, I do this to speak of God's transcendence as a negation of division. For one and three means undivided and whole, the same way in God's nature, one and three are whole and undivided. God is not composed of parts or divisions within His being. Unlike humans, who are subject to composition and division, God exists in a state of pure actuality devoid of any potentiality or multiplicity.[81]

This radical simplicity of God's essence is foundational to understanding His transcendence and omnipotence and has been profoundly explained in the groundwork of Thomas Aquinas, *Summa Theologica: Prima Pars 1-49*. When I say three is one and two is four, I do not mean that God is multipliable—a division of His being into discrete units. Such numerical designations do not add anything substantial to God's *being*. Rather, they serve as conceptual tools for one's understanding, allowing him to grasp aspects of divine perfection within the limitations of his intellect.

The numerical significance signifies the power of God to use numbers to explain Himself to us and not add meaning to His *being*. Thus, we speak of the three divine persons—Father, Son, and Holy Spirit—as distinct numerically whilst affirming their essential unity in God. In a similar vein, attributes such as God's goodness, wisdom, and power are distinguished conceptually, yet they all converge in the divine essence without introducing any composition or division. Thus, we can read from the Scripture that God sees, but His seeing does not imply His power to see sensibly but intellectually. We read that man is created in the image of God, "but as regards that whereby he exceeds other animals," namely his intelligence and reason, which are incorporeal just as God is incorporeal.

Aquinas writes: we draw near to God by no corporeal steps *since He is everywhere, but by the affections of our soul and by the actions of that same soul do we withdraw from Him.*[82] Hence, the less corporeal determination we want to have in God's nature, the more universal and absolute our experience of Him would be and the more properly we would relate to Him. It is not necessary that what we call God must import relation to creatures, particularly how these creatures identify sexually. But it must be imposed from some perfection flowing from God to His creatures. Among these things are not pronouns indifferent to the conventions of sex.

Third, if God is a female deity or can be addressed in a manner unmarked by the distinction of sex, then the Holy Writ shall be the first book to confer such authority. But since neither the Scripture nor any of the Church's magisterium considers God a feminine deity or addresses Him in a manner unmarked by the distinctions of sex, God is, therefore, neither a feminine deity nor a gender-neutral. Many religious texts, including the Bible, refer to God as a Father and use male attributes to describe their comprehension of God. This suggests that God is inherently male and cannot be a feminine deity or gender-neutral. But this he-ness is not based on my arbitrary presuppositions, as we already established.

Although there are sections of the Bible where God employs a feminine metaphor to describe Himself, such as Isaiah. 66:13, it does not inherently suggest a feminine deity nor point to a being that is gender-neutral. Such attributes of God often come with a parallel meaning; in this case, His ability to protect us as a mother protects her offspring. In Psalm 91:1-4, God protects us like a mother hen spreads her wings to cover her defenceless chicks. This enriches our understanding of God as identifying with the human experience in every process.

In Jeremiah 1:4, He is simply "the Lord, who formed you in your mother's womb." And in Deuteronomy 32:6, He is "your father who begot you." Throughout the Old Testament, God is predominantly masculine and is often associated with qualities such as strength, power, and order, as well as negative qualities such as anger, violence, and vengefulness, as in Psalm 94. Whilst it is valid to query why such characteristics are exclusively masculine, the predominant emphasis on God as male is given because of its signification as possessing the initiatory power and sovereignty that are fitting with His relation to His creatures.

No one can say what he does not know. Likewise, no one can say anything about God without implying from the Scripture in which He has revealed Himself countless times. Once one understands and uses the scripture devotional and simple to imply his knowledge about God, whatever he implies would not depend on his predictions and feelings about what he thinks the nature of God should be but on the signification of what his intellect knows about God, i.e. the mode it applies in determining what he understands about God and not even God itself. One thing is for sure: although we possess limited knowledge about God, we can still infer a certain kind of knowledge that, although not entirely comprehensible, remains absolute once one apprehends the Holy Scripture and applies its teachings with discernment.

Fourth, suppose the argument is true that God is a feminine deity or being that can be addressed in a gender-neutral terms; the art of people like Michelangelo and Caravaggio would have clarified that so that nothing can be said of God because neither man nor woman can actually make God who He is except there is imprinter in human psyche who bestows that knowledge. If God is who our limitations and biases portray; the corporeal representation of God through art and literature would have addressed that so that nothing is said of the Creator apart from what we say He is. Whereby this is not the case, it appears that God, in His wisdom during those times past, has revealed Himself in a manner He wants to be called and addressed. Going against it implies personal idiosyncrasies and misuse of human intellect. God made everything in their perfect nature, the same way He is perfect in His own nature.

It would be unfitting for God to confuse us to insinuate conclusions contrary to His revelation. Hence, He reveals and inspires artists and poets to rise above their personal lives and circumstances and speak from the spirit and the soul—as man to the spirit and soul of mankind. Thus, in such cases, as Jung explains, the task forces itself upon us to fathom and explain the very essence of the art because now they are addressing things that spring instead from the dark recess of the human mind that we sometimes discard. These things are not personal, and sometimes, being personal with them is rather a sin. They must flow and not hindered by any form of misgivings—for the artist is his work and not the human being.[83]

Every creative person embodies a duality or synthesis of contradictory aptitude.[84] On the one hand, he is a human being with passions and personal life, whilst on the other hand, he is impersonal and must stay true to the revelation of the creative process. Since, as humans, the artist is capable of error, we must transcend the corruptibility of our human nature and look at the level of his psychic make-up to understand his personality and representation. This psychic make-up informs us about the, the symbolism which are universal patterns of human experience that he carries and brings to life, sometimes at the expense of his own life. In this sense, the personification and depiction of God as a masculine deity throughout history are not because the people of the old times held positions of power and authority in a patriarchal society which mirrored its power structures in religious beliefs and practices, but because the representation is part of the archetypes embedded in us which the artist brings to life.

The existence of these archetypes is a symbolic pattern that shapes our behaviour and experiences.[85] As a consequence, the role of the archetypes in shaping our behaviour, perception and understanding sheds light on this symbolism and representation. The personification and portrayal of God as a masculine deity align with the archetype of the Father imprinted in our minds representing authority, guidance, protection, and discipline.

Etymologically, the word 'type' originates from the Greek word 'typos' (τύπος), which means 'a blow, imprint, or mark[86]'; thus, if the personification and portrayal of God align with the archetype of the Father in the psyche, it presupposes an imprinter, God as we call Him. And even though our knowledge of Him is limited, we constantly use images and symbols to stretch out innumerable things beyond our understanding that cannot be doubted so that they can be taken up, handled and become symbols that ensure life at every moment. The problem as it appears is as Jung opines: Man thinks he shapes these ideas but it is actually these that shape man.

We need to ask ourselves why some religious traditions employ the use of symbolic images to bring to life phenomena and concepts we cannot fully define nor fully comprehend. The symbolic representation of these concepts and phenomena not only suggests the nature of God but offers us some absolute knowledge of His identity as He meets man. Man produces symbolic language to express the ineffable. The conscious use of these symbols is one aspect of the evidence that what we are dealing with is not banal… If there are certain concepts in our beliefs that we cannot understand, then it is incumbent on us to apply humility instead of being arrogant and pretending to have all the answers. True wisdom lies not in feigning certainty but in acknowledging the limits of our understanding. Not all would believe that the Son of God died in human flesh and resurrected on the third day, nor a Virgin conceived and still remained a Virgin after conception. The Christian faith as we know it contains so many logical contradictions.[87] These contradictions can only be understood by those who humble themselves.

The logical contradictions are the wisest and, indeed, the very essence of our faith. As a witness to this, Tertullian avows: "And the Son of God is dead, which is worthy of belief because it is absurd. And He was buried and rose again; the fact is certain because it is impossible."[88] If Christianity demands faith in such paradoxes, it does not follow that this is an arbitrary use of reason or the exhibition of power. The paradoxes are, in fact, the very foundations of Christian belief and one of the most valuable possessions of the Christian faith.

Hence, once a religion like Christianity begins to dismantle its very foundation, especially the paradox concerning God, in favour of inclusivity and uniformity in meaning—as it is now—we become spiritual weaklings and eventually prey to our construct.

The problem is not that man does not want to accept God as He has revealed Himself to Him, but that he has grown prideful and is finding it difficult to return home. He thinks of himself as already the *Übermensch* and cannot submit to anything greater than himself. But even to himself, he lies. Humility is no longer the virtue of Christian belief, particularly in the West; pride and arrogance are. Hence, we return to a crisis of the soul, where the pursuit of self-deification obscures the Divine truth. Many reject the very notion of a higher power, believing instead in their own infallibility and wisdom. Yet we cannot pray, and the mountains move.

To thee, Lord, I do not assert that I know you entirely but rather an investigation to know you more. Open my eyes to the things of your spirit so that I may see things beyond the reach of my knowledge. Give me the wisdom that comes from you, for in you, all things take their title.

We cannot confine God into an often ill-begotten system. The inner man must connect to God—his soul must be in union with God to be able to fathom some of the mysteries about Him and behind His creation. We need an unlearning; that is the process of inner rebirth that comes with crucifixion, death, burial, and resurrection that introduces a new element into the soul. This is the process by which we reform in the newness of our minds. Each of us possesses something that must die. Unless that which might die in us dies, there cannot be real life.

Too much familiarity with God breeds contempt; that is why we are able to impose our limitations and biases on Him and still be happy we did it. God is beyond our limitations and biases. God is not a being whose centre is nowhere and whose circumference is also nowhere. God is rather "an infinite sphere, whose centre is everywhere and whose circumference is nowhere" [*Deus Est sphera inifita cuius centrum est ubique, circumferentia vero nusquam*]. The name God does not define Him. He made it clear in the book of Exodus 3:14 that He shall be called: I AM WHO I AM. Hence, in Judaism, the name of God is written with an asterisk (G*D). The name is not pronounced—the holy name of God is not pronounced to avoid desecration. But it has become a common thing in Christianity to call the name of God, and it is a privilege, of which our wilful blindness to control Him is not only an abomination but also amplifies how demiurge we are proving to be in matters about God.

But who are we to control God? Can we actually know God's mind? God dwells beyond finite understanding in humbleness and simplicity—He is simple and good. There is not a single composite nor complication in God. God is perfect in His nature, and this perfection does not lack any mode of its perfection, Aquinas says. One must let his heart be free from the malice and prejudice that pushes him away from God. Humility and simplicity can help us see God as simple and perfect as He is. God does not like the proud-hearted. Everyone who is proud in heart is detestable by Him.[89]

Pride led man to evil, and he lost his blissful seat in the glory. The same pride may lead man to hell. Those who have insisted they will never speak of God as a spiritual being in spiritual terms but in carnal terms denoting some kind of carnality in the nature of God. Have they comprehended the extent of such 'carnality' using their own logical spices? We forget that a mystery that holds to a different rule cannot borrow materials from the same things it impugns for its own argument.[90] Instead, it will use a different material or deconstruct its own material and emerge from nothingness.

In the same way, He created *ex nihilo*—not out of pre-existing material, out of Himself, nor explosion of a material substance, but by calling things into being out of nothingness and giving them form through His likeness. This is why it is unnecessary either to enquire or to demonstrate whether He has gender or not. For everything about Him seems to be a logical absurdity! And then He speaks to us through the prophet Isaiah: "My thoughts are not your thoughts, nor are your ways my ways. For as the heavens are higher than the earth, so are my ways higher than your ways, my thoughts higher than your thoughts."[91]

Finally, we may want to employ the concept of anthropomorphism and say that it is plausible to assert that the God who created man in His own image and likeness can have a body as such, and can be addressed by the construct of our limitations. As human beings, we bear some resemblance to God and possess qualities that reflect certain aspects of the nature of God. Hence, being male or female is seen as an intrinsic part of God's design, even the one that is neither male nor female. However, being created in the image and likeness of God does not mean being corporeal as we have already established, but in that nature in which man excels over other creatures. Thus, when the Church teaches that *imago dei*, they do so, pointing to the soul because the soul never dies on the one hand, and God cannot be reduced to mere human projection on the other hand.

Human language, concepts and attributes are insufficient to capture God's nature fully. Even if we decide to go by the 'validity' of our own construct, then we are left to conclude that since being male or female is the only concept within God's design, God cannot also take a nature which is contrary to His design. Thus, what we project onto God inhibits deeper understanding and connection with God and obstructs His design.

Now, one may object: Perhaps one may say that not accepting the nonconforming thesis reduces God to a sexual being and demonstrates the extent of our biases that influence our relationship with Him. In response, we should also argue and acknowledge that God's transcendence beyond our biases should not be conflated with interpreting God's nature in alignment with one's own narrow political ideology. Such a line of thinking contradicts the sublime authority of the word of God, which has lived even though its human authors are dead. Since whatever appears male proves to be problematic, the intention of the opposite is dubious because it diminishes the human experience and core religious symbolism that, all things considered, are not merely human constructs. Think of the story of redemption: When God gave us His only begotten Son, He did so by descending low to the place of man, and He lived by all the laws binding man on earth.

We received Christ in solid flesh and blood, fully human and divine. He went through natural birth and death—the law binding man on earth. Tertullian writes, "He had to die in obedience to that very condition which, because it begins with birth, ends in death. It was not fitting for Him not to be born under the pretence that it was fitting for Him to die."[92] God would have done otherwise, but He did not because He has respect for us; he revealed Himself in a way familiar to us! One may find it difficult to accept this submission in order to escape accepting his own ignorance. We choose to maintain our own blasphemies from the examples derived from our spiritual incontinence. If God has maintained unity and clarity in his design, who are we to make a solid authority that strikes a discordant tune?

For whatever reason, one may have conceived the He-ness of God to spring from man's cynicism to uphold patriarchy; it is against the sublime truth of His word—which so persuasively moved Augustine to confession.[93] Furthermore, it seems like a conclusion and a heretical offshoot of Catholicism predicated on the poor perception of the androgyny of Christ and the literary prowess the Holy Writ possesses. As a result, one must seek Marcion to depose his incompetent formulations, which he has furnished with pseudo-theological exegeses and Aquinas to accommodate his profound loss of intellectual assimilation. If God is as many have claimed, such must be its persons—imperfect too; such must be His creation, the heavens and the celestial bodies and things conceived and produced out of it.[94] The world must be a wrong thing; the reality we know must begin in a different chapter. But even evolutionary biology will not agree with such presuppositions, for nothing we say ascribes its truthfulness. Then, as there is no truth to what we say other than the exhibition of our unconscious complexes, we must go back to the principle that as we know them not based on the false manifestations of our concupiscence.

"No material substance is without the witness of its own original, however great a change into new properties it may have undergone."[95] Indeed, some people may be struggling with the He-ness of God. However, our duty is not to act as cultivators and harvesters of their psychic manifestations. God, in His wisdom, manifests Himself in different ways in each of us and in a manner sometimes contrary to reason and tradition. By paying attention to ourselves, we gain insights into the unique work of God in us, understand our behaviours and patterns and work towards personal transformation.

There are certain questions one must live his life in preparation to present them at the Throne of Grace. Before we were formed in our mother's womb, He knew us (Jer. 1:4). Before we call, He will answer, and whilst we are speaking, He listens (Isa. 65:24). Who can count the number of hairs on our body and the treasure of marrow within our bones[96] except for God from whom all things come from?

Only Him knows what is good. Only He can be asked. Only on His door can we knock, and if we can submit our intellect to Him, He will grant us the fullness of His Spirit. He cannot take away our limitations because those are things that are meant to draw us closer to him.

The individual life is a complex terrain, and sometimes, we must refrain from making an emphatic claim that seems to have captured what his life is all about. There is something in him, of him and about him that must be left to the realm of the sacred. Those things in man that are incommensurable, those things that he cannot change in himself or others, must be left alone. He must bear the crucible of his limitations until that very night of purgation, where the Divine Majesty shall purge him from his concupiscence. Indeed, one may ask, but why must he bear it and not live out himself as the world will encourage?

The answer is simple, and it is known to him; indeed, man knows deep down within that no amount of validation from the outer sphere can satisfy the veracity of his longing in the inner sphere. The yearning can only be stilled once the nursing mother takes the child in her arms and begins to breastfeed her. She must drink from her milk lest she remains thirsty. Any man who may try to exploit this deep-yearning soul under the guise of science has the answer, and political liberty is treading on thin water. It may not take long before his incompetent demiurge catches him in a vicious cycle of damnation. He is putting his despicable sophistry in a place that only the Most High has authority over.

Every individual is sacred. He is the centre of created things. He is the bearer of light, seen and unseen. In him must his Creator take the glory and not yet another man who goes down to the dust. Every individual is not his own, and what he actually is must not be sacrificed on the altar of blasphemy.

The infinite dignity of the human person must not be tampered with. Sometimes, he slumbers to try to resolve the tension between what is and what ought to be. Externally, he will always go hungry, but what he actually seeks is not ordinary manna. Rather, he beckons on a union beyond him, which, of course, he can achieve despite his mortal corruptibility but may not if he lacks an equivalent energy that will help find his lost feather. The intrinsic goal of every individual is to live beyond himself, to connect with the God above, the image that makes him complete.

Augustine summarises it by saying that the soul of man is restless until it rests in God. How sooner or later do we understand that something is beyond us? But you, perhaps now, may construe this as a subjective science. But that is true if and only if you have not listened to yourself and see nothing about you that shocks you.

We may forget about ourselves and the extraordinary things we may have experienced for many reasons. Much of the reason is based on the fact that everything in this world seems to make sense. Whether solid or not, every fact must be considered in the final analysis and make up the truth. Saying that some facts should not constitute truth is flawed for the same reason.

And let it be granted that the sole reason why those facts should not constitute knowledge is that the proponent has some sort of 'unconscious bias', as they would describe it. Hence, we are caught in a cognitive dissonance where we must deny what we know and tread rather timidly and cautiously lest we are committed to the mob. But we must, at some point, make our choice or choose our perception in order to survive in this world. God has His grace abounds, and it is ready to guide us through the dark night, but only if we are ready to let go of vain gratification. These include theories that draw us farther from Him. We have to be serious with God so that He will in turn be serious with us. We must be precise with what we ask of Him. We should not worry about the challenges of the world that bring the flesh in conflict with the spirit.

Wherefore it is written plainly in the book of Job that the life of man on earth is a trial, and his days are hireling. It stands, therefore, to argue that so long as we continue to live here on earth, it is only natural that we keep forgetting and falling until we arise never to fall again.[97] But that decision not to fall is one we have to make vehemently for ourselves. Thus, we may once again ask ourselves, what is it that we are taking in that is a matter of ignorance but is corrupting our soul so that it shall not discover God in His nature as He has chosen to reveal Himself? Very quickly, we find the answer; very quickly, we are able to find our imperfections, the foolishness of our heart and the weakness of our state. Very quickly, will God purge us from the impulse of our senses to see the radiance of His glory and His plans for us despite our shortcomings? Very quickly, we would also discover that we have abolished God by projecting our biases and limitations onto Him, the very pillar and essence of our being and must return to Him in order to be saved.

VII
Reflections

I made that solemn decision to join the priesthood. I left everything to answer the call. It was a tough decision; I was never sure of its outcome until I was sure of the outcome that had happened to me. I lost contact with my friends. I was too committed to the call, which I do not see as a problem but as my way of giving my God my all: my being. I do not take things for granted and like to finish whatever I have started.

One of my best friends went through a lot after I left; I never even cared to ask him, but these were also due to the condition of the seminary, which you have already read. My life took a different direction, and so also did the lives of people I left to answer my vocation. In my world, I was busy with the seminary life and the demands of the priesthood. I said to myself that the priesthood was the lot mapped out for my delight. I committed to this course and did my best not to be a scapegoat. On the other hand, I only existed and did not live; the impressions made on me by Fulton J. Sheen academically, spiritually, and humanly never manifested until the reality of my vocation happened.

Immediately, I became freer, more natural, and more understanding of my natural life. It bothers me why this had to be the case, why I felt so diminished within me, given that the desire to become a priest was not a desire induced by a chemical substance. I would not say that I forced it when He wanted it not to be. I left it to sprout within me because I knew it aimed at something.

But God has His way of breaking us away from the things we hold dearly and perhaps subjectively important. Whether we like it or not, we must accept it because He is doing it for our own good. Such is how natural transformation occurs, as told in the story of Abraham, Paul and other great men and women in the Bible. It does not necessarily need our consent to occur because, in one way or another, it has already announced itself through nature.

The Psalm is: "The heavens declare the glory of God; the firmament proclaims the work of his hands. Day unto day pours forth speech; night unto night whispers knowledge. There is no speech, no words; their voice is not heard. Yet their voice goes forth through all the earth, their messages, to the ends of the world…" (Ps. 19:1-6). When this transformation sets in, any thoughtful person will question himself about what really happened to him. And it is undoubtedly the case when God knows we have something in store.

If He believes in you, you have no reason to be afraid. In Isaiah 45:2-3, He megaphoned, "I will go before you and level the mountains; Bronze doors I will shatter, iron bars I will snap. It will give you treasures of darkness, riches hidden away, that you may know I am the Lord, the God of Israel who calls you by name." This divine assurance, inscribed in the Holy Writ, forms the foundation of my being. As the events of life unfold themselves to me, I try very hard to remind myself of the unwavering certainty of divine intervention.

The question I ask myself almost all the time is: Do I regret anything about the way things happened? As a matter of honesty, I would not give in to such thought. It is rather an utter disregard for all the immeasurable benefits I receive during my early beginnings. More extreme is utter disregard for divine wisdom. I did not know where the desire to become a priest came from. It is not transferrable lest it is provable, as many of us would like to think. If someone had explained to me where it came from, perhaps my responsibility would have been to accept it or desire it again, but I could not have foreseen the outcome. Indeed, some things informed my decision, such as the books I read and the pious association I was into. Moreover, I come from a Catholic family; my father and mother were practising Catholics. But how many of these things attest to what informed my decision? Of course, my environment contributes to my nurture and the decisions I make are heavily influenced by my environment.

On the contrary, everything cannot be the product of the environment; otherwise, one is nothing but a perfect construct of Pavlov's classical conditioning, alongside the belief that someone somewhere in space and time is pushing us to act as though we were free. I can say that despite my abysmal lack of knowledge, I had the freedom to take a stance rooted in self-understanding and self-awareness.

Again, I do not know where I would have been if things had taken a different turn, but I see the past and my memory should be able to remember it with gratitude. I remember the sacrifice my family made to see me through. We had nothing, but they sacrificed a lot. That sacrifice is not anything, and I have no regret for it. I also remember those entrusted with the responsibility of caring for me during the apostolic work. Sometimes, they do things out of their own pocket without asking for a refund. They gave me a life they could not afford for themselves. God led us through the struggles of our daily lives. Indeed, there is something to be grateful for in retrospect.

The most obvious thing in my experiences layered out here is that perhaps I am alone, and as a result, I have a different reality. I realised this during my boyhood, which apparently reinforced itself in my adulthood. There are things I believe to be intrinsically wrong, and there are things I believe to be intrinsically good. There are also things with grey areas which surpass my rationality. I have always felt this way, because I see things differently and must hint at them, which perhaps people around me do not know or know but do not want to act on them or do not want to know at all. Indeed, the loneliness that I am talking about does not stem from a lack of human presence, for even if there is a human presence, one would still feel lonely if the person around has no understanding of what he knows.

Instead, the loneliness is from that profound difference in one's worldview from that of others—from what is fashionable and conventional. It is born of the inability to bridge the chasm between one's perception of reality and society's collective consciousness. It is not merely a matter of differing *Weltanschauung* but a fundamental disparity in the pattern of understanding. One's insights and revelations exist on a plane that is beyond what one might say to gain some cheap validation. Here and there, there is pressure from others to have it all simplified into manageable pieces without them understanding what is going on within.

Verily, it is a frustrating paradox to be burdened with what yearns to be shared yet unable to convey it in a manner that is truly understood. Like a gardener tending to a rare and delicate flower in the wilderness, one nurtures the seeds of his ideas, patiently cultivating them amidst external chaos in the hopes that they will bloom and spread their beauty to the world around him. To walk the path of loneliness is to tread upon a landscape painted with the colours of introspection and contemplation. From the earliest memories of this art, I have found myself journeying down this solitary confinement, not by choice but by necessity of how one has been fashioned. In the quiet recesses of my mind, I seem to harbour a keen awareness, a heightened sensitivity to the subtle nuances that evade the notice of the ordinary observer.

It is like possessing an invisible sixth sense, an innate ability to decipher the cryptic messages woven into the fabric of existence. Also, with this heightened awareness comes a weight of criticisms, a burden born of the realisation that his path diverges from others and cannot make way as one may desire. But despite those noises is the sense of purpose burning bright within one's soul. And like the psalmist says: "Your word is a lamp for my feet, a light for my path" (Ps. 119:105).

In a world rife with so much conformity and homogeneity, it is very important that one look inward and discover what seems strange to the outside world. Such things renew to the perfection of the world, and upon devoting oneself to such endeavour, he sees everything in the world, including God. Simultaneously, he imbues himself with the sense of the Divine, thus precluding the possibility of being devoid of godliness. For the ubiquity of the Divine presence is such that there is no conceivable space and time where His essence and presence cannot be apprehended. When one hides such things, the forewarnings which might renew the face of the world, one is basically looking away from the world. To look away from the world or to stare at it does not help a man reach God; but he who sees the world in Him stands in His presence, says Buber.

I understand that with great insight comes great responsibility. Often, one experiences a lack of freedom in places where he would want freedom. I speak not with a sense of superiority but with the humility of one who has tasted the bittersweetness of what I utter—of one who is in the same struggle.

Still, I believe that such experience is the essence of being bestowed with such responsibility. You do not go with the flow but allow yourself to flow; your speech aligns with yourself and God. If such things happen, it is because you are insurmountable and have much responsibility. That comes with so many criticisms. Surely, with time, they will come, and in time, they will disappear. Indeed, you will be seen as a threat, but soon, you will become their greatest inspiration. This is what it means to have a different kind of reality.

A man does not have a different reality if the nature of such reality only speaks to his socially constructed prison. A man has a different reality when it fulfils the elementary meaning of his existence. A man has a different reality when he finds joy in true things rather than in false things.

I am satisfied with the trajectory my life has carved. Its abundant journey has saturated me with invaluable lessons and profound wisdom. Each twist and turn, every triumph and tribulation, has woven together to form a different me. In enduring the tempests and trials, I confronted periods of uncertainty, wherein doubt loomed large and threatened to overwhelm my self-worth. Within the depths of these crises, I have also acquired a light to move forward.

When I think about them, I am overcome with gratitude for the bountiful experiences that have shaped me into who I am. Thus, as I stand upon the precipice of the present moment, I am filled with a profound sense of gratitude for the journey that has brought me thus far. Every triumph and tribulation has shaped me into who I am. I have attained the understanding that life transcends mere happenstance, evolving beyond a mere sequence of arbitrary occurrences upon the picture of temporal flux. Instead, the events of life reveal themselves as a sacred road to the promised land, demanding patience, endurance and trust in God, who sees beforehand how one's path and final image will be.

To embark upon this expedition entails a readiness to confront the unfamiliar and delve into the unexplored realms of the human soul. As you may grow weary in your circumstance, I beseech Him, Lord, that this new light you have acquired guides you and helps you discern the right path for you. That you may find peace of soul amidst the disruption of the peaceful progress of your life.

In the conduct of human affairs during this time of our earthly existence. We must understand that there will be times of cruelty and joy. Now, in those moments of cruelty, it is essential to understand that it is not always about you, and neither is it always about you in those moments of joy. However, one sees, tastes, smells, feels or hears the world and determines in retrospect what he will receive from the world. If one holds the conviction of the world, the true nature of its foundation, one is endowed with the ability to engage with it.

The world cannot be a habitable place to thrive if all one thinks about it is nothing but black vs white or conservatives vs liberals. Assuming I accepted your worldview, how can I even trust my reason to make such an emphatic statement and expect others to believe it? It follows, therefore, that we must take upon ourselves the responsibility of determining our mode of engagement with the world. I can assure you that if we could love the world a little more, then we can grip it and do with it whatever we want. Troubles surely will come in its coaster, but the best approach to them is not to spill hate and fall into despair but to carry our cross ungrudgingly and follow Him. That is the ultimate approach that will make life do our bidding. As we begin to do that, the changes we seek will inevitably steer our affairs towards a more humane existence.

Selected Bibliography

Achebe, C. (1958). *Things fall apart*. Heinemann.

Aquinas, T. (2023). *Summa Theologiae: Prima pars 1-49* (L. Shapcote, Trans.). Aquinas Institute.

Arendt, H. (2006). *Eichmann in Jerusalem: A report on the banality of evil* (1st ed.). Penguin Classics.

Arendt, H. (2017). *Origins of totalitarianism*. Penguin Classics.

Arendt, H. (2018). *The human condition* (Second ed.). University Chicago Press.

Augustine. (1998). *Confessions* (H. Chadwick, Trans.). Oxford University Press.

Becker, E. (1997). *The denial of death* (First Free Press Paperbacks ed.). Free Press.

Browning, C. R. (2017). *Ordinary men: Reserve police battalion 101 and the final solution in Poland*. Harper Collins.

Buber, M. (2010). *I and thou*. Martino Publishing.

Dossymbekova, R., Daulet, F., Kenzhebaeva, A., & Zeinolla, Z. (2015). Linguocultural aspects of numerology in the Kazakh and Chinese languages. *Procedia - Social and Behavioral Sciences*, *197*, 2512–2519. https://doi.org/10.1016/j.sbspro.2015.07.325

Dostoevysky, F. (2014). *Crime and punishment*. Penguin Classics.

Dostoyevsky, F. (2009). *Notes from Underground* (R. Wilks, Trans.; 1st ed.). Penguin Classics.

Fanon, F. (2001). *The wretched of the earth* (C. Farrington, Trans.; Reprinted in Penguin Classics 2001 ed.). Penguin Classics.

Fanon, F. (2008). *Black skin, white masks*. Penguin Classics.

Forsyth, W. (2010). *Hortensius: An historical essay on the office and duties of an advocate*. Nabu Press.

Frankl, V. (2021, May). *Ten theses about the person* (F. Vesely & D. Nolland, Trans.). Viktor Frankl Institut. https://www.viktorfrankl.org/texts.html

Frankl, V. E. (2008). *Man's search for meaning*. Rider.

Frankl, V. E. (2014). *The will to meaning: Foundations and applications of logotherapy* (Expanded ed.). Plume.

Frankl, V. E. (2019). *Yes to life in spite of everything*. Penguin Classics.

Freud, S. (1991). *On sexuality: Three essays on the theory of sexuality and other works*. Gardner Books.

Gibson, J. J. (2014). *The ecological approach to visual perception: Classic edition (psychology press & routledge classic editions)* (1st ed.). Psychology Press.

Glowasky, M. (2020). Naming god: Exodus 3:14-15 in Augustine's narrations in Psalmos. *Scrinium*, *16*(1), 177–187. https://doi.org/10.1163/18177565-00160a11

Gould, M. (2012). *The biafran war* (1st ed.). I.B.Tauris.

Gruen, A. (2007). *The insanity of normality: Toward understanding human destructiveness* (2007 Reprint ed.). Human Development Books.

Grundgesetz für die bundesrepublik deutschland (71 Auflage ed.). (2023). C.H. Beck.

Hillesum, E. (1996). Etty Hillesum: An Interrupted Life. The Diaries, 1941–1943 and the Letters from Westerbork. Henry Holt and Company. LLC.

Jankunas, G. T. (2011). *Dictatorship of relativism: Pope Benedict xvi's response*. St. Paul's Pub.

Jung, C. G. (1956). *Symbols of transformation: Collected works of Jung* (R. E. C. Hull, Trans.; 1st ed.). Routledge. (Original work published 31. March 1956)

Jung, C. G. (1980). *Psychology and alchemy (collected works of C.G. Jung)* (2nd ed.). Routledge.

Jung, C. G. (2001). *Modern man in search of a soul*. Routledge.

Jung, C. G. (2003). *Four archetypes* (R. F. C. Hull, Trans.). Routledge Classics.

Jung, C. G. (2014). *The undiscovered self*. Routledge.

Jung, C. G. (2018). *On the psychology and pathology of so-called occult phenomena*. CreateSpace Independent Publishing Platform.

Jung, C. G. (2019). *Memories, dreams, reflections* (A. Jaffe, Ed.; R. Winston & C. Winston, Trans.). William Collins. (Original work published 1963)

Kant, I. (1969). *Foundations of the metaphysics of morals: Text and critical essays edited by Robert Paul Wolff* (R. P. Wolff, Ed.; L. White Beck, Trans.). Bobbs-Merrill.

Kant, I. (2007). *Critique of pure reason*. Wildside Press.

Kant, I. (2009). *An answer to the question: 'What is enlightenment?'* (H. B. Nisbet, Trans.). Penguin. (Original work published 1991)

Kempis, T. A. (1955). *Imitation of Christ* (Reissue ed.). Random House Publishing Group.

Lagnado, L. M., & Dekel, S. C. (1992). *Children of the Flames: Dr. Josef Mengele and the Untold Story of the Twins of Auschwitz* (Reprint ed.). Penguin Books.

Lewis, C. S. (2001). *The abolition of man* (1st ed.). HarperOne.

Lewis, C. S. (2012). *The problem of pain* (7th ed.). Harper Collins.

Mill, J. S. (2015). *On liberty, utilitarianism and other essays (Oxford World's classics)* (Second ed.). Oxford University Press.

Milton, J. (2019). *Paradise lost*. Independently Published.

Myliu, J. D. (2011). *Rosarium philosophorum: Of the de alchemia opuscula*. Theophania Publishing.

Neumann, E. (2014). *The origins and history of consciousness (Princeton classics, 113)* (With a Foreword by C. G. Jung- ed.). Princeton University Press.

Nietzsche, F. (1973). *Beyond good and evil* (R. J. Hollingdale, Trans.; 1st ed.). Penguin Classics.

Nwosu, J. A., & Otteh, E. (Eds.). (1996). *Katikizim nke okwukwe nzuko Katolik n'asusu Igbo* (Easter ed.). Excel Publishers LTD Onitsha.

Pageau, M. (2018). *The language of creation: Cosmic symbolism in genesis: A commentary* (1st ed.). Create Space Independent Publishing Platform.

Perl, G. (2019). *I was a doctor in Auschwitz*. Lexington Books.

Peterson, J. B. (1999). *Maps of meaning: The architecture of belief* (1st ed.). Taylor and Francis Books.

Platter, J. M. (2020). Divine simplicity and scripture: A theological reading of exodus 3:14. *Scottish Journal of Theology, 73*(4), 295–306. https://doi.org/10.1017/s0036930620000629

Pluckrose, H., & Lindsay, J. (2020). *Cynical theories: How activist scholarship made everything about race, gender and identity - and why this harm everybody*. Pitchstone Publishing.

Rodney, W. (2005). *How Europe underdeveloped Africa* (2009 ed.). Panaf publishing.

Rogers, C. R. (1967). *On becoming a person: A therapist's view of psychotherapy*. Constable.

Rogers, C. R. (1995). *A way of being* (1st ed.). Mariner Books.

Rogers, C. R., & Farson, R. E. (2015). *Active listening*. Martino Publishing.

Saint Ignatius of Loyola. (1951). *The spiritual exercises of saint ignatius. Translation based on studies in the language of the autograph* (L. J. Puhl, SJ, Trans.). Loyola Press.

Shakespeare, W. (2005). *Hamlet*. Penguin Classics.

Shakespeare, W. (2015). *Othello* (Vol. 2). Create Space Independent Publishing Platform.

Sheen, F. J. (2005). *The priest is not his own* (Reprinted ed.). Asian Trading Corporation.

Sheen, F. J. (1997a). *Lift up your heart. A guide to spiritual peace*. Asian Trading Corporation.

Sheen, F. J. (1997b). *Peace of soul; timeless wisdom on finding serenity and joy by the century's most acclaimed catholic bishop*. Asian Trading Corporation.

Sheen, F. J. (1998). *From the angel's blackboard: The best of Fulton J. Sheen* (First ed.). Asian trading Corporation.

Sheen, F. J. (2013). *Those mysterious priests* (5th Print ed.). Alba House.

Solzhenitsyn, A. (2003). *The Gulag Archipelago 1918 -56* (T. P. Whitney & H. Willets, Trans.). The Harvill Press London. (Original work published 1986)

Solzhenitsyn, A. (2008). *One Day in the Life of Ivan Denisovich* (R. Parker, Trans.; 50th Anniversary ed., with an afterword by Eric Bogosian). Signet Classics.

St John of the Cross. (2008). *Dark night of the soul*. Wilder Publications.

Tertullian. (2023). *On the flesh of Christ*. Dalcassian Publishing Company.

Tolstoy, L. (2008). *The Death of Ivan Ilyich and other stories (penguin classics)*. Penguin Classics.

Vatican II. (1965). *Dogmatic constitution on the church: Lumen gentium* (2nd ed.). Pauline Books & Media.

Von Goethe, J. W. (2005). *Faust* (D. Constantine, Trans.). Penguin Classics.

Walter, M., & Rex, D. (2013). *Liber psalmorum: The vulgate latin psalter (latin edition)*. CreateSpace Independent Publishing Platform.

Woodhouse, P. (2009). *Etty Hillesum: A life transformed*. Bloomsbury Continuum.

End Notes

[1] Part of this argument has been borrowed from Forsyth, W. (2010) *Hortensius: An Historical Essay on the Office and Duties of an Advocate.* Nabu Press. For context and the usage of the citation the reader should refer to Chapter 1, page 8-10 on the responsibility and duty of an Advocate and Chapter VII on the sale of Judicial Offices.

[2] In *"The Wretched of the Earth"*, Fanon levelled criticism at the political bourgeoisie for their inadequate involvement in the struggles of the oppressed and their inclination to side with colonial authorities to further their own economic interests. He contended that this class, instead of spearheading the liberation movement, often served as a go-between for the colonisers and the general populace, thereby sustaining the very systems of inequity and subjugation that were meant to be eradicated. Fanon asserted that their dearth of revolutionary awareness and dedication to genuine societal transformation made them complicit in the ongoing exploitation of their fellow citizens. In the foregoing paragraph, I contextualise this concept within Nigeria, where the political middle class, much like Fanon's criticism, often neglects to advocate for the masses' concerns. Rather, they frequently side with the established political elite, favouring their personal financial interests over the true freedom of their own people. Instead of leading the charge for national rejuvenation, this class typically acts as a buffer between the governing elite of the mother countries and the subjugated masses, thus upholding the existing order and sustaining the ongoing cycle of corruption. See Fanon, F. (2001). *The Wretched of the Earth*. Pg. 119–165. Penguin Classics

[3] See, Michael Gould, The Biafran War: The Struggles for Modern Nigeria.

[4] Arendt, H. (2107). *The Origins of Totalitarianism*. Pg. 407. Penguin

⁵ Ibid. 407–408.

⁶ Fanon, F. (2001). *The Wretched of the Earth*. Pg. 119–165. Penguin Classics.

⁷ Ibid.

⁸ Rodney, W. *How Europe Underdeveloped Africa* (2005). Panaf Press. See also ibid.

⁹ Fanon, F. (2001). *The Wretched of the Earth*. Pg. 119–165. Penguin Classics

¹⁰ It is a conventional knowledge that religion is the cause of social menace in Nigeria and not a deep-seated decay in the collective mindset that often leads to widespread feelings of discontent and dissatisfaction. We could deduce this from a scholarly perspective, such as Adeleke, A. O. (2015). *Religion and politics in Nigerian society: Problems and prospects (a philosophic probe). Open Journal of Political Science, 5(3), 239–245*. Beyond Nigeria, whenever the emphasis on the problem of Nigeria is made, religion takes precedence, and it is even compared with other places where religion is supposedly the real problem. See , Massaro, C. (2023, October 23). *Nigeria plagued by ethnic and religious violence as attacks on Christians rise*. Fox News. While it must be acknowledged there is often tension between different religious groups in Nigeria, the Nigerian problem as I perceive it goes beyond a religious problem to insist upon a psychological one in the collective mindset, often manifesting itself in the form of cowardice in decisive moments, pervasive mistrust among ethnic groups whereby one's tribe is preferred over the progress of the state and, the absence of practical links between the rulers and the masses. These issues are cracks in the edifice of Nigeria, far more harmful and prejudicial to national progress and unity than the perceived religious misgivings.

¹¹ Jung, C. G. (2001). *Modern man in search of a soul*. Pg. 234. Routledge.

¹² Erich Neumann, The Origins of Consciousness.

¹³ Ibid.

¹⁴ Ibid.

¹⁵ Ibid.

¹⁶ It appears to be a consensus among African philosophers and is popular among scholars of colonial African studies. For example, Ocobock, P. (2012). Spare the Rod, Spoil the Colony: Corporal Punishment, Colonial Violence, and Generational Authority in Kenya, 1897–1952. The International Journal of African Historical Studies, 45(1), 29–56 suggests that in Kenya and other parts

of Africa, the encounter between Africans and Europeans led to an increase in the range of people and organisations accomplices or claiming the use of violence. Until then, such rights were primarily restricted to traditional rulers, tribal leaders, and specific institutions like the court of law. Fanon, in his book Black Skin, White Masks, makes a similar claim but develops it further into the psychological impact of such encounters. In chapter six, The Black Man and Psychopathology, Fanon writes: "A normal black child, having grown up with a normal family, will become abnormal at the slightest contact with the white world" (p.22; Fanon, F. (2008). Black skin, white masks pg. 122. R. Philcox, Trans. Penguin). By way of analysis, these are symptoms of psychic traumas whose archetypes are linked to the "scene" that provoked them, with both Ocobock and Fanon highlighting different dimensions of the violence—physical and psychological—that colonialism inflicted on African societies. In post-colonial Nigeria, it is instead a truism that the conduct of her internal affairs and the amount of force and violence exerted both by the government on its citizens and among the citizens themselves to maintain control and suppress dissent. Whether through the use of military force, police brutality or political repression, there is a pattern of this violence that can only be explained by seeking the source of the underlying trauma, buried in the country's historical wounds. This trauma has been expelled from consciousness but continues to exist in the unconscious. It always seeks scenarios to assert its presence but in a manner so subtle that it makes it impossible to recognise it as such. If not, how can we explain that even in the absence of immediate threats, the State often resorts to excessive force and coercion against its citizens? How can we explain that in such situations where the citizens are exercising their franchise, there is often a swift and violent response from the State? This phenomenon suggests a deep-seated fear and insecurity rooted in historical *Erlebnis* and collective memories of violence. Above all, it reveals an anxiety within the government regarding its legitimacy and the will of the people—a consequence of repressed true patriotism by an authority symbol, the government charged by the colonial masters with maintaining order and control.

[17] The discussion between the public and private realms of life is taken from Arendt, H. (2018). *The human condition*. University of Chicago Press.
[18] The confessions of St Augustine.

[19] Carl, G. V (1972). *Four Archetypes*. P. 75. Routledge Taylor and Francis Group.

[20] Sheen, F. J. (2005). *The priest is not his own* (Reprinted ed.). Asian Trading Corporation P. 25.

[21] The first line, "Lord I lie open to thy scrutiny" is taken from Sheen, F. J. (1997). *Peace of soul*. Asian Trading Corporation. I chose this phrase whilst integrating the rest of the translation from the Catholic Bible to express the vulnerability and honesty I felt the first time I read the psalm from the book and during those troubling times. It signifies a willingness to be examined deeply not by man but God, inviting Him to evaluate my thoughts and actions without hiding anything. This openness reflects trust in God's judgment and the belief that divine scrutiny is what one primarily needs for growth rather than condemnation from man.

[22] John Paul II, P. (1992). I will give you shepherds = Pastores dabo vobis: Post-synodal apostolic exhortation, 25 March 1992.

[23] The confessions of St Augustine.

[24] Shakespeare, W. (1992). Othello (C. Watts, Ed.). Wordsworth Editions.

[25] Frankl, V. E. (1970). *The Will to Meaning: Foundations and Applications of Logotherapy*, pp. 101–102, Plume.

[26] Pageau, M. (2018) *The Language of Creation: Cosmic Symbolism in Genesis: A Commentary.*

[27] Ibid.

[28] When Nigeria gained independence in 1960, the study of history was flourishing, with widespread inclusion in primary and secondary school curricula and high enrollment in universities. However, post-independence brought new challenges beyond colonialism and dependency on European Ideals, and nationalist history struggled to address these modern issues. First, history was seen by the government as irrelevant to Nigeria's contemporary problems, viewed as too abstract and outdated compared to the perceived practicality of science and technology in a globalised world. Additionally, amid the nation's economic and socio-political crises, history lost appeal as a marketable field. The government has also faced accusations of suppressing historical studies to avoid accountability—an issue seen as valid, though debated. Moreover, nationalist history lacked a scientific approach, and some Western institutions reportedly

discouraged African nations from teaching the humanities. These challenges became apparent in the 1980s when history education sharply declined in schools. In 1977, the Federal Government implemented the National Policy on Education, modelled after the American system, adopting a 6-3-3-4 structure. This policy soon incorporated history within social studies in primary and junior secondary schools, later replacing it with government studies at the senior secondary level. History was formally removed from the primary and junior secondary curricula by 2009/2010. In 2017, following advocacy by the Historical Society of Nigeria (HSN) under Prof. CBN Ogbogbo's leadership, history was reintroduced into school curricula by the Minister of Education, Malam Adamu Adamu. See, The Abolishment of History in Nigerian Primary and Secondary Institutions: The Aftermath, 1983–2021 by Oluwafunmilayo Obasa. The extent to which the re-introduction of history has moved beyond policy and into actual classroom practice remains to be examined. See Moga Ezekiel, Alaku, M. E., & Abade, A. J. (2023). Re-echoing the place of history in the curriculum of secondary education. Journal of African Advancement & Sustainability Studies, 29(2), ISSN: 3125-5521.

[29] Here, I am alluding to Kant's metaphysics of Morals. Then, the reference

[30] In *The Undiscovered Self*, while discussing religion as the counterbalance to mass-mindedness, Jung essentially argues that while acknowledging the State's moral and factual claims, one recognises a higher, transcendent authority to which both man and the State are ultimately accountable. This belief, Jung argues, grants the individual a profound sense of inner freedom, as their ultimate allegiance lies not with the temporal, fallible powers of the world but with a higher divine order. Thus, even if one argues that God be removed from the constitution of the State, the reality remains that such an omission does not diminish the reality of divine authority. God's sovereignty is not contingent upon human law or political system recognition."

[31] Frankl, V. E. Ten Theses about the Person. Translated by Franz and David Nolland. https://www.viktorfrankl.org/texts.html.

[32] Frankl, V. E. (2008) *Man's Search For Meaning. Rider*.

[33] The Pontifical Council For The Family The Truth And Meaning Of Human Sexuality. This reference is among the website references listed in my selected bibliography. Please help me check and cite it accordingly.

[34] Jung, C.G. (2014) *The Undiscovered Self*, Routledge Great Minds, p. 16.
[35] Buber, M. (2010) *I and Thou*.
[36] Ibid.
[37] The Truth and Meaning of Sexuality.
[38] Ibid.
[39] Ibid.
[40] Ibid.
[41] Ibid.
[42] St Augustine (1991) *Confessions*, Oxford World Classics.
[43] *Dark Night of the Soul*.
[44] Critique of Pure reason.
[45] Ibid.
[46] Ibid.
[47] *The Imitation of Christ*.
[48] St John of the Cross, *Dark Night of the Soul*.
[49] Here, I am alluding to John Milton's invocation in his book, *Paradise Lost*. The full quote reads: What in me is dark, illumine, what is low in me raise and support; That to the height of this great Argument, I may assert thy Eternal Providence and justify the ways of God to men.
[50] Fanon, F. (2008). *Black Skin, White Masks*. Penguin.
[51] Myliu, J. D, *Rosarium Philosophorum of the De Alchemia Opuscula*.
[52] John Stuart Mill, *On Liberty, Utilitarianism and other Essays*.
[53] I think the most striking literature that has caught my attention so far on this matter is Capécia, M. (1948). I am a Martinican woman (as cited in Fanon, 1952). Penguin.
[54] Hannah Arendt, *The Origins of Totalitarianism*.
[55] See, Arendt, H. (2107). The Origins of Totalitarianism. Penguin.
[56] Kant, I. (1969) *Foundations of the Metaphysics of Morals*.
[57] This phrase has been attributed to Augustine in his Tractates on the First Epistle of John. See Tsamadias, N. (2020). Affective attunement, psychotherapy, and the nature of the human encounter. PhilArchive. Similarly, in correspondence with Hannah Arendt, Heidegger ascribed this statement to St Augustine: "I love and I desire your existence." Arendt partially implores the phrase in her writing to prescribe the condition for dealing with the contingency

of human existence and the relational aspect of identity. See, Arendt, H. (2107). *The Origins of Totalitarianism*. Pg. 394. Penguin. This phrase encapsulates the notion of loving someone while wishing for their continued existence and without being able to give a definitive reason for such affirmation. In making this appeal, it is concurred that such a form of love aligns with acknowledging a shared ontological foundation between the self and the Other and should be the assumption on which political life is predicated.

[58] See, Arendt, H. (2107). *The Origins of Totalitarianism*. Penguin.

[59] Ibid pg. 395.

[60] Ibid.

[61] Here, I allude to Gothe's *Faust* Part 1.

[62] Jung, in his book *The Undiscovered Self*, reached a similar conclusion. However, the difference between his scholarship and mine remains the fact that I am investigating the insistence on sexuality and black identity. My scholarship in this aspect and being able to prove that this ideology is religious is first and foremost based on my observation of the matter and Jung's scholarship.

[63] In a commencement speech delivered by Solzhenitsyn, he mentioned that there is a split between our words. In his words, "The split in today's world is perceptible even to a hasty glance. Any of our contemporaries readily identifies two world powers, each of them already capable of utterly destroying the other. However, the understanding of the split too often is limited to this political conception: the illusion according to which danger may be abolished through successful diplomatic negotiations or by achieving a balance of armed forces. The truth is that the split is both more profound and more alienating, that the rifts are more numerous than one can see at first glance." See *A World Split Apart*, June 8, 1978. I must emphasise that my acquaintance with Solzhenitsyn's discourse only occurred subsequent to my own formulation of comprehension regarding the era.

[64] The word *Kpim* is an Igbo word meaning essence, the core of something. It is borrowed from Iroegbu, P. (1995). *Metaphysics: The Kpim of philosophy*. Owerri: International University Press. Therefore, God as the *kpim* of everything is to say that God is the all-encompassing essence of everything—the central unifying reality from which being and meaning are derived.

[65] Arendt, H, *The Origins of Totalitarianism*, p. 254.

[66] St John of the Cross, *Dark Night of the Soul*.

[67] Jung, C. G. (1988) *Memories, Dreams and Reflections: An Autobiography*, William Collins, p. 182.

[68] See Pro Eligendo Romano Pontifice (2005) Homily of His Eminence Card. Joseph Ratzinger.

[69] Frankl delineates between two distinct forms of leisure: centrifugal and centripetal. While centrifugal leisure propels one outward towards distraction and dispersion, centripetal leisure draws inward, fostering introspection and meaning-making. Through this dichotomy, Frankl invites his reader to contemplate the profound significance of how we engage not only with our leisure time but also our interaction with the world, pinpointing its potential to either scatter our focus or deepen our existential understanding.

[70] Etty Hillesum, *An Interrupted life*.

[71] Kant, 1. (2009) An answer to the question: What is Enlightenment? For enlightenment of this kind, all that is needed is freedom. And the freedom in question is the innocuous form of all freedom to make public use of one's reason in all matters. p. 101. Penguin Books.

[72] Augustine, of Hippo, Saint, 185–196 & 228–245. (9780199537822). The Confessions of Saint Augustine. Oxford University Press.

[73] Kant. 1. (2009). An answer to the question: What is Enlightenment? For enlightenment of this kind, all that is needed is freedom. And the freedom in question is the innocuous form of all freedom to make public use of one's reason in all matters. Penguin books.

[74] Carl G. Jung (1953) *Psychology and Alchemy*, 2nd edition, p. 22.

[75] Carl G. Jung (1953) *Psychology and Alchemy*, 2nd edition, p. 22.

[76] See, Panicola, V. R. (1968). Christianity & the androgyne: Reflections on sexual difference and complementarity. Dominicana, 53(3), 314–329. Retrieved from Dominicajournal.org.

[77] Ibid.

[78] Jung, C. G. (1953) *Psychology and Alchemy*, 2nd edition, p. 22.

[79] Ibid.

[80] St Augustine (1991) *Confessions*. Oxford World Classics.

[81] St Thomas Aquinas, Summa Theologica: Prima Pars 1–49.

[82] Ibid.

[83] Ibid, pp. 22–23.

[84] Ibid, p. 35.

[85] Aquinas, T. (2023) *Summa Theologiae*. Aquinas Institute. Question 3, Article 1, p. 25.

[86] Jung, C. G. (1953) Psychology and Alchemy, 2nd edition, p. 22.

[87] Jung, C. G. (1933) *Modern Man in Search of a Soul*, United Kingdom: Routledge Taylor and Francis Group.

[88] Ibid.

[89] Jung, C. G. (1964) *Man and His Symbols*, United States of America: J.G. Ferguson Publishing.

[90] Jung, C. G. (1953) *Psychology and Alchemy*, 2nd edition, p. 22.

[91] Tertullian, *De Carne Christi*, chapter 5.

[92] Tertullian, *De Carne Christi*, chapter 6.

[93] Isaiah 55:8-9.

[94] Tertullian, *De Carne Christi*, chapter 5.

[95] Ibid.

[96] St Augustine (1991) *Confessions,* Oxford World Classics.

[97] Job 7:1.